Cornhole Pool, Hot Springs, Arkansas, 1865

Courtesy of Garland County Historical Society
Hot Springs, Arkansas

Fire
in the Springs

A tale of star-crossed immigrants

Lisa Schliff

Fire in the Springs
A tale of star-crossed immigrants
by Lisa Schliff

Published by
Wilks Publishers

Cover and Interior Design: Nick Zelinger, NZGraphics.com
Editor: Kate Dumont

ISBN: 979-8-9866101-1-5 (print)
ISBN: 979-8-9866101-0-8 (e-book)
Library of Congress Control Number: 2022913901

First Edition

Printed in the United States of America

For my mother and father

*"I will not allow my life's light to be determined
by the darkness around me."*
~Sojourner Truth

*The Jew came to the unknown from afar,
With sore feet, with a grieving heart,
Pack on shoulders, stick in hand,
Into the new, the free gigantic land.*

From *Kentucky* by I.J. Schwartz,
translated from Yiddish by Richard Helfer

1

Gliewitz, Germany
1858

On an early spring morning, just past dawn, Rosalia Wolfson and Annaleya Steinberger trudged downtown to the fish market together. They clutched their wool shawls to keep the brisk vernal breeze from blowing them open. White bonnets framed their faces but couldn't prevent a few stray locks from flying out from under them. Each had a thick, coarse cotton shopping bag lined with newspaper, and pfennigs in their apron pockets. They were under orders of their respective mothers to select with discrimination the freshest, tastiest whitefish or herring they could find at the lowest price. As they passed the brickyard, a group of masons in black overalls and stained, tan shirts taking a beer break made kissing noises and leered at them.

"Ach, I would love to go over there and kick them in the shins," Rosalia groaned.

"Don't you like the attention?" Annaleya teased her. "Now that we aren't children, the men notice us. Especially you, *sheyna*, with your golden head of hair."

At thirteen, Rosalia Wolfson had only one friend, Annaleya Steinberger. She had argued with every other girl in the neighborhood. Even Annaleya exchanged cross comments with her now and then, but she loved Rosalia well enough to overlook their spats. Their looks contrasted comically as they trudged through the town of Gliewitz arm in arm. Rosalia's short strides could barely keep up with Annaleya's long ones. Her fine blonde hair, escaping in strands from underneath her white bonnet, made Annaleya's long, thick, frizzy copper braid appear positively red as a tomato in contrast.

"Don't be silly! It's you they're ogling now that you have a bosom. I have practically nothing there," Rosalia griped, grasping her shopping bag tightly to her chest. She imagined the eyes of the brickyard masons penetrating through her clothes to the flatness of that area and laughing.

"Well, you will get a bosom soon enough. But look at you, like a tiny, beautiful doll. Who wouldn't be attracted? All the boys in yeshiva are."

"Those boys? They are still children themselves. And idiots. Especially my cousin Daniel. Oh, I can't bear him. He teases me so much when his family comes for dinner, and when we go to his house, he tries to get me alone and then pushes and shoves me."

"That means he's attracted to you, *sheyna*."

"I will show him some attraction. Maybe a crack on the head with the butter churn. Won't he like that? That will give him something to talk about to his friends, especially Jacob. He gives me the creeps. I think he'll grow up to be a *ganef*, a thief. He was already caught stealing something from the Rabbi, a gold ring or something like that."

"That's just idle gossip."

They turned a corner and the shopping district of Gliewitz splayed out before them. Vendors with carts called out their wares, and vendors with stands overflowing with fruits, vegetables, cuts of meat and seafood piled goods into customers' bags and wagons. The two girls veered sharply to the left where they knew the fish seller always stationed his stand. They had to stop abruptly and wait for a rattling buggy drawn by a tough, huffing brown mule to cross in front of them.

"Ach, the smell of fresh mule droppings. What a way to start a morning," Rosalia moaned.

"Stop complaining. There are fragrant odors here as well. I smell Frau Becker's fresh baked bread and pastries. Let's buy one each if we have a few pfennigs left at the end."

The girls stood elbow to elbow, eyeing the catch that Herr Weiner had on display. Large fillets of sturgeon gleamed in the morning sunlight. Perch, rainbow trout, and walleye stared with one dead eye out, scales wet and shiny.

"I will have three of those trout. What a good price! And a little bag of herring, bitte, Herr Weiner," Annaleya requested politely.

"Why so costly the herring?" Rosalia scowled. "Last week it was half that."

"Last week was last week," replied the fish seller as he filled Annaleya's thick leather tote with trout wrapped in butcher paper. "These herring I imported from Denmark." He paused to scoop up the very herring he was praising for Annaleya's smaller bag. "They are the best, the tastiest. Might go up even higher next week, who knows? Depends on the Danes and import taxes." He grinned and winked at Rosalia, wiping his chapped, swarthy hands on his apron. His dark eyes moved across their faces and down. "You are both growing up so fast! I remember when your mamas held your little hands while they shopped."

Both girls blushed and giggled. When Rosalia finished her purchases, they strolled across the town square to Frau Becker's bakery and bought a small pastry each to share with their mothers when they got home. The cobblestones of the downtown district rolled uncomfortably under their thickly soled, black leather boots. They walked in the shadows cast by blocky three-story apartment buildings to escape the increasingly stiff wind. Then they reached the dusty, unpaved dirt roads of the Jewish quarter, where familiar, small clapboard homes squeezed together. Neat little gardens sprouted around most of these poor abodes like multi-colored salads waving and curling in their loamy beds. Rosalia eyed the gardens that were visible from the front and side, comparing them to her own. She loved to work in Mama's garden, digging her petite, roughened hands into the soil, planting seedlings, watering and observing their daily growth with anticipation.

As they rounded the final corner to their respective houses – Annaleya lived just down the block – they almost collided with two boys running towards them.

"Daniel! Look where you are going," scolded Rosalia her cousin once she realized who was jogging away down the street. "Why aren't you and Jacob in yeshiva?"

Yeshiva was for boys only, led by the Rabbi and sometimes the cantor. They studied Torah and Talmud, deciphering the strange lines and dots that comprised the written Hebrew language. Rosalia watched with envy and longing after breakfast as her own two younger brothers, Henry and Jake, walked out the front door with their satchels and study books every morning except Saturday, which was reserved for Shabbat services.

Daniel slowed down and turned back towards Rosalia, with Jacob not far behind. His long, curling black payes framed both cheeks. At fourteen, he was much taller than Rosalia, but who in town wasn't?

"Rosie?" He used his affectionate nickname for her. "Don't tell your parents you saw me. They'll just tell my parents, and then I'll get in trouble." He strode over to her and Annaleya, leaned down and attempted to kiss Rosalia's lips. She ducked and stepped backward.

"What is wrong with you? I should scratch out your eyes and put them in your mouth! Get away from me."

Daniel's chestnut eyes narrowed and his plump lips hung in a frown.

"Where I am going, you cannot imagine in your craziest dreams."

Then he shrugged and sauntered off to join Jacob again.

"There is something evil about that boy," murmured Annaleya.

"I would have to agree. What is wrong with him, trying to kiss me like that?

"He has a crush on you. It's obvious."

"Well, the feelings aren't mutual. I wonder where they're going that is so special?"

"I wouldn't have the slightest idea. Let's follow them."

The girls watched from the corners of their eyes as Daniel and Jacob walked hurriedly down the street, their identical, long black wool coats flapping behind them. Yeshiva had just let out two blocks away, and Daniel, the tallest and most boisterous of the class, and his best friend Jacob Levy, shoved the younger boys in front of them out of the way. They had been called to the Bar Mitzvah a year ago, which made them 'men' in a ritual sense. They stomped down the street together, scuffing their leather boots along the unpaved road. Rosalia and Annaleya watched from a short distance to make sure the boys wouldn't spot them. Then they ran to catch up as the boys turned a corner. Daniel was bragging loudly, so it was not difficult to overhear their conversation. *As usual,* Rosalia told herself with a roll of her deep azure eyes.

"Come on, Jacob, let's go find the gypsies living under the Neisse River Bridge," said Daniel, pulling on his left payot, curling the dark sidelock around his finger.

"Gypsies? Hold onto your pockets, I hear they steal for a living."

"I'll cuff any of them who tries to take my pfennigs! Right in the face."

He punched his fist into the air.

"Oh yeah?' taunted Jacob. "I'd like to see you try to fight a gypsy. You'll be dead in a minute with a knife in your heart. That's how they fight."

Daniel grinned and shook his long black side curls and sneered,

"I'm too fast for any of them."

They continued down the street and turned a corner.

"Did you hear that, Annaleya? They're going to the Neisse River, where the gypsies have set up camp. Do we dare follow them there?"

Annaleya shifted her bulky bag nervously. "I don't know. Maybe the fish will spoil by the time we get home. That may not be a good idea."

"No, the fish will be fine. Herr Weiner put them on a small block of ice in our bags. That's why they're so heavy."

"Yes, but the ice is melting! See it dripping on the ground?"

"I'm sure the fish will keep for another half hour. I'm dying to see what kind of mischief Daniel and Jacob are getting into."

Annaleya shrugged and followed her friend as they shadowed the boys around the corner and down the street, ducking behind the occasional white elm or overgrown gooseberry patch.

They all hurried down Kaiserstrasse Avenue, where the one-story, clapboard houses looked more dilapidated. As they continued east, the houses became smaller, spaced farther apart, with sagging porches, splintered roofs, missing steps. Finally, they came to the bridge over the Neisse River stretching like an indigo velvet ribbon embroidered with delicate white lace rivulets. Under the bridge, three Romany wagons were lined up below an embankment. The wagons were decorated with brightly colored banners, swirls of green, turquoise and vermillion, that hung attached to steel hooks from each top corner. Three thin, saggy-spined black and white dobbins stood tied up nearby, munching in their feed buckets. Not a person was in sight.

Rosalia stopped abruptly to avoid being spotted, and Annaleya almost slammed into her. They crouched behind an old, ivy-covered fence running along the embankment and peered cautiously above it toward the bridge. The boys were tiptoeing around the gaudy wagons, and periodically glancing behind their shoulders, and at those moments Rosalia and Annaleya sank behind the fence. Suddenly, a flap of the middle wagon was flung aside and a woman with long, unbrushed ebony waves of hair like twisted yarn, stuck her head out.

"Hello, young mans. You want something?" she asked sweetly, staring at them with large eyes the deep grey of wet river stones, a firm line of black kohl drawn above and below each lid. Silver hoops dangled at her cheeks, reflecting the sun in sudden glints. She scooted nimbly out of the gypsy wagon and stood before them with muscular arms crossed under her swarthy-skinned bosom. Daniel and Jacob stood frozen, staring back silently.

"Look at this woman," Rosalia hissed in her friend's ear. "No bonnet, hair flying around. And her neckline is very, very low. Shameful!"

"Quite low. How I would love to dress like that sometime."

Both girls giggled softly.

The Roma woman lowered her chest so that the boys could catch a glimpse of her cleavage just forming a swollen Y at the edge of her scoop-necked mustard and rose-colored dress. She stepped easily out of the wagon and approached them, hips swaying in an exaggerated motion.

"Do you see the hair?" squeaked Rosalia. "It's all the way down past her bottom! Now she is saying something to the boys." The two girls strained to hear, their heads now above the fence line. The gypsy's voice, loud and vibrant, floated up the embankment.

"You like to buy something for your mothers? I have sweet perfumes for them." Her German was heavily accented by the consonants and vowels of the Roma language, but the girls could still understand her. She smiled broadly, showing several glinting golden front and canine teeth. The girls gasped as the gold reflected the sunlight like tiny beacons in her mouth.

They saw Daniel suddenly reach out and touched her left breast.

"Get your hands off me!" she scolded angrily, shoving him backward with surprising strength. Immediately a large bulk of a man leapt out of the wagon, hurled himself at Daniel and knocked him to the ground. He began hollering at him in Romani and stepping on his neck with a heavy brown leather boot. The girls watched as Daniel gagged and attempted to grasp the offending boot to lift it from his throat. The boot stayed as firm as the leg of the irate Roma appended to it. Jacob flushed a deep red, turned and scurried up the embankment, legs churning like leaping trout. When he had completely disappeared, the boot rose and released Daniel. He pulled himself up and spanked off the dirt that had been ground into his black wool coat. The husky Roma man immediately turned on the teenager, bellowing in broken German,

"I break you neck the next time I see you, boy!"

A shimmering, gaudy gold headscarf was wrapped around his brow like a circus bandage. He elongated his neck so that his face was only inches from Daniel and scowled, round eyes flashing, eyebrows like black slashes pointed at the bridge of his ample and slightly crooked nose. Behind the fence, Rosalia was covering her mouth tightly with one hand, trying to stifle the laughter that bubbled up. She could feel Annaleya stiffening beside her.

"I don't know why this is so funny to me," Rosalia whispered to her friend. "He is awful to do that."

"It's not funny, it's hateful. I want to go home now." Annaleya's deep set hazel brown eyes filled with tears, and she grabbed her tote bag.

Suddenly Rosalia realized that a small group of people were gathered nearby on the broad wooden bridge overlooking the river. A short, hefty bell of a man in a heavy, long black coat made his way down the embankment like an oversized crow to Daniel and the gypsy man.

"What is going on here?" he asked, his voice high-pitched and imperious. One hand held down the embroidered yarmulke perched on his head, under which a few strands of salt and pepper hair curled tightly.

The gypsy woman ducked back inside the wagon. Her husband turned to Rabbi Schultz, anger contorting his swarthy features.

"This …. this devil boy, he put hand on my wife, he insult her!"

The rabbi backed away several steps and cleared his throat, pulled on his scraggly frosted beard, glanced away for a moment.

"I do not know what happened, I was not here. But Daniel is a good boy and would not do such a thing. "Daniel," he turned to the disheveled boy who was slowly backing away from them. "Did you touch the lady?"

"No, rebbe. He's lying. He threw me on the ground and tried to steal my money!"

Rabbi Schultz and the gypsy squared off face to face.

"I will kill your son if I see him again!" hissed the gypsy, the tails of his gold headscarf blowing in the sudden gust of wind that was passing through. The rabbi touched his dark felt top hat.

"He is not my son. But he is a son of this town. There will be no killing, Hashem forbid. You come into our town and make trouble. Daniel did not touch your, your……wife. Leave!" He pulled his short and wide figure up to its maximum height and spun on a booted heel, stiffly walking away and back toward the bridge. But the gypsy did nothing, only stared at the disappearing figure of the Jewish community's religious leader. He shook his head, ambled over to his bony white mare, whacked her hard on the rump, and clambered back into the wagon.

"You go along home now," the rabbi turned and called sternly to Daniel.

"Yes, Rabbi."

Daniel walked hurriedly until he reached the far end of the bridge. The chilly Neisse River flowed below it, growling like a large hungry bear. Then he slowed down and began clambering up the embankment. Rosalia grasped Annaleya's hand and they both ran back the way they had come, looking for a corner to turn so that Daniel wouldn't spot them. They didn't stop running until they arrived at Annaleya's house. Trying to catch her breath, Rosalia gave Annaleya's hand a squeeze as they parted at the gate of the Steinburgers' rickety garden fence.

"Don't tell your Mama, Papa, or anybody, what we saw."

"We don't need to. The Rabbi and his friends on the bridge will not be able to keep it to themselves anyway."

"True. But I want to be the one to tell. I would love to get Daniel in as much trouble as possible."

Annaleya shook her head and flipped her russet braid with a pale, freckled hand, looking unhappily at her best friend. Still, she gave her a kiss on the forehead and disappeared behind her front door. Rosalia turned away and immediately felt a pounding weight, a heavy bulk whack into her. She fell on the ground and her shopping bag went flying into the street. Squinting up toward the glaring sun, she saw two glaring brown eyes and a scowling face hovering over her. Jacob Levy hissed,

"You better not get Daniel in trouble, or there will be vengeance! I saw you and Annaleya spying on us behind the fence!"

Shaken and flushed, Rosalia jumped up and quickly smoothed her dress and apron. Her golden hair was spilling out on one side from under her bonnet.

"Ach! How dare you touch me? We saw you run off like a coward when Daniel got in trouble!" Rosalia was shouting now, unable to hold back a wave of fury.

Jacob reached down and yanked the strands of hair that had come loose to Rosalia's shoulder, then stomped off down the street.

2

osalia tiptoed past the kitchen door, not wanting to explain to anybody why she looked so disheveled. Voices were floating through the house, one Mama's and after a few minutes she recognized her Great Aunt Eva's voice. She stopped in the parlor and sat down on the shabby, dust-colored sofa, leaning her head against the frayed antimacassar. Stretching out her legs that barely reached the floor, she listened attentively to the conversation in the other room.

"But the temper! You would never think such a *sheyna maydeleh,* such a pretty girl, could steam up like a pot of boiling water that way."

That was Great Aunt Eva, who was always criticizing her. Eva Lowenberg was related to Rosalia through her mother Dora Wolfson's side of the family. She was short and squat, with hair as white as an egret feather. She walked as little as possible and was frequently out of breath.

"She will outgrow it. She is still a child. Maybe Edith will rub off on her a little."

Mama. Always defending her.

"Who will outgrow what?"

A deep male voice. That was her father! He must have come in the kitchen from the back door. She could smell him all the way into the parlor, reeking of fermented hops from the Schmidt Brewery where he worked.

"Oy, what a start you gave us!"

Mama again.

"I'm just finishing the chopped liver and chicken kreplach soup. Aunt Eva is staying for dinner tonight. Where is that blue-eyed daughter of ours? I sent her out shopping for fish hours ago."

Suddenly Rosalia remembered the bag filled with trout, herring and ice. It was dripping all over the parlor floor. Mama would kill her!

Isaac Wolfson leaned over to kiss his wife and straightened up abruptly, staring at Rosalia round-eyed, with the comical grin that she loved because it twisted his face to one side and made him look silly.

"Rosela, where have you been?" asked Dora, sounding perplexed, relieved and angry at the same time. With a sinking feeling in her gut, Rosalia saw her mother's eyes slide downward to the dripping canvas bag in Rosalia's right hand. "Oy vey."

Isaac smirked. "While you women take care of that mess, I'm going to get ready for dinner."

Dora whisked the fish into the cold closet and handed Rosalia a rag to wipe up the puddles of water that the ice had converted into on the warm kitchen floor.

"I don't have to be a genius to figure out that you did not come straight home," she said sternly to Rosalia. "Did you stop at Annaleya's house to visit? Because you stayed way too long, young lady. Couldn't you have put the bag of fish – what kind did you get, by the way – in Frau Steinberger's cold closet until you left there?"

"I did not stop and visit with Annaleya at her house," Rosalia spat out the words like dirty crumbs. "We ran into cousin Daniel and Jacob Levy, they were rushing off somewhere, so we followed them. They went to the Neisse Bridge and talked to a Roma Frau, then Daniel put his hand on her…." Rosalia took a deep breath and tapped her own slightly budding chest.

"What is this? What is this?" wheezed Aunt Eva, chins shaking above her embroidered white collar. She often repeated herself.

"Then the husband threw him on the ground and almost killed him!"

By this time Dora had carefully placed bowls of hot chicken kreplach soup on the table and was calling Isaac, Rosalia's younger sister Edith and the boys to dinner. Jake came running in first and practically tipped his chair over in his eagerness to sit and eat. Henry followed behind and tried to imitate his older brother, as usual. Rosalia rolled her eyes at her two little brothers. They were becoming more annoying every day. Isaac returned to the kitchen table, wiping his hands on an old kerchief, and Edith followed behind, pulling her chestnut curls into a bun at the nape of her neck and working a wooden fastener through the bun as she sat complacently next to her sister. Rosalia sighed inwardly as she looked up at Edith and felt tinier than ever. Would she ever gain any height before she reached adulthood? Jake was almost catching up to her.

"Baruch ata Adonai," intoned Isaac somberly, starting off the mealtime prayer. That always settled the children down as they followed along in Hebrew. When it was time to eat, everybody began chattering at once as they scooped up the delectable chicken-stuffed dumplings and tasty broth. Great Aunt Eva kept looking over at Rosalia, shaking her head from side to side as if ponderous and weighty issues were tipping it to and fro. She would catch Rosalia's eyes and look at her quizzically. Finally, like a bird no longer able to suppress its squawk, she said to Rosalia,

"So, little Liebchen, why did you and Annaleya follow your cousin? What would possess you to do such a thing? Because now you've seen something you shouldn't have seen, and the whole town will find out about this. And you know his father, your Uncle Benjamin, will beat the daylights out of Daniel when he finds out."

"Rosalia is in love with Daniel, that's why!" Jake giggled, and Henry giggled along with him. Flashing him a dirty look, Rosalia retorted,

"Nothing could be further than the truth. I can't abide him! He's a devil, putting his hands on that Roma woman. And he lied to the Rabbi about it. I'm just sorry the husband didn't tan his hide until he couldn't sit down for a year!"

Jake and Henry stared at each other wide-eyed, then grinned and gaped at Rosalia like a pair of matching mechanical dolls.

"Now you've done it, Rosalia," scolded Dora. "The boys will tell their friends and it will be all over town. Jake, Henry, you must promise me and your father that you will not breathe a word of this in yeshiva."

The boys began eagerly spooning more chicken soup into their mouths, one spoonful after another. Dora sighed. Isaac said to them sternly,

"You children will keep quiet about this shameful thing for the honor of our families. Do you want to shame your Uncle Benjamin and Aunt Julia?"

Rosalia caught her brothers' eyes and stuck out her tongue at them.

"Ma! Rosalia stuck her tongue at us!"

Dora threw her hands up in the air and squeezed her cotton napkin in one clenched fist.

"Dinner is over for the kinder. Go to your rooms and let the grown-ups finish supper in peace."

Rosalia and Edith pushed away from the table clumsily, kissed Great Aunt Eva on her heavily powdered, wrinkled cheek, and decided to sit together in the garden behind the house. They each grabbed their embroidery hoops, thread and needles, and hurried outside to the weathered little pine bench that their father had painstakingly constructed long ago. A steady breeze shook the nearby pines and endowed them with whispery voices. The sky was dusky and on the verge of inky darkness, so they carried an oil lamp with them. Edith brushed a soft chestnut curl out of her face and tilted her head toward Rosalia as they sat down side-by-side.

"You know what you have done, don't you?"

"No, what are you talking about?"

"Don't play coy with me, Fraulein Wolfson. I am your sister. I can see right through you."

"Oh, you mean following Daniel? Rest assured, dear sister, I am not in love with our cousin. Nothing could be further from the truth. In fact, I suspect it is the reverse. I detest him." She couldn't bring herself to tell Edith about the kiss.

"I'm not considering the love or lack between you two. It's what you did tonight that I'm talking about. You told everybody at dinner what you saw, and you know how gossipy Great Aunt Eva is. She will tell all the ladies she knows, which is almost everybody in the Jewish quarter. It will get back to Uncle Benjamin and Aunt Julia, and…."

"Ya, ya, that's probably what will happen. And then," Rosalia was almost whispering now, "Daniel will get a beating. That's what he deserves." She narrowed her eyes at Edith and furrowed her brow. "I hope he gets a few beatings!"

"Well, you are just mean, little sister. I knew you had a temper, but now I see you have a mean streak too. I'd better steer clear of you from now on."

"Nien, nien, I have no mean streak. It's Daniel who is the mean one. And his creepy friend Jacob. I don't trust that one either. He kind of threatened me today, after sneaking up on me."

"Ach, then you'd better look over your shoulder, and often."

Rosalia glanced over her right shoulder, smirking, but it had gotten so dark as they sat and embroidered, with only the light of the oil lamp to light their work. She could see almost nothing but the faintest outlines of the walnut and apple trees bordering the garden. But she did hear something, a distant growl, a faraway crushing of dried leaves and pine needles on the forest floor that stretched beyond the streets of the Jewish quarter.

"A bear! Let's get in the house."

And both girls ran.

3

Winter roared into Gliewitz mercilessly, with snowbanks blocking doorways and icy wind cutting through leather coats, woolens and boots. Rosalia was in the barn, a thrown-together edifice the size of a lean-to, the chilly morning after her fourteenth birthday, cleaning the mess made by the four goats they owned. The he-goat, a bully in spotted brown and white fur, always scared her, lowering his sharp little horns and jabbing at her. His mate, a sweet white animal, had blessed the Wolfsons with two female kids, so they would have no lack of goat milk in the future. Trying to dodge Devil, Rosalia's nickname for the male, she picked through the hay with fingers shoved into an extra pair of her father's huge, torn work gloves, throwing into a pile the stones and thistles that the goats had shaken off their coats or dragged in and scooped out their droppings with a hand shovel. The barn door creaked slightly, and two figures slipped in. She heard movement behind her and assumed it to be Papa coming to milk the animals.

"Rosalia, come over here. I have something to tell you."

"Good morning."

She recognized her cousin Daniel's voice and then Jacob's. They were fifteen now and cockier than ever. Daniel, curly black frizz dancing across his head, nodded to her familiarly and smiled. *A strange smile, not friendly. What is he up to?*

Used to attention from boys, she shrugged and turned back to her task at hand. The only sound was the rustling of Rosalia's fingers as they combed through the hay. An occasional "ping" echoed faintly through the barn whenever she dropped a stone in a nearby tin bucket. The air of the barn was filled with the musty odors of goats and cows mixed with the sweet, grassy scent of hay. Then she heard the sound of footsteps coming toward her.

"Why aren't you in yeshiva today?" Rosalia finally asked, not looking at the boys. "My brothers went this morning, so I know you should be there too."

The boys shuffled closer to her. Daniel coughed and cleared his throat.

"We're taking a short cut."

Looking at the barn floor, Rosalia could see one scuffed brown shoe very close to her old gray work boot. She felt a small tingle of alarm run across her chest.

"What are you talking about, 'short cut'? Yeshiva is all the way on the other side of town. You're going to miss the whole class and the Rabbi will pull your ears."

She looked up exasperatedly at the two boys, swatting a large, buzzing black fly from her face. Jacob moved behind Rosalia and grabbed her around the waist. Daniel pulled her coat off in one quick motion, and Rosalia began struggling with them. Her dress billowed up in her face in a cloud of fabric like the wash blowing in the breeze on Mama's clothesline.

"What, are you crazy?" she shouted. But the boys ignored her shouts words that echoed in her own ears and bounced off the barn walls like a warning shot. She couldn't escape their grasp no matter how fiercely she shoved and kicked at them. Jacob held her from behind, her arms pinned at the small of her back. Daniel leaned over and buried his head in her chest. Now the tiny lavender flowers and leaves of her dress pattern backlit by a ray of sunlight were all she saw as Daniel's hand reached inside her bloomers. She felt the hand, warm and knuckled, rummage around and open up, all the fingers and thumb pressing against her thighs, then pulling down her bloomers and underpants. She felt his finger go where it shouldn't go, in the secret place between her legs that she knew must be saved for a husband, even though they didn't speak of those things in her family. Daniel's breath gusted into her ear like a strange animal exploring a cave. It made her stomach lurch as she squirmed to get away from him . Rosalia tried to hold the tears inside, but like a spray of milk from the cow's udder, they tumbled down her face, tickling her skin as they dripped. The boys snickered and shoved her onto the hay-strewn wooden floor of the barn, leaning their weight upon her until she felt she couldn't breathe.

The barn door creaked and squealed on its rusty hinges, and heavy bootsteps thudded, vibrating the planks underneath. The two boys leaped up, leaving Rosalia rumpled and sobbing in a heap, desperately pulling her dress down. They moved in two different directions, Daniel pushing back his brunette curls and then shoving his hands in his pants pockets.

"What is going on here?" bellowed Isaac as he strode toward his daughter's shuddering form on the floor.

"We are late for yeshiva, Uncle," Daniel called out as the boys fled, giving Isaac a wide berth and dashing out the barn door. They continued to run, legs pumping furiously and high leather shoes kicking up the dust and dirt of the yard beyond as Isaac stared angrily at their disappearing backs. He lumbered over to Rosalia, who had already stood up and was smoothing her work dress down, brushing off strands of hay in fluttery, nervous swipes. She patted at her hair, pulling tresses behind her ears, and kept her eyes peering down at her father's familiar, rugged dark boots.

"What did those boys do to you," Isaac whispered, fearful of the answer he might hear.

"They … pushed me down, that is all, father. I am fine."

"You don't look fine." Isaac's baggy, slate-gray eyes peered into Rosalia's jewel blue ones. "I know what boys can get up to. Why were they in my barn with you when they're supposed to be in yeshiva? If you don't tell me, I will find out from them."

"Oh, no, no, no father, please please," Rosalia stammered and cried at the same time, her azure eyes brilliant with tears. "I tell you, they pushed me down on the floor. I don't know why. I must go in the house and help Mama with dinner."

She tried to rush past her father, swinging far to the left and aiming for the welcoming light outside the barn door, but Isaac reached out his husky arm and grabbed her as quickly as a frog's tongue yanking an insect out of the skies. "You had better be telling me the truth, daughter."

He released her arm, and she rushed into the house, the rustling of her dress against her legs filling her ears, the fabric that had just been flung up over her head to expose her secret place. She hated the traitorous fabric, the treacherous garment. Suddenly she couldn't wait to tear it off and burn it and don a different dress. Would she ever feel innocent again? Rosalia tiptoed into the house and to the room she shared with her sister and sat in a corner shivering. Her mind roved like a wild dog, into the yeshiva where Daniel and Jacob would brag about what they had done to her, down the streets of the town where its inhabitants would be gossiping about her and the boys, between her legs where the travesty had occurred. She felt dirty, but not like the time she had fallen on cow manure in the meadow behind her house. This was not just cow dung on her skin and clothing, it was a filthy secret invading her interior and oozing outward. Would others see it?

Rosalia couldn't recall the rest of that day, except as a murky haze that seemed to follow her everywhere. She found herself seated at the dinner table with her family but couldn't remember how she had gotten there. A large wooden bowl filled with tzimmes was on the table, so she knew she must have helped Mama with dinner. Her parents were reciting the prayers, so she joined in robotically with her siblings. Then Mama began serving the tsimmes, brimming with potatoes, prunes, carrots and lamb. Everybody but Rosalia dug in heartily. She had no appetite. Isaac eyed her suspiciously.

"Rosela, eat! Or else you'll get sick and Mama will have to care for you. She has enough to do!"

Rosalia obediently placed a few morsels of carrot and potato in her mouth, chewed and swallowed.

"Excuse me, I don't feel well."

She walked slowly to her bedroom clutching her stomach and curled up on the bed. She stared out the window in the dark and knew that it was snowing now, even though the falling crystals were silent. They shimmered, tiny, in the weak light of the lantern Papa had left on outdoors. She pretended that she was a snowflake and had no other purpose in life but to melt away.

She awoke the next morning still on top of the bed. Edith was sound asleep next to her, but under the covers in her nightie. Rosalia realized with a start that she had fallen asleep in her day dress and was still in it. She breathed a soft sigh of relief that she had changed into a different dress after what had happened to her. Outside the tiny snowflakes had transformed into a raging snowstorm. She doubted that Papa would even try to ride the wagon to Chapwork in such inclement weather. Still, the donkey and hens had to be fed, the goats milked. She could hear her parents moving around in the kitchen, so she waited until she heard Papa go outside to the barn. Usually Edith and Rosalia took turns caring for the livestock, but on a day like today, Papa would do those chores. She was glad for the heavy snow, but she wondered how she could possibly not ever go into the barn again. Her chores took place there as well as in the house. She slid out of bed, brushed her hair and smoothed the wrinkles out of her yellow and white day dress, then tiptoed into the kitchen.

"Good morning, are you feeling better?" Mama asked.

"Yes, Mama. I'm fine."

"Papa tells me your cousin Daniel was in the barn yesterday and you say he pushed you down. When this rotten weather is gone, I'm going straight to Uncle Benjamin and Aunt Naomi to give them a piece of my mind. Where are their son's manners?"

"Please forget that it happened, Mama. Please."

"Well, I don't know why I should. Daniel will get the spanking he deserves from his father, even though he's fifteen already. If he's going to act like a child, he should be treated like one."

"Please, Mama. Don't go to Uncle Benjamin. It was nothing."

"If Mama doesn't go, then I will," Rosalia's father weighed in. "Oh, never mind, Dora. Benjamin and Naomi and the kinder are coming for Shabbos dinner next Friday anyway. We can tell them then."

"Papa, no, I beg of you. And that way you will ruin Shabbos evening."

"Rosalia's right about that, Isaac. We must wait until after Shabbos."

The week before Shabbos crawled for Rosalia, every day one day closer to the misery of seeing Daniel again. She decided to be very ill that day, take to bed and miss the Shabbos meal altogether. The snowstorm lasted three days and finally subsided on Thursday, which dashed Rosalia's hopes that Uncle Benjamin would keep his family home on Friday. Her cousin would be here in the house. But of course, they visited back and forth throughout the years. Did she think that would stop because of what had happened in the barn?

She woke up early on Friday morning and stared out the window. The sky was just lighting up with thin shafts of sunlight rising over the horizon. The snow that had painted the land white was melting and leaving behind its special gift of muddy pools and icy chunks. This wouldn't be enough to stop her cousin from coming to dinner tonight. As she moved around the bedroom gathering her dirty laundry to hand-wash now that they could go outside, Edith awoke with a yawn and a stretch.

"Gut Morgen, sis. I am so hungry! Eggs and buttered bread sound very nice right now."

Rosalia smiled briefly at her sister and said nothing. Her appetite had disappeared.

"Are you well? So quiet and not eating. We are all beginning to worry about you."

Rosalia shrugged and murmured, "I am fine, don't worry." Then a pause. "Actually, I am feeling a little bit sick. I woke up with a headache."

Edith jumped out of bed full of energy and ran into the kitchen. Rosalia could hear her telling Mama and Papa what she had just said and smiled inwardly. The first brick of her ruse to avoid dinner tonight was already being mortared into place by her gullible twelve-year old sister.

By dinnertime, Rosalia was firmly ensconced in bed with a cup of chicken broth on a tray. She dozed throughout the day and tried to fall back to sleep when Uncle Benjamin and Aunt Naomi called through the door, then entered with their younger son, Avram. It was easy to hear all the conversation in such a small house, so Rosalia listened with a tight chest and fluttery stomach. Hallos were exchanged and inquiries of the health of all family members. She heard Papa say,

"Rosalia is a little under the weather today, so she's staying in bed. Say, where's Daniel?"

"Maybe you didn't hear, but the rest of town seems to know. Our young man got into some bad mischief with the Roma people down by the bridge. We heard the story from Rabbi Yeshivatz. He got a good whipping last week, and is not allowed to come visiting with us until all this gossip dies down."

"These young ones...."

Rosalia stuffed her fingers in her ears to keep from listening to the voices in the kitchen. She was relieved that Daniel wasn't there, but it pained her that his parents and brother were in the house. The fragrance of Mama's cooking diffused the entire house, and Rosalia finally got her appetite back. Unfortunately, it was too late to get up and pretend a remarkable recovery. She would wait until her relatives left and then sneak into the kitchen for a bit of whatever was left on the counter. She took two small strips of cotton cloth from her sewing basket, twirled them into balls, and was just about to stuff them in her ears. Without warning her bedroom door swung open. Aunt Naomi and Uncle Benjamin stood in the doorway, both dark-haired, dark eyed, short and pudgy.

"Get better quickly, niece," whispered Aunt Naomi in her low, hoarse voice.

"We will tell Daniel that you missed dinner, just like he did," said Uncle Benjamin. "He likes you so much and is sorry that he couldn't come."

4

Winter finally gave way to spring, which was in full luster, dyeing the landscape a multitude of hues where there had been only a drab gray and white palette. The glittering snow melted, revealing rooftops and cathedral spires, pines and lilac bushes, cobblestone avenues and dirt roads throughout Gliewitz. The Wolfsons were feverish to spend more time outdoors than in, and without wearing the layers of wool and insulating undergarments that kept them warm in the winter. Still, there was a tremendous amount of work to be done on their little plot of land. They owned only one donkey, four hens and four goats, but the amount of manure the beasts produced in a day was astounding and had to be swept daily out of their little barn. The hens were laying more frequently now that the weather had warmed, and eggs had to be gathered every morning. The vegetable garden in back needed weeding and planting, and the manure had to be spread and dug into the soil to produce robust spinach, peas, carrots, potatoes, cabbage, and an assortment of herbs.

Rosalia prayed every day and night that Papa and Mama wouldn't demand to know why she avoided the barn. She pondered as she lay in bed when the others were sleeping, arranging and re-arranging her words to develop a myriad of excuses why to not enter the cursed structure.

Rosalia was pulling weeds, on her knees in an old, soiled day dress and even older scuffed boots when a shadow draped across her hand and the row of carrots she was working on. She glanced behind her and met Edith's glare.

"Do you think you are a princess? The boys and I have been cleaning out the animal stalls for months with no help from you. I don't understand why Papa allows you to get away with this."

"You can clean the dirty animal caca!" Rosalia hissed at her sister. "Or ask the boys to do it. That's where boys belong anyway. Up to their necks in caca!"

"I cannot bear your angry words," Edith responded, glaring with rounded copper brown eyes at her. "I'm going to tell Mama and Papa how you are speaking to me."

"Go shit in the river!" Rosalia hollered, red-faced. "I have no time to work in the barn. I have enough work, cooking with Mama and tending the garden. And you know I'm studying English every day now so that I can tutor and teach. I want to do more than marry and raise children."

Edith's eyes narrowed. She tossed her thick, dark curling tresses and firmly planted her hands on her hips.

"Nu? What is eating at you, Rosalia? You have been grouchier than a black bear in an outhouse." Their favorite expression. "You are worrying Mama and Papa, too. We all know you have a big temper, but none of us has seen you smile in a long time. You must tell me what is on your mind. What is bothering you?"

Edith's words crushed Rosalia with fear. She swallowed and looked down at her hands, roughened by farm work. She could no more articulate the attack upon her body and even more profoundly, upon her spirit, than sing a Torah passage. She glanced up again quickly, her sky-hued eyes moist.

"There is nothing bothering me. Except you, you lazy ganef! Stop stealing my clothes."

She turned her back to Edith to keep her from noticing the tear that was, unbidden, making its way down her cheek. Still, she couldn't prevent a tiny sob from welling up from her throat. She prayed that her sister hadn't heard it. She was on the verge of weeping but tightened her eyes and throat to keep the dam of taut muscles around them securely shut. She wasn't ready (would she ever be?) to reveal to her sister the profound revulsion she felt, not about the messy and malodorous donkey droppings, but about the barn itself. She seized a clay flower pot and hurled it against a nearby rock where it smashed and broke into several pieces. Edith's copper eyes widened with astonishment.

"Oy, you are in for it now, Rosie," she warned her sister, shaking her head and backing away. "Papa will punish you for this, no doubt. You cannot break everything we own to let us know you are angry!"

Rosalia shrugged haughtily, well aware that Edith's words were true. She would most definitely suffer castigation in some way for the breakage. But she didn't care, and in fact, wished it upon herself. Maybe punishment would somehow cleanse her, relieve her of the relentless dirtiness she felt inside.

The month of June ended, and the wealthier inhabitants of Gliewitz prepared to to depart for their summer visits to the northern Baltic seashore and the healing baths in the south of Germany. Rosalia's family only noticed the rise in temperature, the sunnier, longer days, and the garden harvest. Papa's salary at the Schmidt Brewery, although more generous than the earnings of their neighbors who were itinerant peddlers wandering the streets and nearby villages with their wares, could not afford a trip for the Wolfsons. While Rosalia ambled through town buying backache medicine for Papa from the apothecary, she gazed dreamily at the coaches and carriages of the wealthy rumbling across the cobblestones as their fine horses towed them to destinations she couldn't even imagine. She wished fervently that she could climb into one of those elaborately carved and transports outfitted with sleek, spirited steeds and leave this horrible little city. Once, not very long ago, she had loved her home; now it was a blight that she desperately wanted to flee. Despair building in her like a dark river current, she headed home with the valuable ointments, carefully tucking them into her knitted carrying bag to keep them safe and hidden.

At home, she saw Henry filling a bucket of water at the well pump with Jake dancing around him, taunting him in a singsong voice.

"You're the runt of the litter," he sang out teasingly. Rosalia knew he had just learned the word 'runt' after the cat, semi-feral but occasionally friendly, had given birth to a litter in the barn. Rosalia still hadn't seen the kittens, although everybody else in the family had gone to admire them as they suckled on their mother's teats.

Henry, older and stronger, but no less foolish, sloshed some of the water out of the bucket and soaked Jake's shoes and socks. Jake began to cry.

"Stupid, I hate you," he shouted at Henry, clenching his little fists and banging one of them on Henry's shoulder.

Rosalia was stunned. The boys seldom fought, so this was unusual. She lacked the spirit to admonish them. They could fight all day and still their lives would not be ruined like hers. Just then the boys looked up and saw her. They stared at her silently for a suspiciously long period of time. Rosalia grew uncomfortable, and then downright fearful. Had her brothers heard anything about her from their cousin at yeshiva? She didn't dare ask them. Jake suddenly shoved Henry, and the bucket flew out of his hands, spilling the contents on its trajectory to the ground. Just then Rosalia heard the back door creak open.

"Boys! Stop your rough play, fill that bucket and bring it to me now."

The door slammed shut. Averting her gaze from her brothers, she went in the front door and straight to her bedroom. The aromas of Mama's delicious brisket and potatoes infused every corner of the house, but they didn't appeal to Rosalia. Her stomach was clenching and spasming, and the little appetite she had built up disappeared as she thought about the possibility that Henry and Jake had heard about her shame in the barn. Why wouldn't boys talk? Girls did.

Dinner was another interminable stretch for Rosalia. Once again, she picked at her food and ate little.

"Shayna, you are going to disappear if you don't eat," murmured Dora, wagging her head like a davening rabbi. "I can see you have lost more weight, and you can't afford to. You barely fill out your clothes these days."

Rosalia, attempting to mollify her mother, stabbed at a small piece of brisket and shoved it in her mouth. She chewed it slowly and deliberately, trying to make it last.

"I know why Rosalia isn't eating," piped up Henry, large black eyes bright and piercing as he stared at his eldest sister.

"Why is that, boy-who-knows- everything?" asked Papa.

"I can't say," Henry almost whispered this time, shaking the ebony curls that framed his face and clearly regretting his original boast. Rosalia froze in her seat, staring at Henry for several seconds, and then looking down at her barely touched plate. Her mother and father, both bewildered, watched the two of them grow uncomfortably quiet.

"I, for one," growled Isaac, pressing his hammy hand to his thick chest, "want to know what is going on with you *kinder.*"

Dora nodded in agreement, and they both waited with wide eyes glued on Henry's face. Instead, Rosalia rose abruptly and announced,

"My stomach hurts, please excuse me. I must lie down for a little while."

She hurried to her bedroom before Isaac or Dora could protest. Her mind whirled with frightening clarity. As Rosalia had feared, Daniel and Jacob must have boasted to the boys in yeshiva about their attack on Rosalia in the barn. What else could explain Henry's behavior and words at the table? And if Henry had heard the story, no doubt every boy in yeshiva had heard it as well. She was not so naïve to imagine that the story would be confined to only the Hebrew and Torah students. It would infiltrate the ranks of older siblings, cousins, and finally the elders would get wind of it. If this were true, Daniel had unquestionably rendered her unmarriageable in the town of Gliewitz. Humiliated and horrified, Rosalia vomited on the floor the little dinner she had managed to swallow, and then continued to retch in great dry heaves. She knew that the entire family could hear this, as everything was audible through the thin walls of their little house, but there was nothing she could do to keep it silent. Dora rushed into the bedroom with a mop and pail with Edith close behind her. They both gaped at Rosalia's impossibly pale skin, and Dora exclaimed,

"You are sick! Oy vey, we will get you into bed after I clean this up. No, don't help, just rest there, I'll get it. Edith, get some rags to wipe up the floor and come back with some chamomile tea for your sister. What could you have? I hope nothing serious. Please, dear God, not the consumption."

They settled her into bed with the hand-quilted covers drawn to her chin. Rosalia was relieved to fool them this way. They could believe she was coming down with something and that way they all would forget Henry's declaration that he knew something about her. Rosalia saw Isaac peeking in on her from time to time, creases of consternation lining the little crescents of cheeks that thrust above his full, wolfish beard. Eventually she fell asleep despite the ugly, churning thoughts grinding through her mind.

In the morning, she saw that Papa had left her a stein of watered-down beer to slake her thirst and settle her stomach. Rosalia allowed herself to be pampered and tended to for several days, feigning dizziness and digestive pain. Her fine blond tresses remained unbrushed and in braids, little strands curled along the edges of her face bejeweled with perspiration. She stared at the ceiling when Isaac and Dora entered to check on her and she ignored Edith entirely. Her little brothers made no appearance at all, to her great relief. Finally, growing restless, she could feign illness no more.

"I am feeling much better now," she declared the afternoon of the fourth day after taking to bed. "I think I need to move around a little and eat something."

Dora smiled ecstatically to hear this.

"Thank God. I was just about to bring the doctor to the house."

Isaac had planned to slaughter several hens in the coop as payment, but instead only sent one to its untimely death and fate as broth in Dora's matzoh ball soup. After another day of recuperation, the four walls of her and Edith's bedroom were beginning to lean in on Rosalia. She was ready to go out into the fresh air and do some farm chores.

"Rosela dear, let us go together to the town square. I must buy some herring from the fish market. A walk will do you worlds of good," Dora insisted.

Arm in arm, Dora and Rosalia walked to town each with a knitted tote. Rosalia couldn't help but admire her mother's youthful looks despite the gray strands that striped her dark locks. Dora had grown chubby over the years of childbearing, but her smooth, unlined face remained as attractive as ever. When they reached the fish stand in its usual northeast corner of the town open-air market, they surveyed the fresh catch arrayed in lined nets that rested on wooden blocks.

Iridescent scales gleamed on river salmon from the Rhine, perch, pike, carp, and herring. The fish vendor, Morris Wiener, was wiping his sturdy fingers on his white apron. He caught Dora's eye and winked.

"Hello, Frau Wolfson. What can I get for you today?"

"How is the herring today, Mr. Wiener? Is it very fresh?"

"Caught this morning, Frau Wolfson. Couldn't be fresher. Same goes for the pike."

"Hmmm. Well then, give me five or six of the herring. That is all today, as we must also replace a broken candlestick."

Dora glanced behind her at Rosalia, who winced at the memory of flinging it. The fish vendor saw her at that moment and Rosalia suddenly noticed that his expression had subtly shifted from jovial to serious. His swarthy, tanned and wrinkled brow furrowed, and he stared at her face, then swept his eyes downward. He knows, she realized with a shock. She stepped back one pace and watched the town square whirl around her. Her mother, unaware of Wiener's ogling, seized her daughter's arm to support her.

"Rosalia has not been well this past week," she explained to him apologetically. "Let's go home right away, *shayna,* and back into bed."

But that was not all. In the next few weeks, Rosalia felt eyes upon her and whispers and murmurings when she passed neighbors. First it was just the schoolboys, and no adult paid attention to their frivolous chattering and tales. Then, some of the adult town members spoke in hushed tones, stopping suddenly when they caught sight of Rosalia walking into the town market or dry goods store. At first she thought it was her imagination, but then she took note of the fact that she didn't notice any such behavior when the passersby were German gentiles of the town. Of course not! Being Christian churchgoers, they wouldn't know who she was or hear the gossip that spread from Daniel and Jacob in *yeshiva* to their classmates and then to their families. However, it seemed that nobody had carried the tale to her parents. They were in the dark about the gossip, or certainly they would have confronted her with it.

One muggy afternoon as spring heated into summer, somebody knocked on the Wolfsons' front door. It was a Saturday, and most of the Jewish community were returning from Shabbos services at the synagogue. Rosalia was still alone in the house, having refused once again to attend services. No amount of persuasion or threats from Dora or Isaac could sway her. The knocking filled her with dread.

"Who is it?" she called out crossly.

"Rosalia, it's Annaleya. We haven't seen each other in so long, and I miss you. Please let me in."

Annaleya. She missed her dearest friend fiercely but was fearful of facing anybody in town by now. She struggled with the urge to order her friend to go away and leave her alone, but her loneliness and isolation had built up over the months and were too much to bear at this moment. She flung open the door, put her arms around Annaleya, and pulled her gently into the Wolfsons' parlor. Annaleya rolled her bright hazel eyes at Rosalia and the two girls sat together on the saggy brown sofa. Rosalia gazed fondly at her friend, taking in the familiar russet braids framing a rotund, rose-cheeked face and draped down the front of her pale green day dress. Annaleya was big-boned and tall for a girl, but still managed to retain a delicate femininity that Rosalia admired. They squeezed each other's hands.

"How are you feeling, little sparrow?" Annaleya's smile dissolved into a furrow of concern across her freckled forehead. Rosalia couldn't speak for a minute, not prepared to answer such a simple question asked by someone with whom she had once shared all her secrets. Finally, she forced herself to respond.

"Not so well, pretty swan. Things are not so good with me." Rosalia forced herself to hold back the well of tears that suddenly sprang to her eyes. Annaleya nodded her head, seeming to understand. But what did she know? Rosalia's heart thumped in fearful anticipation of her friend's next words.

"Roselah, there is talk about you. Ugly talk. I tell people it can't be true, but nobody listens to me."

A regatta of tears sailed down Rosalia's face. She was living a bad dream over and over, with no chance of waking up and discovering that her life was the same as before.

"I heard from my brother, who heard from Jacob Levy, your cousin Daniel's best friend. They are saying terrible things about you. Is this why you aren't coming to services? Your mama and papa tell everybody that you are sick and they don't know what it is. But I see that you aren't. Roselah, are you pregnant?"

Rosalia's eyes grew round with surprise, and she felt like the air had been knocked right out of her stomach. She could hardly breathe. Annaleya leaned forward and hugged her like a bear enveloping a little ragdoll. She whispered in Rosalia's ear,

"You can tell me anything. I will protect you with all my heart."

Rosalia finally caught her breath when Annaleya released her from her tender embrace. She frowned with anger, then looked sideways at Annaleya like a cat about to pounce on its prey. She began to say something, but suddenly couldn't help the smile that replaced her frown. The idea that she was pregnant was so far off, that she started giggling. Then she bent over and laughed, unable to stop. Annaleya gaped at her in disbelief, and then joined in the irresistible hilarity, although completely confused as to why. Just as quickly, Rosalia stopped laughing and began crying.

"Ach, you are making me crazy. Please tell me why these boys are telling tales about you. What happened? Or didn't happen?"

Rosalia spent several minutes composing herself, burst into another brief round of laughter, and calmed herself again. Then she inhaled deeply, shuddering a little, and told her friend exactly what had occurred that winter morning in the barn.

"Ari tells me that Daniel claims he violated you, and Jacob backs him up because he was there holding you down. They make it sound like you are no longer pure."

"Not completely violated, no. But they are right, I am no longer pure. Daniel put his hands on me where only the husband should. Do you understand?"

A brief nod.

Rosalia realized at that moment that in the telling and retelling, Daniel and Jacob had embellished the story until it became in their imaginations not just touching her private parts, but a rape. Daniel's false version had rendered his cousin unmarriageable. Was this his and Jacob's idea of revenge for the gypsy incident? Rosalia knew that she was now considered damaged goods and there was no future for her as a wife and mother in Gliewitz. Her ruination was complete, sealed like the names in the Book of Life.

5

As the last light of the sunset glowed on the horizon on the last Friday in August of 1858, the Wolfsons stood around the dinner table, which was covered with an elegant white linen cloth, an heirloom passed down from Dora's grandmother. The kitchen was close and warm, and a small brick stove in the corner glowed from within as the hot, reddened coals slowly winked out. They stood around the table and lit the two Shabbos candles flanking the challah plate in the center of the table, intoned the prayers and settled into the simple, hard-backed wooden chairs that Isaac had built long ago. The candles' flames cast flickering shadows that shafted the log walls of their home. A pale blue cotton napkin covered the ceremonial, braided loaf of challah bread tucked underneath. Dora, Rosalia and Edith solemnly recited the prayer over the candles. Isaac intoned the prayers over the wine and uncovered the glossy challah loaf.

"*Hamotzi lekhem min Ha'aretz,*" he spoke the ancient Hebrew prayer reverently, blessing the grain of the earth, the bread. Rosalia scowled, feeling ungrateful. When the prayer was finished, Isaac cut the bread and distributed equal pieces to each family member. At last they sat down noisily and chattered as they served themselves and one another the deliciously scented food that Mama had prepared.

After a few small bites of chopped goose liver, Rosalia once again pleaded an aching stomach and a headache. Dora sent her to her bedroom with a small bowl of beef barley broth. She could no longer bear to be in the company of her own family, shamed as she was by her memories and the gossip circulating about her in town. Despite her self-inflicted isolation, she left the door slightly ajar so that she could listen to the conversation. Every day she dreaded would be the day that somebody would reveal to her parents the gossip about her.

"The Prussian gentiles are as black-hearted as ever," she heard Isaac say. "Oy, they still get drunk and some are becoming more than mischievous, they are murdering Jews with little or no provocation. I was on my way home from work in the wagon with two silver candlesticks next to me in the flour bag. You remember, Mama, we borrowed them from Aunt Eva, I was bringing them back to her. A uniformed guard stops me on his huge white horse and calls out, 'Ugly Yid, what's in the bag?

"Oh no, Isaac, the candlesticks?"

"Don't interrupt, Dora. Let me finish. So I show him what's in the bag. He says, 'Give me those silver candlesticks and I won't run you through with my saber.' Then the other guard, just as shikker, reeking of hard liquor, leans forward and says, 'Let's just take the candlesticks and kill him. Then we have two treasures!' Both were in full military uniforms, one on a white horse, one on a black, as proud as King Wilhelm on his throne." He paused, Rosalia knew, for dramatic effect. That was his style. She could hear the mare outside stamping a hoof and shaking her reins, a muffled tramp and jingle coming through the thin walls.

"So what happened? What happened then!" clamored Jake and Henry.

"Well, my children, I say to the guards, 'Certainly, sirs. Take the candlesticks, I give them to you with pleasure. They are only silver plated, not solid silver. But if you want them, they are yours.' They then laughed and pointed their fingers at me. 'We don't need your junk,' they say. I bow respectfully and off they ride, bouncing their rear ends on their saddles. They still don't know that the candlesticks were indeed pure silver. And there's a lesson here, kinder."

There was silence for a moment. Rosalia tipped her head toward the kitchen to hear.

"You cannot figure out the lesson? The moral, such as it is? Henry?"

He stuttered, "N-n-n-o, Papa. I don't know. Oh, yes, I do. Save the spirits drinking for Shabbos and holidays."

"Ah, that is part of it, my wise child. The other part is…." Again a moment of silence. Papa loved to create suspense. "Don't let your actions be guided by pride. We defend ourselves from the Prussian soldiers with our humility and wiles, not our arrogance. Pride against pride, we will always lose. Remember that."

Henry grinned, his freckles widening across the plains of his cheeks. The two brothers giggled and shoved each other back and forth until Mama cried out, "Enough. You are driving me crazy, you two *shlemiels!*"

More laughter broke out around the table. Rosalia shut her eyes and pulled a sheet over her head as she listened to the banter of her family through the thin walls of her bedroom. Not very long ago she would have been at the table too, partaking of the food and listening to Papa's stories.

A knock at the front door stopped all the chatter, and Isaac called out nervously, "Who's there?" Henry and Jake began to cry and whimper a little, and Mama whispered, "Don't be silly, there are no soldiers going around knocking on our doors."

Rosalia heard the front door creak open slowly.

"Ah oh, oh dear," Isaac whispered loudly. "It's……" Pause. The silence was filled with Jake's whimpering.

"Cousin Avram! And looks like he's got a friend along, too."

Rosalia could hear her mother laughing with relief. A visit from a relative living in another town was considered a blessing, and it enlivened the family. She couldn't help but slip out of bed and peer into the parlor. Avram Steiner walked inside, long coat swinging against brown leather boots. She remembered visiting him and his wife, and seven children a few years ago in Oppein to the northeast. He looked much older now, lines creasing his long, narrow face and crisscrossing his forehead. To her surprise, a younger man followed behind. Rosalia could just catch a glimpse of his profile: short of stature, a cute, rounded nose, a strong jutting chin with a wisp of brunette beard. They disappeared into the kitchen.

"I apologize for interrupting Shabbos dinner, but the wagon broke down and we came into town much later than we expected." Avram was Mama's cousin on her father's side. She recalled Mama telling the family that she grew up playing with him in the nearby town of Oppein. Delightedly she said, "Please come, sit and eat with us. Who is your friend?"

"This is Carl Gersman. He is joining me on our travels. It's becoming more and more dangerous to travel alone. King Wilhelm's troops are drumming up stronger sentiment against Jews. They have attacked a number of peddlers traveling alone from one town to another." Avram shook his full head of frizzy umber hair and laughed bitterly, unsmiling. "As if we offer any competition for the rich Prussians. Carl is apprenticing with his father, the kosher butcher in Oppein. From time to time when that work is slow, he joins me to load the wagon with goods and sell what we can in the outlying towns."

"You are a young one," Rosalia heard her mother comment. "How old are you? Who are your parents?"

"Very nice to meet you, Fraulein Wolfson. I'm twenty-four. My mother is Esther Heller Gersman. My father is Dov Gersman."

Oy, Mama, always so nosy when a young man shows up. Rosalia tiptoed down the short hallway to the kitchen door, peering in from the side to escape detection.

Carl looked at Avram and then back to Dora, eyes lowered. *A little shy,* thought Rosalia. *That is nice. I like that.* She walked to the kitchen table, slowing her pace deliberately.

"Hello, Cousin Avram. It's so nice to see you again. How is your family?"

"My wife is well, but one of the children has the consumption. Our eight-year-old, Miriam. Please pray for her."

Isaac and Dora murmured their sympathies. Avram stared at Rosalia and smiled. Then Carl looked up at her just as she turned her gaze to him. His eyes were a deep oak that lorded over a smooth, sweet face peering out through the tufts of a youthful light brown beard and mustache. She was drawn to his lively, self-confident voice, his pleasant expression, the sparkle of intense interest in his eyes.

"Who is this lovely *sheyna*?" asked Avram, grinning at Rosalia. "Is this my little cousin Rosalia? You have grown almost into a woman. Last time I saw you, you were just a little girl playing dreidel."

Rosalia shrank from his gaze, and then glanced curiously at Carl, who at that moment was staring intently at her. As they regarded each other, there was silence around the table. The two then both stared down at the table in tandem.

"Look, Rosie is red in the face!" taunted Henry.

Without warning the memory of Daniel's attack sliced through the moment like Papa's sharp butcher knife, and she crumpled inside like a slaughtered calf.

"Sit, please, all of you," insisted Dora, gesturing to a rickety pine bench that Isaac had brought in for their guests from the woodshed. Rosalia slid into the chair that had remained empty since she left the table only minutes before. *It seems like hours.* Avram and Carl sat side by side on the bench that Dora had carefully positioned directly across from Rosalia. The dining table was now crowded to discomfort, and elbows were bumping each other.

"Listen, I have some news for you!" exclaimed Avram, smiling broadly. "Carl and I are going to the United States of America. We have both been saving our marks and pfennigs for three years or more. We will leave in three months, after we both have enough money to purchase passage on the steamship leaving the port of Hamburg. America is giving away land free, a law they passed called in English words, the Homestead Act. Lots of land! We are going to start a kosher butcher business, in a state called 'Arkansas'. Carl's brother Samuel owns a dry goods store and can employ us a little, help us get settled. Then when we are able, we will add a butcher shop to the back of his store. That way we draw in more customers for each other."

"Samuel wrote me a letter not long ago," interjected Carl. "There still is no kosher butcher in his little town. The Rabbi does it for now, but he would be happy for that job to be taken over by somebody else."

"Free land sounds like a dream come true," sighed Isaac. "But we hear a little bit the news from the United States, and things are not perfect there. People there are divided about slavery of the African people in the cotton plantations. I hear some are even talking of fighting over this. Do you really want to go at this time?"

"It's a chance we are both willing to take," Avram responded, glancing at Carl for affirmation. Carl nodded.

"We think they will somehow resolve this problem without fights. They are a people of a written Constitution that all must follow, not subject to the whims of a monarch as we are."

"Yes, a monarch who hates the Jews, and makes it worse for us than any others," added Dora. "Except the gypsies."

"People they call in English "pioneers" are still going westward to seek gold. That's not for us, but Samuel takes advantage of their gold fever and sells them the tools and dry goods they will need to get to the state of California, or wherever they want to settle down and live. Arkansas is a stopping point for the settlers, trappers and miners travelling west. And this is a place that holds no grudges against the Jews, and treats them fairly, so I hear. At least, compared to our own country. We will have freedom in Arkansas to observe our religious practices without threats and live anywhere we desire. We can send our kinder to schools and universities. We can even vote in an election for a president to lead us. This is a whole new way of life."

"What is the name of the town your brother lives in?" asked Rosalia, surprising herself by speaking up.

"It's called Hot Springs. Rich people go there from all over America and even Europe to soak in the curative spring waters. Samuel writes me that they also shop in his store. He is doing well," Carl answered her. She couldn't help but notice that his warm oaken eyes were taking in her features, roving subtly from brow to chin and then southward.

Avram pulled a small package out of his pocket and opened it, spreading out the contents for the Wolfsons to view. Small, dark rectangles the color of the earth lay against the white of Avram's linen wrapping.

"And what is this?" asked Isaac, gray eyes twinkling. "Dirt pastries?"

Ach, me first, I want to eat the dirt pastries," yelled Jake.

Dora admonished him, "Sit down, get your hands away from those things, and hush up, let Cousin Avram tell us."

Esther and Rosalia rolled their eyes at each other, united in the ongoing endurance of their youngest brother's outbursts.

"These little gems are known as 'chocolate,'" continued Avram. "The fruit, called a cocoa bean, comes from South America. Into the crushed and powdered bean goes butter, oil and sugar. The butter makes them dairy, so we cannot eat them at this meal with the beef. I have brought them for all of you to taste. In the finer cafes of Berlin and Hamburg, I hear they serve it melted, sweetened and hot in a drink called cocoa."

After profuse thanks from the Wolfsons and another hour or so of eating, drinking, discussion about the coming signs of war and Jewish diaspora in Europe, Rosalia and Edith cleared the table. Dora prepared a corner of the parlour with pillows and a blanket for the visitors to sleep on.

"You don't need covers on these warm August nights," Dora assured them, and the men nodded in agreement.

The next day, after a simple morning meal of Dora's fresh baked rye bread rolls with cherry marmalade and hard-boiled eggs, the Wolfsons were ready to taste this new and mysterious food. Each of them took a tiny piece, the boys shoving theirs eagerly into their mouths, and the sisters nibbling timidly on the edges of theirs. Dora and Isaac waited and watched for their children's reaction.

"Mmm," said Edith, "Chocolate is delicious. I've never tasted anything like it."

Rosalia nodded her agreement silently, peering at Carl and then looking away quickly when their eyes met. The chocolate slid down her throat like a caressing waterfall of sugar and sensuous, rich pleasure. The boys and Edith begged for more, which gave Dora and Isaac the courage to take a small bite. They chewed slowly and then smiled at the same time.

"So do you like these magical chocolates?" Avram queried his cousins. "Carl and I plan to import and sell them in Samuel's store. We both feel the same way, none of these chocolate delights would we offer for the goyim here in Germany. They don't treat us well enough to deserve the pleasure."

"Well, you know, Avram," said Isaac, pausing for emphasis, "Many Americans are German gentiles too."

"That is true, cousin. I believe that living shoulder-to-shoulder with people from many other countries, being treated equally by the government, will make us all equal. What an amazing idea! This is a land where we will be free. And eat chocolate."

"But what of the slaves?" Isaac asked. "We read about them in the newspapers. The owners of the slaves, of course, want to preserve slavery. They make big profit working those people they stole from Africa, yes? But there are Americans who oppose this way of making a fortune. And they are becoming more outspoken. What will you say about slavery when you get to America?"

"I will certainly keep my mouth shut when I first get there. It's foolish to stick out your neck when you don't even know where they're hiding the guillotine. How do I feel about it? It's wrong, we all know that deep in our guts." Avram patted his paunch.

Carl murmured, "Weren't our ancestors slaves in Egypt? Don't we celebrate being freed from that terrible bondage year after year on Passover? If we Jewish people don't object, we are hypocrites."

The hair on the back of Rosalia's neck tingled. She had a strong premonition that she was somehow connected to this conversation, to the strange and new country across the Atlantic Ocean, and at least to one of the men in the room.

6

Hot Springs, Arkansas
1859

A splintered, nag-drawn wagon jostled along the curving road lined with green ash and black gum trees striated by the golden afternoon rays of the sun. The Ouachita Mountains rose gently on either side of the road. Carl Gersman adroitly avoided the ruts, maneuvering the dray left and right as he guided the worn out, huffing beast. Large and small bundles in the bottom of the wagon jounced from side to side and sometimes skyward when the wheels rode a bump. He was heading into the town of Hot Springs, his final destination after a long journey across the ocean from Europe to the dense and bustling city of New York and then southeast. He reveled in the mild spring breeze that ruffled his hair hanging unkempt below his torn straw hat. He had to squint his eyes as he rode into the sunlight.

After changing marks for dollars in New York, he had journeyed by stagecoach over the Allegheny mountains, on the roughest roads he had ever traveled. He shared a bateau with a French fur trader down the Ohio River to the broad and murky Mississippi. At the mouth of the Arkansas River, he hopped off the Mississippi steamboat and boarded the Catawba, a steamer which brought him to Little Rock. There he purchased a pathetically thin, swayback white and black speckled mare (he couldn't afford the sturdy and reliable mules in town) and a rickety, well-used buck board cart, with half of his precious savings. He named the mare Vashti, a reference to a queen in the Book of Esther, his favorite story. He hoped to fatten her up a little once they settled in with his brother Samuel and his wife, Gussie. In the late winter of 1856, Samuel's parents, relatives and close family friends had scraped together some of their savings to buy him and Gussie a train ticket to the port of Hamburg, and another ticket to board a steamship for America. This was their wedding gift for them. Samuel was robust and muscular, and it was only a matter of time before Prussian officers would forcibly conscript him in the army. Carl hadn't seen Samuel since waving goodbye to him at the train station three years ago.

Today Carl was sniffing the fragrant pines and magnolias infusing the air and looking ahead at unfamiliar landscape as he drove the cart toward his final destination. Bird calls echoed through the treetops, some similar to those he had heard in the German forests, and others alien and unsettling.

A lanky yellow dog appeared on the roadside, tail hanging and ears low to the ground. Around the next curve stood a small tarpaper shack. Clothing hung on a rope line like fallen flags in the still air. More little shacks appeared and faces dimly appeared in windows glancing out at him as he rode by in the jangling cart. Barefoot children with stick-thin legs and dirty faces stopped running and playing in front of the hovels to stare. Then the road ducked into a narrow, flat valley flanked by wooded hillsides on both side of a very long main street that disappeared around a curve. Eventually, he arrived at the center of town. Men and women riding horseback or driving carts like his passed in both directions. A gangly, towheaded boy walked across the road with a bulging sack. *Potatoes,* Carl assessed with his peddler's eye. Buildings with signs over the doors were open for business.

"Hallo, good afternoon," Carl tipped his hat and greeted an elderly couple riding in a small black buggy beside him, using the little English he knew. They waved back at him and smiled.

He came to a hillside spewing thin streams of pale vapor from rushing streams of water. Were these the hot springs that the town was named after? Surrounding the small, wispy clouds of steam was a veritable village of small wooden houses and outbuildings, that appeared to his eye to have been hastily built. They adorned the hillside like odd, square plants blooming in tans and whites. Porches with long benches and chairs flanked the front door of many of these structures. They were rough and hand-hewn. However, two buildings stood proudly among them, large two-storied structures with carefully lettered signs. 'George & Weir Bathhouse,' Carl read as he rode by. 'Mitchell Bathhouse,' the other one proclaimed in black lettering on a white-painted board.

He could tell the mare was getting tired and thirsty by the way she shuddered slightly with every step and frothed at the corners of her tough, rubbery mouth. It was timely that he spotted a clean creek rolling along the main street. He pulled the beast over and watched her slurp up the creek water as if breathing air. Then they continued, following a small, creased and wrinkled hand-drawn map that his brother had mailed to him long ago.

He spotted Samuel in front of a small log cabin, tethering his own large, sturdy mule to a tree.

"Here I am, over here!" Carl shouted into the air as he approached Samuel, who looked up from his task and broke into a broad smile.

"Little brother, you are so big! Taller than me! Why did it take you so long to get here?" Samuel hollered back, even though they now were standing close enough to hear each other easily.

"The Ohio River, a demon in disguise, was trying to drag the paddleboat down to the bottom before I could make it to Little Rock."

Carl stopped the cart at the foot of the path that led to the house, jumped down and ran to grab his brother in a bear hug. They kissed on both cheeks and looked at each other, then hugged again.

"That's a beautiful mule you got there, brother. I bet he works hard and steady for you. Nobody in Oppein owns such a magnificent one. Life in America treats you well, nu?"

"The mules here are much stronger and of better stock than the horses, I'll warn you of that right away. Here in America is not a stroll in the Garden of Eden like it seemed back in Germany. Hard, hard work is in store for you. But you will notice more freedoms than you could ever dream of in Prussia." He paused and wiped away a tear. "Finally, mishpocheh has come to town for us. Kinfolk! But where is cousin Avram?"

Carl hung his head, a pain grabbing at his chest as he thought of Avram's last days on Earth. Samuel was expecting to greet him too, and then after a brief visit, Avram planned to continue on to New York and import specialty items to Samuel's dry goods store.

"Ach, my letter didn't get here soon enough. Sad to say, Avram died of consumption just a few months before our ship was to set sail, along with his daughter Miriam. He struggled with it for quite a while, and I had to stay away from him for fear of getting it too. I have traveled all this way alone."

Samuel pressed his thin lips together under a full dark brown mustache streaked with silver and looked down at the ground. Suddenly subdued, he murmured,

"We will say a Kaddish prayer for him at shul."

The brothers stood silently for a few minutes, heads hung down and shoulders drooping.

"This is a blow for us in many ways and even more so for his family. We will write to them and send them something from the store. Still, life must go on. Come inside and say hello to Gussie. You haven't seen her since our wedding in Oppein."

The brothers punched each other gently in the ribs, ducking their heads to wipe away tears. Once inside Samuel's little log cabin, Carl gazed at the smoky, pitch-dripped walls and carefully mounted brick hearth and stove that were the heart of the room. A pale-cheeked, chubby woman with thick dark tresses tied up in a bun stirred a pot of stew. The aroma of chicken, potatoes and onion infused the air and Carl's eyes teared up again. He hadn't smelled anything like that in his months of journeying. She turned and smiled at Carl.

"I yearn for a decent kosher dinner! I had to eat salt pork and sausage on the way over, trayf that we Jews shouldn't eat. But I was too hungry to say no, and there was nothing else."

"Hashem will forgive you," Gussie remarked. "We must keep living above all else. We wouldn't want you to starve to death before getting here."

Soon the family was gathered around an unpolished, rough-hewn oak table that evening with a steaming platter of chicken stew in front of them. Carl's eyes roved from wall to wall as Gussie served dinner. He looked down approvingly at the sawn and planed poplar floor, then around at the round log walls, and up at the lofty raftered ceiling. A small, elegant tapestry hung from a nail near the front door, likely a family heirloom from Gussie's grandparents. Steel hearth tools leaned against one another in a corner, coated with ash and soot. He reveled silently in the ambience of family and the warm dwelling that stood between their vulnerability and the wilderness.

Samuel recited the Hebrew prayer and Gussie served her husband and brother-in-law the warm, tasty meal. Carl looked down at his plate.

"What is this? Orange potatoes?"

Gussie tittered softly.

"Hah, brother Carl, those are sweet potatoes. Better get used to the color because you will see them in many dishes here. Lucky for us, the flavor is wonderful."

"Tell me about Mama and Papa, and all the family. You know I haven't seen them in a long time," sighed Samuel.

Carl smiled softly in recollection and scratched his neck.

"Papa is fine, still as strong and hard-working as the ass and dray he drives around the countryside. But Mama, she's …" he shook his head sadly. "I haven't seen them in four months, but Mama wasn't well when I left. She coughed day and night. She might have caught the consumption from cousin Avram, may his soul rest in peace. Our sisters are in good health, may they live long. Anna is to marry next year, the betrothal has been arranged with Joseph Goldfein, the cantor of our synagogue. It is a great honor."

A prolonged silence followed as they all brooded over Carl's sad news of their mother.

"Even so, with all that passed, what a heaven you have carved into the forest of this land!" Carl exclaimed. "And a beautiful wife. God bless Papa for making the arrangement with Gussie's parents. I dream of a family in a home on our own land."

"Do you have a maideleh in mind, Carl?" queried Gussie, tilting her head and brushing back a loose wavy lock of dark hair.

"As a matter of fact, I do."

"Tell us, brother, or I'll pester it out of you," warned Samuel.

"Her name is Rosalia, daughter of Isaac and Dora Wolfson. They live in Gliewitz, that small city with all the beer breweries not far from Oppein. She is only fourteen, beautiful, smart, but strangely, no marriage match had been successfully made by the shadchen there in town. Before I left for America, I spoke with her parents and we are betrothed now. But the price of a second-class ticket on a steamship is very steep, so they will send her here when they have saved enough money for the journey. They can't afford to send a companion with her either, so we don't want her in steerage. That would be risky according to accounts made by others who had to suffer traveling in what amounts to the boiler room of the ship."

"Mazel tov!" cried out Samuel and Gussie at the same time. Samuel asked him, "How long do you think before she can buy the ticket?"

"Her parents assured me that I wouldn't have to wait more than a year."

Carl tugged on his beard and smiled, eyelids half-closed. Then his eyes popped open.

"Oh, I have a question for you, and Mama and Papa want to know back home as well. People in Europe worry about the fight over slavery in this land. Do you think there will be a war between the slaveowners and the government?"

"Gussie and I don't approve of slavery. Our ancestors were slaves in Egypt, and that was cruel and wrong. Colored people, that's what the white goyim call them, are treated very badly. A white man can kill his slave and never have to answer for it. They separate mother from child and sell the child to another plantation owner. There are no plantations here in Hot Springs, they are found in the northern and eastern regions of Arkansas. Still, people in this town have slaves as personal servants, and it is not much better. Even a few of our more prosperous Jewish families have a personal slave or two. Fights and arguments are growing more intense between the abolitionists, who want to end slavery, and the slaveowners. From what I read in the latest newspapers, President Buchanan favors the slave owners. I see trouble ahead."

The candles burned down to the holders, and the smell of burning tallow made everyone wrinkle their noses. They all rose to go to bed. There was a bedroom down a short hallway for Samuel and Gussie, and a small horsehair mattress covered by a gray woolen blanket on the floor in front of the hearth for Carl. As he eased slowly down onto the mattress and stretched out, he felt like a prince in a castle. Compared to sleeping in his wagon or in the corner of a boat with his worn wool coat for a blanket, this was great luxury. The cool night air of April seeped through the front window slightly ajar and gently caressed his nostrils as he cozied into the bed. Carl peeked out the window with heavy-lidded eyes, exhausted, trying to spot a star or the moon. He saw two stars, large and brilliant in the jet-black sky. As he slid irresistibly into slumber, outside somewhere nearby the unrecognizable scream of an animal wandering the night raked his ears like a sharp claw.

The next morning, Carl awoke to the aroma of coffee and eggs with onions. Over breakfast, the brothers discussed land for Carl to build on. Samuel had been able to purchase the land from the government at a dollar an acre soon after he arrived.

"It would have been twenty-five cents an acre if President Buchanan hadn't vetoed some kind of law from Congress. Instead, all our savings are gone buying the land, but it is worth it. Now nobody can throw my family off our own land! We have a deed and it is recorded by County Clerk. We'll fence off an acre of my land for you, and you can pay me the dollar when you have it. Or you can even work it off at the store. So what is family for?"

Carl longed to tell his brother how his heart felt like it was bursting through his shirt and his head was swimming with joy, but he couldn't speak. Instead, he grabbed Samuel and gave him a tight hug, just like a bear might give her cub. Samuel pushed him away.

"Don't get sentimental on me, little brother. I'll tie your bootlaces together and watch you trip. Besides, we have work to do. Let's take a walk around the six acres. We'll find the perfect acre for you to build your house on. Then we'll draw up a deed."

Carl found his wide-brimmed straw hat among his pile of possessions in the corner of the cabin. He put it on and then tipped it politely to Gussie, who was scouring the breakfast dishes in a tin pan full of soapy water.

"Gussie, you are the cook of my dreams. Thank you for the best breakfast I have had since I left the Old Country. May I never lay eyes upon it again."

She smiled briefly. Could Carl be imagining the tension that trembled at the edges of her mouth? As the brothers left the house, Carl caught from the corner of his eye the sight of a scowl on Gussie's face. Was it directed towards him or Samuel? Or both of them? He couldn't tell.

7

When she had a brief moment of leisure time between day-long chores and dinnertime, Rosalia loved to hunt for insects in the garden. She discovered that beetles of all varieties tended to hide on the undersides of leaves. Flipping them over, she would delight at surprising the tiny round or long black and brown bumps with wings and waving antennae, then she would shake them to the ground. Imbued with curiosity but not destructiveness, she would poke at them delicately with a twig until they flew or crawled away.

Sometimes her friend Annaleya would join her. They would inspect the bushes for damselflies, firebugs, leaf beetles, and bugs they couldn't name on warm summer nights, huddling like a pair of bear cubs teaming up to pounce on their next hapless victim. When the sun began to slide behind the distant hills to the west, their mothers would call to them to come in and help prepare the evening meal. They would jump up and wave goodbye, Rosalia's blonde waves streaming and Annaleya's carrot-hued braid bouncing as they parted and ran home.

After the assault in the barn, and the vicious and inaccurate stories circulated about it, Annaleya was forbidden to play with her. The days and months stretched before Rosalia in a kind of solitude that both soothed and frightened her.

She felt protected, drawn into an intangible cave where nobody demanded explanations. In her dreams, the tiny insects she hunted were now hunting her. Her thoughts were tangled up in the veined wings and undulating thoraxes, the multi-faceted little eyes and waving legs, of those creatures she used to delight in. She wondered why they would not leave her alone. The shadowy grotto had become a home for her mental meanderings. Rarely did she leave the darkness of it, and even more rarely did she leave her house. Even as she toiled alongside her mother and sister, ripping and resewing hems, tatting lace, mixing batter for the Rosh Hashanah honey cake, rounding up the goats, her mind was not present to her family members.

One icy winter night Rosalia heard her father come in and stamp his boots on the little shmatte rag at the front door. In earlier days she always ran to greet him, but not lately. She hung her head over the potato soup and wished that she were invisible. His footsteps thudded and creaked across the bare floor of the sitting room. Then she felt and smelled his breath directly behind her, very close.

"Good evening, Papa," she mumbled, sniffing at the potato soup as if too engrossed in its progress to look up.

"Rosalia, my daughter, we must talk. And, though it breaks my heart into pieces, Mama must hear this also."

Her heart began to hammer against her chest. She tried to will herself to faint, but that didn't happen. Had her father caught wind of the gossip about her and Daniel? She shrugged her shoulders at him, as if there could be nothing of importance they could possibly discuss about her, an insignificant girl.

"Now, Rosela," he commanded her in a stern voice.

Scowling, she joined both parents in the sitting room. The boys, tumbling about on the floor, were ordered into their bedroom, the loft above the kitchen. Edith was placed in charge of tending the soup and tzimmes for dinner.

"I heard a very ugly tale about you from Frau Dovkin, the neighbor. She actually stopped me to ask if I knew about you and your cousin Daniel. That many others had heard he was boasting of violating you. I do not know how to say it nicely. And I'm sorry you must hear the word. Is this true?"

Dora's face flamed red, even her ears and neck.

"Isaac, you know what a horrible gossip Sara Dovkin is! How dare she say such things about our daughter? Why would you even listen to her? Why, I'll march over there now in the cold and dark to tell her what is what!"

Rosalia couldn't look at either of her parents. Instead, she stared hard at her hands clenched together in the lap of her dun wash dress. There was a brief silence, and then she decided that she must draw courage and speak.

"Papa, Frau Dovkin is both right and wrong about this."

"Don't speak in riddles to me, just tell me the truth," Isaac retorted crossly.

"What I mean is this. Do you remember when you found us – Daniel and his friend Jacob and me – in the barn a few months ago?" Isaac nodded mutely. "Daniel did not vio … violate me," she stammered. "He did put his hands upon me." She couldn't go on.

Mama was tearing up now, she could see the gleaming of it in her dark eyes. "What do you mean? You are still a virgin, yes? But still, where did he touch you."

Rosalia cast her eyes down again, too embarrassed to describe what had been done to her aloud to her parents. She sensed in their tense and pained expressions that they had already figured it out.

"I will kill the boy, and make his parents pay," murmured Isaac in a quiet fury.

"No, you will do no such thing. They are our relatives. My own sister's son. All the more shocking to hear this. We must talk to them, and then make sure to protect Rosalia from him at all times. It will be difficult, but the boy brought this upon the families with his vulgar behavior."

"You realize that no shadchen in town will help us to arrange a marriage for her, don't you?"

Dora smiled her implacable smile, the one she saved, Rosalia had noticed, for situations that seemed impossible to resolve. The *shadchen,* the matchmaker, ruled the roost of marriageable girls and paid attention to the gossip in town.

"We will figure something out," she said.

One night late in the autumn of 1860, Isaac had just gotten home from work smelling of hops and yeast as usual from the long workday spent among the vats of beer that he loaded onto wagons for transport to other towns. Sometimes he delivered hundreds of bottles to a nearby city, hooking a company wagon to a mule and hauling them lonely miles at a time. There was talk of a railway line that would be built through Gliewitz in the future, but who knew when? Until then, he would plod along with the horses and the boxes of beer buttressed against one another with ample cotton padding to keep them from breaking.

As Isaac, Dora and the children slid into seats and paused to pray before Dora piled her sumptuous beef stew and sauerkraut onto their plates, Isaac cleared his throat and announced, "I have important news to tell all of you."

The boys cleared their throats in mimicry and stroked invisible beards, bonking their heads together and then yelling, "Ouch!" in unison. Edith and Rosalia glared at them impatiently.

"I wrote to Carl Gersman in America and he answered us. Rosalia will go there to marry him." He proudly flourished a crumpled letter from his back pocket and waved it in the air. "My darling daughter, you will soon be in an exciting new land. I think the travel and marriage will heal you."

Rosalia felt her cheeks heat up like two beeswax candles aflame. Papa was wise, but would his prediction come to pass? Would her mind be healed by an unknown future fraught with perils? Halfway through a bite of stew, she dropped her fork into the plate and stared wide-eyed at her father. She heard that Mama and Papa had approached several different shadchens in Gliewitz to make a match, but nothing had come of their efforts. This had only added more grist for the gossip mill. She tried to recall the face of Carl Gersman, whom she had seen only once, long ago at the dinner table. His features were unclear and generalized in her memory, but she did remember that he had looked handsome to her, and she was pleased to think of him as her future husband. He wasn't an older man with whiskers and gray-flecked hair like Moises Klein, the glassworker, who had married Annaleya just last spring. There must be twenty-five years difference in age between them, but only eleven between her and Carl.

The boys and Edith gazed at Rosalia with wide eyes, making her feel like a royal princess.

"You're going to America? I want to go too!" yelled Henry.

"Hush, you are too loud, Heinie," Dora admonished him. "One child leaving is all I could take. You're not going anywhere. Besides, Rosalia must wait until next spring to travel when the weather is clear and safe."

Henry pouted and then shoved Jake. Rosalia watched them and realized at that moment that she would probably never see her family again. Her life would begin anew in a distant country, a wild country with – what did they call them? – "Indians". Fear gripped at her stomach, but fascination tantalized her mind. She struggled to reconcile all the emotions and thoughts that tumbled about like the foaming rapids of a river.

"Do I have a choice?" Rosalia almost whispered. "I have no future here. I might as well leave."

A wave of fury arose within her at the injustice of the situation. Daniel should be the one to leave his family and friends, not her. She lifted her face and stared angrily at her mother and father, and then banged her fist on the table, making every dish, bowl and utensil on it jump. She opened her mouth to speak, and then closed it again, realizing the futility of any words she could possibly say. She actually felt better than she had since the day she walked out of the barn in shock. Her protective, chilling little cave was receding, giving way to an odd commingling of outrage and excitement.

That night Rosalia and Edith whispered together for a full hour in bed together. Rosalia could see that her younger sister was delighted to have her to speak with again.

"You are going to sail on a steamboat!" Edith hissed to keep their parents from hearing their conversation. "You will see America, and the *goyim* there, and the black-skinned people who are slaves, and the brown-skinned people who are Indians. Will there be many other Jews where you are going?"

"I don't know," murmured Rosalia back. "There must be some. And there must be a Rabbi, or who will marry me and Carl? Papa must write a formal letter of acceptance to this marriage arrangement. Maybe he can ask Carl in the letter."

"Do they have lions there?"

"No, silly, lions are in Africa. But I think they have mountain lions, smaller but also very fierce. And bears living in the woods, the same as here."

"Then you must learn to shoot a rifle to protect yourself. Here we are not allowed except for the boys that go into the military. Oh, I will miss you so much, and I will come to visit you one day when I am older. I promise."

"And I will miss you. And Annaleya." She grew teary thinking of living the rest of her life without being able to reunite with her dear friend.

They continued to whisper fears, reassurances, expectations, promises, until their eyelids drooped shut against their will and they fell asleep.

Rosalia awoke early the next morning, and slipped quietly out of bed, careful not to awaken her sister. She changed quickly from her muslin nightgown into a presentable cotton day frock and prayed fervently that Mama wouldn't demand a multitude of chores that day. She had an errand to run in town and had to gather up the bravery to be seen in public regardless of how people behaved toward her.

Dora was up and working in the kitchen before anyone else arose, taking plates out of the cabinets and ingredients from the cupboards to prepare breakfast. A pile of fresh eggs from the hen coop was already piled on a towel, ready to be fried. Apples, cored and peeled, were bubbling softly in a pan over the stove fire.

"Well, well, you are up very early this morning," exclaimed Mama as Rosalia entered the kitchen. "And you might as well get used to it. You will be preparing meals for a husband and children soon enough."

Rosalia reddened slightly at the thought.

"Would you like me to pick up something in town, Mama? I can do chores when I return."

Dora gave her instructions for several shops that she needed to visit, with a list of items to purchase. Rosalia combed her hair and then braided it into a long plait. Like a tawny lion's tail, it fell below the brimmed hat she put on for trips to town. It wasn't more than a two-mile walk to the center of Gliewitz, past the brickyard, the shingle factory, one of many printing houses, and the brewery where Papa worked. A dancing breeze batted at the lines of laundry drying outside apartment windows and played with her hat. Old men with long white beards played chess at tables set outside cafes. Women and girls walked purposefully in and out of stores with bulging cotton bags. The center of town was the rare venue where Jews mingled with gentiles. At last she spotted Hamstadt's Books, a street-level store next to a bakery in a five-story brick building. The four levels above were taken up by modest apartments.

Rosalia was entranced by the bookstore whenever she entered it. She yearned to become educated enough to read any book on the shelf, to learn and understand the contents. Bernd Hamstadt, the bookstore owner, had lent her two books in exchange for a bottle of Schmidt lager that she had wheedled out of her father. She had struggled through Jane Austen's *Pride and Prejudice,* translated into German, and then read it twice more. It had taken her a very long time, but she welcomed the escape into another world where she was looking in on the lives of others that were completely different from hers and were so enchanting. Still, she noted, the elegant ladies had their problems with the men.

She had also tackled a German translation of *Moby Dick* and found it too difficult. Nonetheless, she refused to give up and read it to the end in a state of confusion. Jewish girls were not formally schooled, but they were given a modicum of education by private tutors if the family could afford it. She knew there were changes afoot in Prussian society, that rules were being eased and laws being changed for the better, albeit slowly. She intuited that there would come a time in the future when a formal education would be available to all girls, and when that time came, she wanted to be at the head of the classroom instructing them.

The bookstore had a section of books in English, but as Rosalia leafed through them, she knew they were too difficult for her. Bernd Hamstadt, the German bookstore owner, recognized Rosalia and strode over on long, lanky legs.

"Hello, tiny fraulein of my heart," he said with a soft smile. "I have not seen you in my store for a very long time."

Rosalia was aware that Bernd was attracted to her. Because he was a Christian living in a distant neighborhood, he hadn't heard a word about her sullied reputation. He was married to a young German woman from Dusseldorf and now they had a newborn son. Despite his burgeoning family, he appeared to still harbor great attraction for Rosalia.

"Herr Hamstadt, do you have a good book that teaches English?"

He guided her to a section of language books and pulled a thin volume from the shelf.

"This is a very good primer; I have one at home and am learning a little English myself. I predict the United States will be doing more business with Europe, and I want to be ready for it. But you, fraulein? Why would you want to learn English?"

Several patrons standing nearby leaned closer to the pair to catch the answer. They might have some spirited town gossip to share at the dinner table that night.

"I am going to America. There I will marry a man who is betrothed to me, and there will be my new home."

Both Bernd and the eavesdroppers made astonished noises, clucking and swaying their heads. Rosalia turned her head slightly, and from the periphery of her view spotted the other customers. She realized instantly that the news would be all over town and regretted her indiscretion. She should have invented a story to explain her sudden interest in English, but it was too late now. *Oy, what does it matter now? Soon I will be gone from here, and I will never see Gliewitz again.* She paid for the English instruction book and hurriedly left the store. Her light brown woolen shawl flapped about her shoulders in a brisk wind as she kept her gaze on the street ahead, looking neither left nor right.

The winter months of 1860 brought deep snow to Gliewitz, and there were days so brutally raw and harsh with biting winds and blizzards that the town businesses, industries and schools ground to a halt until the storms abated. Rosalia spent most of those days curled up with her English book once she had finished her chores and housewifery lessons for the day. Her mother was instructing her in embroidery for her trousseau and cooking for the Pesach Seder and the high holy days. Although she knew much of the cooking from watching and assisting her mother in the cramped kitchen, Dora wanted to show her certain herbs, spices, and cooking steps and techniques that she didn't know yet: how to enhance the chicken broth for the matzoh ball soup, bring a fluffy texture to the gefilte fish, blend the horseradish with a dab of cream, spicy enough to bring tears but not so burning hot that it is inedible. The entire household was abuzz with the prospect of Rosalia leaving them to marry a pioneer in America. This was the primary topic of discussion in their friends' and acquaintances' homes throughout the town while the furious wintry weather whipped into a frenzy outside.

In late February, Dora peered out the front door excitedly as she and her neighbors watched the familiar chestnut roan mail horse snort through light snowflakes and shake his dark mane, towing the delivery wagon along the narrow street towards the Wolfsons' house. The postman hopped out and handed Dora a letter. Despite the gelid temperature, several neighbors slipped out of their homes and were gathering around the wagon at a polite distance. A mail delivery was a community event in Gliewitz.

"Could it be a letter from Rosalia's intended in America?" muttered Frau Kohlmann loudly enough for the group to overhear, her plump double chin bobbing above the thick knitted wool scarf that buffered her from the elements.

"Most likely a love letter," sneered Frau Dovkin, "Or perhaps the man had a change of heart." She was thin, pale and always deeply disappointed that her two daughters still were not married. Both of those matches had been ruined when the intended husbands were conscripted into the Prussian army and taken away late in the night last year. Dora shook her head in disgust at Frau Dovkin but said nothing.

"Ach yes." "Oy, maybe so." "What else could it be?" The inquisitive crowd nodded sagaciously, shivering and murmuring to one another.

Meanwhile, Dora accepted the letter, thanked the postman graciously for doing his job in such frigid conditions, slipped him a bottle of Schmidt ale and shut the door quickly. She turned the letter over and over in her trembling hands. The return address was from Carl Gersman in Hot Springs, Arkansas. After a few quiet moments of prayer, she forced her footsteps to Rosalia and Edith's bedroom door and tapped hesitantly, then peeked in.

"Roselah, please come out, there is a letter from America for you."

Rosalia had been bundled in bed with a knitted wool shawl around her shoulders, studying English as she had been doing for the past several months as often as she could find some free time. Her mother knew that she was applying herself diligently to this task and seldom disturbed her moments with the English primer. Now she heard through the door her name and the word 'America'. Edith was sitting on the end of the bed knitting, and both girls immediately jumped up and flung open the bedroom door. Dora stood before them with the valuable missive extended.

"You are going to be a married woman soon, so you can open your own letter," Dora said proudly to her daughter. Rosalia tore open the letter and read it eagerly with her mother and sister looking on:

17 October 1859

Dearest Rosalia,

May G-d give you good health. I just recovered from grippe and a fearsome fever. I credit my rapid restoration to the thought of you coming to Hot Springs to be my wife, along with herbs and witch hazel that the people here use for illness. These days I must stay with my brother Samuel and his wife Gussie.

Please be reassured that there is a congregation, although no temple yet. That will come later, we all believe. For now, Rabbi Schechter holds services in the parlor of his house.

Rosalia glanced up from the writing as Edith leaned in to read with her and Dora said, "So? What, what is he writing to you? Tell us."

"Let me finish!" Rosalia yelled in frustration. She glared at her mother and continued reading, this time aloud.

My parents are happy to hear that at last I am getting married, and that you are to be my bride. My parents approve and so does my big brother here in Hot Springs. Please, I ask you, if at all possible, to call on them and meet them in Oppein before you board the Atlantic steamship in Hamburg.

Please tell your mother and father that Simon and Rosa Meyer will meet you in the Port of New Orleans, Louisiana, when you arrive from Hamburg. You can stay with them while you all prepare to take a stagecoach (this is what they are called in America) to Little Rock. They are good, observant Jews and trustworthy. I do not want you travelling alone in our new country, which has civilized cities and towns, yes, but also wilderness and untrustworthy fellows wandering through, looking for mischief and trouble to make. I do not want you to fear coming here, but at the same time, we must act with caution in a place that we did not grow up in and still know little about.

I am glad that the shadchen and your mother and father wrote to arrange a marriage between us. I am dreaming of the time that you arrive, and hope that you feel the same way even though you must leave your family and homeland. I beg your forgiveness in this regretful circumstance. May you learn to love Hot Springs in the future as much as you love Gliewitz now.

I pray that G-d protects and keeps you and your family well.
Your Betrothed,
Carl Gersman

Dora observed Rosalia's hand trembling slightly as she read the final paragraph of the missive. She sensed intuitively just how wrong Carl was about Rosalia's feelings for Gliewitz.

"You will visit Carl's parents as soon as the weather improves," Dora said importantly when Rosalia stopped reading. "Your father and I will help you make travel plans."

The next day Rosalia was up early and on her way through the stinging cold morning air to the bookstore, clutching her English text. Herr Hamstadt had promised to practice English with her, and he was the best English speaker she knew. They practiced in a rear corner of the bookstore sitting in two fancifully-carved, high-backed Biedemeier chairs. He corrected her grammatical errors and encouraged her to practice the new vocabulary of each unit, which had lists and lists of words of various categories. This day she was applying to memory a long row of verbs.

"It is hard to imagine this town without you in it" sighed Hamstadt, lapsing into German. "My heart is lighter when I see you come marching in here."

Rosalia answered him in English, "The boat … no, I think it is a steamship, a special, huge boat, yes? The steamship will carry me into the United States of America. I will not to see you again."

"No, Rosalia, you made a mistake. I will not see you, there is no "to" after "I will not"."

"Ach, so confusing. Will I ever learn this complicated language? Here you say "to", there you don't say "to", and I make no sense of it." She had lapsed back into German with a frustrated sigh.

"Don't give up, liebchen. You are speaking very well and you are an intelligent fraulein."

Suddenly he leaned forward and kissed her lips. Rosalia gasped and stood up quickly. Hamstadt smiled at her as she stared at him, dropping her English textbook to the floor.

"I am betrothed, and you treat me like this? You should be ashamed."

She left the shop hastily but knew it was too late when she glimpsed the reflection of Frau Dovkin in the front window-pane of the bookstore. Frau Dovkin had seen the kiss. What was she doing in front of the bookstore? Had she followed her? Rosalia rushed past her, cheeks ablaze and braid flying behind her. She felt mortified and blameful of herself for not having foreseen this possibility. She should have looked behind her on her way over. Moreover, she knew that Herr Hamstadt was fond of her. She shouldn't have placed herself in a situation where they were alone together in close proximity. *Shame on you, Rosalia. You are dirty, damaged goods and he knows it. Frau Dovkin knows it. Everybody knows it.* Warm tears suddenly streaked down her cold, bright pink cheeks. She couldn't wait to leave Gliewitz. Thank Heaven Carl did not know about her tarnished reputation. Hopefully, he never would.

8

Hot Springs
1859

Samuel came to help his brother whenever he could take time from his dry goods store. Carl knew that Samuel's building skills were far superior to his. They had learned from scratch in their hometown constructing simple outdoor structures: the typical small barn, chicken coop, outhouse and so on. However, Samuel had built his own cabin with the aid of an able local carpenter, John Crabtree, who had taught him secrets of the trade from the foundation to the roof.

On a mild August morning, the brothers began cutting down trees, both to create a clearing for the cabin, and to provide for its logs. Samuel brought a two-man crosscut saw from his store inventory. They stood at each end of the wide, sharp-toothed tool and worked back and forth together, pulling and pushing as the slash through the trunk of an oak grew deeper and deeper. Their coordinated action reminded Carl of their horseplay together as children, pushing and shoving, pushing and shoving. He couldn't help but grin at the memory.

Although he savored the scents and bright noises of his brother's family, he lived apologetically from day to day, feeling like an intruder. He struggled with the envy that rose up like a distant wave cutting through his heart. The dream of a rosy-cheeked, industrious Jewish wife and children to love and raise seemed far from being possible when he took inventory of his life. He thought about Rosalia Wolfson back in Gliewitz, her enchanting cornflower eyes gleaming at him across the Shabbat dinner feast he had shared with her family. Even though they were betrothed, she was far from here, and Carl now knew what it would take for her to travel this distance, particularly if she journeyed alone. The perils that would face her made him shudder. Purchasing tickets in a foreign currency, speaking and understanding English, boarding the correct transportation, adjusting to the new foods, and the loneliness had taken its toll on him. She would have to tolerate all of this and more as an unaccompanied woman. He prayed that somebody, an older woman or perhaps a male cousin who could protect her, would travel with her.

Some of the other Jewish immigrants in town pitched in to help Carl build his home as time allowed them, arriving with hammers, saws, shovels, and square-headed nails. They would hop down from their drays, tie up their mares or mules, and shake Carl's hand with great enthusiasm as they circled the land to view his progress. They taught Carl building skills that he hadn't yet acquired. His knowledge of building was limited to the small animal shelters and outhouse he had helped his father with in Oppein. Carl had already met many of them at the home of Rabbi Jacob Schechter, a tiny, slender man with a massive light brown beard and matching mustache, for Friday evening and Saturday morning Shabbos services. Most of them were from somewhere in Prussia, but few of them had been born and raised in Oppein, Carl's hometown. Nor was anybody from Gliewitz, he had discovered over time. This would be disappointing for Rosalia, and he had ached for her, knowing the homesickness that she would inevitably endure.

Abner Fleishner, a short, bald and stocky neighbor to the north of Samuel's six acres, came often in the mornings to share the hard labor of pit sawing. Carl, younger and stronger, would grab the crosscut saw from below and Abner would push from above. They both donned large-brimmed straw hats to keep the sawdust from flying into their faces as they serrated through the poplar log balanced on two makeshift sawhorses. Talking was impossible, as the sawdust would fly into their open mouths. After four or five hours of steady sawing and planing the logs smooth, they would stop for a brief lunch, the two of them sitting on large, flat rocks or logs on the ground, legs stretched out. Then Abner would leave to tend to his own affairs, giving Carl an affectionate pat on the shoulder and a wave as he left. By early winter they had finished pit sawing all the logs and were now gauging and undercutting the floorboards.

The Stern brothers came once or twice a week, whenever they could get away from their clothing store for a few hours. There were three of them, twins and an older brother, all in their twenties like him, dark-skinned, tall and muscular. They would help with the foundation since they had those skills Carl was lacking, laying joists evenly on top of wooden blocks. They excavated and poured a foundation, used the fallen timber of walnut and oak trees, fashioning logs to set one upon the other for the walls of his new cabin. Carl wanted his new home to be elevated so that it would stay dry during winter storms and freer from insects and vermin. He couldn't afford the high-class building foundations that wealthy folks could: stone masonry, some even with a fancy food cellar, nor would he settle for a flat foundation with a lowly dirt floor.

One late summer morning, as the remaining dead leaves fluttered their trajectory from tree limb to frosty ground, a pale, thin horse rider clopped slowly down the rough path to Carl's acre of land. Carl's solitude that morning was only interrupted by the occasionally nickering of Vashti grazing nearby in a fenced-in plot of weedy land. Carl whirled around, startled, and looked down the path at the horseman approaching. His black riding suit almost disappeared against the ebony flanks of his mount, and if it weren't for the circle of white collar that poked up around his neck, he might have looked like death personified coming to pay him a visit.

The rider's watery, faded gray eyes were drawn to the half-built structure: a post and beam foundation, partially framed walls and an oak shingle roof. The incipient layout of a vegetable garden sprawled to the right of the house, with the promise of seedlings hinted in the carefully measured rows of tilled black soil.

"Hail there," he called out to Carl. He shifted the bible tucked under his gangly arm.

"What you say me? You say me go to hell?"

"My Hebrew friend, I said *hail,* but yes indeed you speak the truth. Hell is where you will go unless you accept the Lord Jesus as your savior. I come to save your soul and share the gospel."

"Ach!" Carl grinned triumphantly, tugging on his short dark beard. "You want me believe your religion? Or go to bad place forever? Go away. I'm very busy finish my house."

Carl silently cursed his poor language skills. His English had improved slowly in two months. The gaunt, austere-looking Reverend swung down from the saddle and tied his horse to a nearby buckeye tree. Taking his dull gray coat off dramatically, he announced, "I am here to assist you in the construction of your new home. In exchange, will you listen to what I have to say?"

Carl stood speechless for a moment, staring in surprise at the stranger.

"I like you help," he responded with a shrug. "Vat is you name?"

"I am Isaiah Upton, servant of the Lord. My church, the First Baptist Congregational, is in nearby Cottonwood, and my congregation will welcome you with open arms if only you will convert to Christianity and believe in Jesus."

Carl sighed. It wasn't the first time an itinerant gentile 'man of the cloth', as the Southerners called them, had tried to proselytize him or the other Jews living in Hot Springs. It happened with such regularity that it simply became accepted as a passing rainstorm might briefly interrupt outdoor chores, then once gone, those chores resumed.

"Pick up shovel, Mr. Isaiah, and help me move big rocks behind house. I don't need Mr. Jesus. I need man with muscles and hands to work. You help me, I fix you a little bit food for break time. Good trade?"

Upton scowled at Carl and said ominously, "Your soul will surely perish, and you will suffer the fires of hell unless you repent of your sins and accept the Lord Jesus. Get down upon your knees! Accept your savior!"

Carl shook his head and beamed broadly. "The Jewish people don't get on our knees. We stand to pray."

He turned his broad back to Upton, revealing sweat stains that had soaked through his thin, brown work shirt. This intruder was like a pesty fly, buzzing and landing on people's noses. Carl swung his shovel into the ground, deepening the hole that would soon contain the footings for a front porch. As he dug, looking downward and paying no attention to the pastor, he suddenly heard a thunking noise behind the house. Looking up, he saw Reverend Upton toting a pile of rocks in his wheelbarrow and dumping them in a heap behind a cottonwood tree.

"I will help you with your work, sir, if it gets me one step closer to saving your soul!"

"Don't worry about save my soul. Save rocks for garden retaining wall."

The two men worked until late afternoon, speaking only to give or get instructions for the construction of the outhouse. Although Carl rankled at the preacher's attempts to convert him, he appreciated the fellow's building skills and knowledge of tools. He loved the scent of the pine and oak as they were planed, smoothed and sawed into the desired shapes and textures. He felt a certain power when he gripped the handle of the hammer, the steel of the saw. He felt at one with the world while he was troweling mortar onto bricks for a fireplace. His chest seemed to grow a little bigger when he stepped back to see the results of his work and his future cabin starting to take shape out of thin air. Shovels and nail heads clanged in a cacophony of sound that echoed off the surrounding tree trunks. The two men labored side by side like old buddies, but Carl wasn't fooled; he knew this Christian stranger's ultimate goal was to lure him into his church. He didn't mind working shoulder to shoulder with Upton as long as the man kept his mouth shut. But how would he finally get rid of the fellow, whom he knew would persist in his Christian lectures like the weeds in a meadow?

Their gnawing hunger and the weariness in their joints and hands forced them to drop the tools and sit side-by-side on a log, legs outstretched in their grimy boots. Carl opened a tote sack full of roast chicken legs and feet, a thick slab of rye bread, and a macaroon that Gussie had prepared for him that morning. He shared all of it with Isaiah Upton, who ate gratefully after insisting on Christian prayers before they took a bite. Isaiah had a flask with wine in it, and Carl spoke the Hebrew prayer when Reverend Upton was done.

"You are a man of the Old Testament, Carl," Reverend Upton murmured respectfully. "From your people come my people. We want you to reunite with us once again in the Bible of Jesus."

This pushy man. How do I make him go away now?

While they were eating, a rustling in the allspice bushes that bordered the path to Carl's building site attracted their attention. Samuel emerged from the shadows of the green ash trees behind them, stout in his gray work overalls and suspenders.

"Brother, am I glad to see you," Carl called to him in German. "Do you know this fellow? Maybe you can convince him to leave."

In English, Carl said, "Mr. Isaiah Upton, please meet my brother, Samuel."

Samuel sat down heavily on the log and leaned over Carl to shake Upton's hand. Then he turned to his brother and proclaimed dramatically in German,

"A letter came for you this morning from your sweetheart Rosalia."

"Sweet news you bring me, brother. My first letter from her after our betrothal. I wrote her three, maybe four months ago and have been waiting and waiting. Now I'll have a hard time concentrating on my work until I get home and read it."

Reverend Upton swung his eyes from one brother to the other with a puzzled expression. Samuel briefly translated their conversation in German for him, and Upton smiled a wide smile that stretched out his narrow, hang-dog face, the lower half dangling a scraggly white beard and unkempt mustache.

"You will enter into holy matrimony, then, brother Carl? I can only hope you will marry your bride in our church, so that you may be united for eternity in heaven with Christ."

Samuel scowled at Upton, but Carl simply laughed. He was too joyful to allow this fool to ruin the moment. He tried to imagine what Rosalia could have written to him. Would there be any hint of affection? Joy at their future union? Perhaps a date of departure for America. Distant noises beyond the grove of black gum and ash pulled him out of his reverie, sounds recognizable but not explainable. The sound of gunfire reached their ears, but that wasn't unusual. Hunters fired to bring down game at all hours of the day. What made it strange was the accompanying sound of men's voices, loud and abrasive.

"Men hunt," commented Carl in English, "and yell very loud. Why? This scare away the animals."

Samuel squinted into the sky as if the answer were there, shaking his head slowly. Reverend Upton looked down at his dust-covered shoes. Their strained expressions puzzled and disturbed Carl. He sensed something ominous yet couldn't imagine what it could be.

"This is what it sounds like, my brother," Samuel spoke solemnly in German, "when a group of men make what they call in English, a 'lynching'. It is always the white men attacking one poor shvartze, the dark-skinned man. They wrap a rope around his neck. They hang him from a tree to kill him."

"What?" yelled Carl, almost in shock. "This is no better than where we come from. I thought there were laws in America. Where is the constable and deputies? Why aren't they stopping these men from doing this."

"My Jewish friends, this is the devil laying hold of what should be good, white Christians. Although the Bible tells us that the Negro is cursed and inferior to the white man, that does not cancel out the commandment that thou shalt not kill," Reverend Upton said sternly.

Carl could only understand half of what Upton said. He ran over to Vashti, mounted her quickly, and galloped off in the direction of the commotion. The noises began to fade, and he panicked that he wouldn't get there in time; Vashti was no racehorse. The trail he was on ended at a dirt road, and on the other side of it was a clearing with men on horseback. Carl slowed Vashti to a trot and edged toward the clearing. The men, all white goyim as Samuel had predicted, were riding into the woods in different directions. There must have been five or six of them, Carl figured. He entered the clearing and spotted something swinging from the high branch of a black gum tree, something long and dark. His mind wanted to transform it into another shape. It was an animal, wasn't it? But he knew in his heart, and his brother had forecast it, that this was a human being. A shvartze murdered almost right under their noses in the middle of the woods. Five or six against one, an unfair fight even in the Old Country. His veins swelled with grief and fury, and he felt nauseated. He pressed himself forward and rode up to the body. It had been twitching but was now still. The right hand and left foot had been sliced off. Pools of blood darkened the weeds and grasses below it. He gazed in horror for several minutes, and then heard a sharp click behind him. He turned toward the noise and found himself looking at the double barrel of a rifle, pointed at him by one of the lynchers on horseback.

"Don't tech that if ya don't wanna dah too," hissed the man, glaring at him with narrow, pale blue eyes. He wore a wide-brimmed leather hat low over his forehead, almost hiding platinum wisps of hair. Carl moved his horse slowly away from the hanging body, keeping his eyes on the man's face.

"Why? Why you do this? And why you cut off hand and foot?" Carl tried to keep his voice from trembling but could not.

"This boy is a cousin to John Brown, the slave in Virginie who tried to stir an uprisin' at Harper's Ferry. We think they need a little reminder who's boss," sneered the heavy-jowled man, tipping his wide-brimmed hat to reveal a shock of blonde hair streaked with grey. "Git a goin', stranger, afore we string you up too."

Carl turned Vashti around as quickly as he could make her move and rode her back to the house, shaking uncontrollably from head to toe. When he saw Samuel and Reverend Upton awaiting him, he dismounted and related what he had seen to them. He tried not to sob but couldn't prevent it.

"We must go to the constable, Sam, and report this right away. Those men should be arrested and taken to prison for their murder."

He wiped embarrassedly at tears, smearing his face with the dirt that was on his hands. Reverend Upton asked,

"What's he saying, Mr. Gersman?"

Samuel didn't bother to translate for Upton.

"The constable won't do anything to bring justice for the slaves. That is the way things are around here, and you will have to get used to it. For all we know, some of the men you saw could be deputies or their friends."

Upton was swinging his head back and forth, white locks of hair swaying in tandem, and pressing his bible tightly to his chest.

"Our Lord and Savior Jesus will surely receive that poor black soul into the kingdom of God. May he be at peace for eternity."

"That is fine for eternity," Carl said angrily, "but what about right now, today? How we live in peace together when this happen? And nobody go to jail?"

"Carl, please calm down," Samuel attempted to soothe him. "Let's go back home. You can read Rosalia's letter. Right now it is dangerous to be near the scene of the crime. Those men could easily kill us, too."

"I don't want to read her letter now," Carl said, still feeling slightly queasy. He and Sam mounted their animals and walked them towards home, leaving Reverend Upton alone in the woods.

Gussie was waiting at the front door for them. She had the sealed letter in her hand and was beaming. When she saw the expressions on Samuel and Carl's faces, she stopped beaming and raised her eyebrows.

"Nu? What happened to make you look like somebody fell in the well?"

Samuel briefly related to her the story of the lynching. She shook her head and frowned.

"I spit on those evil men." She aimed at the ground and followed through, letting fly an admirable missile of saliva. "But what can we do about it? We are outsiders here still, and the white goyim will turn on us with any excuse."

Carl took the letter from her hand and sat on the garden bench to read it. His brother and sister-in-law slipped inside, and he was grateful for the privacy.

"To Carl, my betrothed" it began, and he savored the notion of Rosalia writing such a greeting, grinning and nodding his head. *"May G-d keep you safe and healthy far from your birth home and parents, may they live long. My parents are in good health and so is my sister Edith and my brothers, Jake and Henry. Also in good health are our aunts and uncles and cousins. Except for my dear Great Aunt Eva Wolfson who suffers from galloping pneumonia and we are all worried and pray for her night and day that she will survive the illness. Edith is betrothed to Herr Frank Heller, a dairyman. They will marry in a year and a half. We are all very happy for her."*

Carl grew slightly impatient with the banal details of her first paragraph, scratching at his mustache and shifting his weight on the bench. Still, that she was apprising him of family news indicated that she was preparing to take him into her family. This thought warmed him.

"I am tutoring English to some German children in town who want to do well on their exams. The money that I earn from the tutoring I am saving for passage to America. My father is also saving his money for my journey. He likes you very much, and so does Mama."

Carl smiled widely and looked up at the sky before returning to the letter. "Thank you, Hashem, for blessing me with their approval."

"We thank you kindly for giving some of your hard-earned savings to Papa. This will help to buy the tickets for train and steamship. However, they are very costly and we will need more time to save before I can start out on my trip. I beg for your patience. Perhaps in one year and a half we will buy the tickets. I may be lucky enough to leave after Edith's wedding. Then I can look forward to my own.

Please write to me as well and tell me about America and Arkansas and the little town of Hot Springs. Is the land there truly free if you build a house on it? Or is this just a false rumor? Does everybody own a gun? Are the Jews treated well? And anything else you think might be important for me to know.

I remain,

Your Betrothed, Rosalia Wolfson"

The weeks and months ahead passed quickly for Carl in a nimbus of work. He cleared part of the acre Samuel had sold him for gardening, a chicken coop, outhouse and barn, continued to work on the cabin, honed his kosher butchering skills on an occasional rabbit or hen, and still managed to work at Samuel's Dry Goods Store. He paid his brother the dollar he owed him for the land after earning enough at the store to save a little money. The prospect of owning his own abode on his own land drove him to a level of toil he had never achieved in the Old Country. Hard work was what kept the Jews surviving through oppression, deprivation, and diasporas, his parents often pointed out. It was something that could not be taken away from them unless they were stricken with injury or bad health. Until now, he had never realized how true this was.

The months passed like gusts of wind as Carl divided his time between working at Gersman's Dry Goods store and building his new log cabin. He was driven doubly by his desire to give Samuel and Gussie back their privacy when he moved out and his desire to shelter Rosalia in as fine and comfortable an abode as he could possibly construct. Already eight months had gone by since Carl's arrival in Hot Springs, and he still had much to finish on the house in which he dreamed they would spend their married lives. Rosalia's occasional letters from Germany bolstered his spirits, and he wrote back to her as often as he could spare the time.

"Dearest Rosalia,

May G-d bless you and your family with peace and good health. It was a joy to hear about Edith's wedding to Herr Heller. I can only express my great sadness that you must wait for your own wedding to a Person (myself) so far from home, that she would marry before you. We must be patient and depend upon G-d to bring us together as soon as possible.

The house is almost finished. I pray every day whenever I am working on it that it will fill your heart with delight. Many good men in town have helped me, teaching me construction skills I would never learn on my own, sharing tools, working side-by-side with me. We will be sure to invite all of them to our wedding, and to thank and praise them.

I am in wonder that more than a year has gone by since I got here. Now it is 1860 and a man named Abraham Lincoln, from the state of Illinois, was elected President of the United States. Have you read about him in the newspapers in Germany? He is opposed to slavery of the colored people in this nation. Because Samuel and I have light skin color and are not shvartze slaves, we can vote. Therefore, I voted for the first time for Mr. Lincoln, because I know that slavery is wrong and he will put an end to it. It makes me proud to choose a President for my new Country. He will take office (that is how they say it) in March 1861."

Still many more days and weeks passed like birds winging across the sky, and Carl and his helpers labored on. They raised the walls using vertical boards, covered them with weatherboarding for protection, laid down ash flooring, notched and nailed and shingled. Carl worked on the house every day except Shabbos and when the winter weather became too icy, or lightning raked the skies. When spring gradually sent its hints of color and warmth to Arkansas, the Wolfsons still didn't have enough savings for Rosalia's transportation. The week that Carl finished the roofing, the Confederacy was formed and announced in the newspapers. The week he laid out the last of the roof shingles, President Lincoln was installed in office. One April morning Abner was very late. Carl began to worry, as he was a steadfast and punctual fellow. Close to noon he caught sight of Abner hurrying down the leaf-strewn path, his old leather rucksack of tools jouncing on his broad back.

"I'm sorry to be so late. Everybody in town is talking about what happened. I couldn't go two steps without some-body stopping me."

"What happened?"

"You know that Confederacy that got started back in February? It was in all the newspapers."

"Yes, but Arkansas isn't part of that. At least not yet."

"Those *meshuggah,* crazy slave owners attacked a fort named Fort Sumter in the state of South Carolina. With rifles. They are making war with their own country!"

9

April 1861 – April 1865
Civil War Letters

May 21, 1861

Dear Rosalia,

May this letter find you and your family in good health and at peace, thanks to G-d. We must pray for peace in this country of America. Southern slave owners who don't want to set their slaves free fired cannons on a fortress called Fort Sumter in South Carolina. That is another state, there are maybe as many of them as in Prussia, and I learn their names through the newspapers and talking to Samuel and my new friends in town.

President Lincoln ordered a blockade of all the ports in the southern states that made this rebellion called 'Confederacy'. Fortunately, that means you could still come to the United States through the huge New York Harbor. But then you will have to travel over land southeast to Arkansas, and that is a very difficult trip, especially for a lady. I should know, as I endured it in 1859. The port of New Orleans is the closest port to Arkansas, but the President blockaded that one too.

I must apologize for the small amount of money that I sent to help your parents purchase the ticket last month. A large portion of my earning is going into building us a strong, decent house to live in. I will do my best to send more this month.

This conflict must end soon, and then you will come. Happiness fills me when I think of our future marriage. Please keep hope within your heart and in your prayers that these battles between the Southerners and Northerners will end quickly. I remain,

Yours in Faith,
Carl

August 16, 1861

Dear Rosalia,

I have heard nothing from you since my letter of May 21. I pray to Hashem that illness or bad luck has not befallen you to keep you from answering me. My brother Samuel and his wife Gussie continue to reassure me that it is this terrible fighting between the North and the South that slows down the mail delivery. I hope this is the reason.

Even though Samuel and I are opposed to the system of enslavement of the shvartzes, the darkies they call them, we do not voice our opinions for fear of being attacked or ambushed by the residents here who are in favor of such a thing. And I must admit, our business is doing excellently because of it. The outfits marching into Little Rock and Rockport to enlist in the Confederate Army are buying our shelves bare.

The little village of Hot Springs has no army troops, barracks or forts. Even so, the way of life here is being badly affected by this war between the states. You are safer waiting in Gliewitz for it to end before you embark upon your journey. I write this with grief in my heart, as my dream of marriage to you must be delayed in such a strange and dramatic fashion.

Nevertheless, with patience and fortitude I believe that we both can wait out the war. Until then, I pray for you and your family to be comforted by G-d and at peace.

Yours sincerely,
Carl

November 5, 1861

Dear Carl,

Your letters to me have arrived extremely late, as I can note from the dates on them. Please forgive me for delaying in answering them. My family were all so extremely occupied with preparations for Edith's wedding to Herr Heller. Edith walked to the chuppah in a very charming lace-trimmed silver and lavender dress that Great Aunt Eva lent her, saved and stored since her own wedding. The bubbes cooked delicious platters of beef brisket and potatoes for the guests. Mama made three or four excellent strudels and apple cakes. Papa bought beer and wine for all. (except the children, of course!) The wedding was quite beautiful, and I was only sad that you were not in attendance. I caught Papa crying! For happiness, of course.

My mother and father are quite alarmed at the war going on in the United States. Of course, they forbid me to travel to America now. It does not matter, though, as we have yet to save enough money for my second-class passage on the steamship. Thank you for sending money to us to help with the ticket, but please do not send more at this time. We are fearful that it will be stolen in the mail, especially now that there is war. I can hardly believe that civil war is happening in the United States, nor can anybody else in Gliewitz. Still, as Papa pointed out to me, where there are slaves, there is no true freedom. We learn that from the Book of Exodus, don't we?

I am still tutoring English to the children of the wealthy Germans in town, and my earnings go into the "ticket to America" jar in my bedroom. Some have plans to send their children to the United States, although those plans must wait until the war there ends

Now that Edith is married, this room is mine alone, a pleasure even though I do miss my sister's company. My best friend Annaleya is also married and will have her first child in June of 1862. I feel very alone and find that writing to you brings me solace. Please forgive me for writing my feelings to you so boldly.

I pray that Hashem blesses and watches over you during this dangerous time.

Yours in Peace and Faith,
Rosalia

March 12, 1862

Dear Rosalia,

I was so happy to get your letter, especially since its arrival was very slow, but that must be expected now that there are battles in the land of America. In February thousands of soldiers on both sides died in battles in Tennessee.

Friends of Samuel write from Little Rock that Governor Rector of the State of Arkansas moved the capital and all of his important records to Hot Springs. This is only temporary. He is afraid of the Union Army coming to Little Rock to take over.

That doesn't mean that we have peace in this little town. We do not at all. Groups of outlaws are invading the town, Northerners and Southerners both. They rob people at gunpoint and set buildings on fire. Samuel's store has been robbed three times now, with a pistol pointed at Samuel's head. Now I have a rifle for the first time in my life, I traded for it at Herr Keller's Guns & Arms Establishment. It is a simple one, not fit for army fighting. Herr Keller refers to it as a 'frontier rifle'. Still, it will do for self-defense, which is becoming more and more necessary in town.

I am forced to conclude that you and I must abide this turbulent time of war in America until we see one another again. Until then, I remain,

Yours in Faith,
Carl

July 27, 1862

Dear Carl,

I pray that this letter reaches you, Samuel and Gussie soon. I cannot describe how worried and fearful I am that you and your relatives are in such danger in – of all places – the United States of America! Robberies at the barrel of a gun, fires, soldiers fighting, ach! Mama and Papa are biting their nails to the quick thinking about you. Please, I beg you, continue to write and let us all know that you are well in body and soul.

I am still tutoring English and getting better in the language. You will be amazed at how much English I know and will be able to speak when I arrive in Hot Springs. Are you fluent yet? I have seven students, which makes me busy almost every day. I spend much time alone in my room preparing lessons, correcting exams that I must administer regularly to satisfy the parents. Do the schools in Hot Springs need teachers? I would like to teach children when I have settled in. Will you allow me to do so after we are married?

Please forgive the length of this letter to you. I do go on, don't I? Well, so many of the girls in Gliewitz my age are married or preparing their dowries and weddings. I have only Mama to pass the time with. My brothers, who seem to be getting bigger every day, are still making pranks and roughing each other up. I stay away from them most of the time. And so, I think a great deal about my upcoming adventure, a journey across the ocean and life in a new nation where freedoms for all people (except, it seems, the shvartzes) are protected by the government.

Yours in G-d's Blessing,
Rosalia

October 18, 1862

Dear Rosalia,

I am writing to you from New Orleans, State of Louisiana, where my relatives and I have relocated. We are staying temporarily with Simon and Rosa Meyer of Gliewitz, whom you know as they are friends of your family. They are very fine people, and graciously share their small apartment with us until we find one of our own to stay in. Samuel and I are selling the inventory of his store to earn our living in this city. We go door-to-door around the city, and also visit the troops in temporary barracks. The enlisted soldiers have very little currency to purchase our dry goods, but the officers always buy something they need from us. The North made upon the South something called a 'blockade' which leaves the South unable to import goods. Because of this our goods are in great demand. Still, once we run out of inventory, we will have to figure some other way to survive in New Orleans until we can re-establish Samuel's store again back in Hot Springs.

If you sent a letter to the Hot Springs post office, I am sorry to say there is no retrieving it at this time. The town of Hot Springs is on fire. Bands of outlaws called by the southerners here called "Bushwhackers" set the fires after they rob the stores of money and goods. Residents who haven't joined the armed forces (on either side) are fleeing for their lives. Samuel's store was robbed once again, but thanks to Hashem, nobody set it on fire. Our houses were still standing when we left with all we could carry in our trunks onto the stagecoach out of town. I can only pray they will still be there undamaged when we return. It is good that you are not here yet.

New Orleans is an interesting place. I hope you get a chance to tour and view it when this war is finished and you can sail into its port. People living here speak many different languages. They come from many places around the world. The food here is very hot and spicy, with surprising flavors I have never tasted before. Most of it is delicious, but sometimes it is too spicy for my tongue. The Meyers bought regional spices and foods to make it for us. We have dinners of spicy catfish, bread pudding desserts with rum sauce, breakfast of pastry called "beignet" (a French word), which are fried dough balls rolled in powdered sugar.

Do not give into despair, Rosalia. This chaos and war cannot go on much longer. The Union Army is vigorous and relentless under the command of President Lincoln and they will beat down the Confederate Army. It is very obvious to anyone who thinks about it with clarity of mind. Please send future correspondence to the Post Office in New Orleans. As ever,

Yours in Prayers and Hope,
Carl

March 2, 1863

Dear Carl,

All the Jewish community of Gliewitz awaits your letters and the letters of other émigrés to America. Through them we hear news of the war there. Even though some of that news is old by the time we get it, we still hear more details of your lives during this bloody fighting than we read about in the newspapers here. Plus the newspapers don't get everything right, we suspect. Now my family, our relatives and friends and the Rabbi all know what is happening to your little town of Hot Springs. We are all terribly upset about such violence and wrongdoing to residents who are not even in the military. We all wring our hands over your exodus to another state, another city where you are protected. (I hope!)

We did read in the newspapers that in January of this year President Lincoln signed a law to free the slaves. He calls it "The Emancipation Proclamation." We are happy for the slaves who are now free. Just like what happened to our forefathers in Egypt. Except no plagues, unless you want to count the war as a plague, which it is.

The only news I can think to write is that we have enough money to purchase my passage on the steamship. Still we must save a little more for one train ticket to Hamburg. Papa will accompany me to the train, but I must make my own way across the city and board the ship on my own. I am frightened of that, even though Papa wrote out very specific directions to help me and we go over them from time to time. But when will my time come to leave? We can only pray that the fighting will end soon. I remain,

Your betrothed,
Rosalia

November 29, 1864

My Dear Rosalia,

Your letters over the past year have kept my heart light. When one arrives, it is a golden day for me and I thank Hashem and pray for Him to keep you and your family healthy and safe in Germany. I hope you feel the same about my correspondence to you. They are slow in arriving, but they do finally arrive.

In the midst of this War Between the States, there was an astonishing thing. It was an American election for President of the United States. Can you imagine the freedom to vote for the leader of your country? In Prussia, we have no such choice. King Wilhelm was born into the position of ruler and our relatives there must bow down to him and his children.

I write this almost with disbelief: I voted for Abraham Lincoln, to re-elect him. And he won! The vice-president will be a man named Andrew Johnson. I don't know much about him. But many of the people here in Hot Springs voted for Lincoln's opponent, General George B. McClellan. Our vote is secret, and it's a good thing because people might stop shopping at Samuel's store if they find out we voted for Lincoln. He is not very popular in the Southern states where there used to be slavery, and that includes Arkansas.

You may wonder how could Carl vote when he is not even a citizen of that country? I will tell you: I had to file a 'Declaration of Intention' with the Court. It is not a royal court, but a court of law. Then I was qualified to vote! The papers I filed show that I intend to become a citizen, which I do. I have to live here five years, and since I came in 1859, I can become a citizen now. You will become a citizen also, but you still can't vote, being a woman, of course. Don't worry, I will vote for both of us!

With hopes for our future together,
Carl

April 30, 1865

Dear Rosalia,

So much news to tell you, I hardly know where to start. The war between the states is finally over, after four long years.

Grievously, less than one week after Mr. Lee's surrender, somebody killed President Lincoln. This is a President of the United States who was re-elected for a second term! The Meyers have been crying for days over it. I overhear many White Southerners talking, and they are happy he was assassinated. The Negroes here in Hot Springs keep their thoughts to themselves, but I'm sure they grieve for the man who set them all free legally. I must force myself to write this to you, as I wish it weren't true. By the time you get this, I am sure you will have already read about it in the local newspaper, so I will not tell you the details.

Samuel, Gussie and I are preparing to leave New Orleans and return to our homes in Hot Springs. The Meyers have agreed to meet you at the Port of New Orleans when your steamship arrives. They will escort and accompany you to Hot Springs in a stagecoach (not quite the same as the coaches in Prussia, as you will see).

The years ahead look free of war and filled with blessings. I remain,

Yours in deep devotion,
Carl

10

When Carl returned to Hot Springs in May of 1865, the civil war had been over less than a month. He found his cabin in ashes. Only the cement foundation and brick fireplace still stood, scorched and forlorn. Samuel and Gussie's house remained intact, but not untouched. Every possible item they had left behind when they fled the town had been stolen. Gersman's Dry Goods had been raided and emptied, and then torched. Carl and Samuel spent the better part of May rebuilding the store, as it was their livelihood. They were able to use the original foundation and salvaged wood from the forest floor to build a ramshackle shop.

Their neighbors fared no better; their homes were burnt to the ground. Many other stores in town were also in ruins. A dozen shop owners defending their businesses were killed. The few women who had stayed behind to protect their land were raped and killed. Only the government buildings had been left alone, protected by Union troops when the capital was temporarily shifted there in 1862.

Despite the ruination left behind, Carl had something to celebrate. The Homestead Act of 1862 had been passed, so now he could acquire free land. With Samuel to guide him, he filed an application with the federal government.

"No, I did not take up my arms against the United States government," Carl declared as he scribbled laboriously to fill in the answers in English. He stopped writing and lifted both his arms up in the air.

"No, silly," Gussie laughed. "Arms in this case means weapons."

"And yes, I am over twenty-one years old," Carl continued, laughing also. "Honestly, I feel like a hundred some days."

"Good, you are finished. Now sign at the bottom," Samuel pointed his index finger at the last line. "You now are almost the owner of your own five acres of American land. You have to improve it."

"Oy vey. I have to start from the beginning once again to build a house. I never imagined this would happen, neither the good nor the bad. So we must be grateful. God bless President Abraham Lincoln who signed this Homestead Act."

Carl's land lay as near to Samuel's acres as they could find, just a mile and a half away. When Carl wasn't helping at Gersman's Dry Goods Store, he was in the woods building another cabin. This time around, he had many more construction skills since he had already built one before the Civil War. Abner Fleishner, a neighbor and close friend of Samuel's, came every Sunday to help Carl. Carl reciprocated when he could, as Abner was rebuilding on the plot where his house had been torched during the war.

"Why?" Carl moaned one day as he, Samuel and Abner finished setting bricks for the fireplace and the sun began to set. "Why did people destroy this town and hurt and kill people who were not soldiers? And even kill the women and children?"

They were resting together after a long day of work, a Sunday when Samuel closed the store. They pondered Carl's heartfelt question, each puffing tobacco-filled pipes and sipping small cups of the crème de menthe that Abner had brought back from New Orleans to wind down for the evening.

The growing darkness coaxed out several stars directly overhead like bright little eyes blinking down at them. Two or three owls were hooting back and forth in the walnut orchard. The fragrance of newly blooming honeysuckle was strong enough to overpower the husky smell of their burning tobacco pipes.

"Little brother, the men who came through here, they have a special name given by the white Christians. There are two names that I heard of before we left Hot Springs back in 1859. Some are called Jayhawkers, men from Kansas who are Unionists and anti-slavery. The other kind is called Bushwhackers, and they were on the Confederates' side."

"Where do they get those funny names?" Carl interrupted.

"The Jayhawker name comes from a mix of two birds, the jaybird and the hawk. Get it? They are loud and noisy, and they hunt and kill. Rabbi Schecter has been teaching us the names of the birds of Arkansas, and he told me this."

"That I understand. It is a perfect word for those murderers and thieves. What about the other word, Bushwacker. All I know about it is the word 'bush', a big plant. Makes no sense to me."

"The word signifies somebody who will ambush you by surprise. A man without the courage to fight in the army and out in the open. A violent prowler."

"But no matter the side to us, they became violent and greedy when they came into Hot Springs and saw our stores and banks," Abner remarked. "They took advantage of the war to steal from us and then burn the town down like it was kindling waiting to be lit. They just went crazy, lost all sense of right and wrong with the war going on around them. The only buildings left standing were a few bathhouses over at the springs, some houses like mine, and the bakery. The cemeteries were not touched. Some wealthy fellow name of Hiram Whittington, a well-known gentleman in Hot Springs. His house was left to stand, although ransacked. Also, ahem," Abner coughed, making his double chin shake, "still standing in the woods on the outskirts of town is a brothel. We can only imagine why that was not damaged."

Carl stared silently into his cup of crème de menthe as his brother and Abner laughed and joked.

"Why do you think that rich man's house wasn't burned like so many others?" Carl asked as their laughter subsided.

"He played it smart. He gave a hundred dollars to the Hot Springs Cavalry Company. They protected it."

The men chuckled and sipped their drinks. That moment of levity, however, lasted for only a moment.

"Now I must start over building my house," grieved Carl. "as if I just got here from overseas. Do you think the federal government people will not count the years of war against me? I am only allowed five to finish a dwelling."

"Don't forget, and don't pity yourself," admonished Samuel, "Almost everybody is hanging on the same tree branch. I am lucky, that is true, that my house is still standing. But I must replace every stick of furniture, tools, kitchenware, everything we left behind. Still, I will be helping you, and so will our friends, to build back what was lost. We will live life poorer with all that we lost during the war. All of us. In time the store will do more business and we will prosper."

It was late spring and fields that should have been planted already with crops stood brown, bare and unturned in the mild Southern breezes. In the aftermath, farmers planted late to reap whatever crops they could. Everybody in town worked frantically from sunup to sundown to restore what had been destroyed by the bushwhackers and jayhawkers. Hammers and saws rang and screeched all day, in every neighborhood and district. People whose homes had been spared put in part of their daily toil helping others lay new foundations, cut down pines and oaks and clear their crowns, plane and place logs, craft doors and windows.

After a hard but pleasurable day's labor, Carl would take a detour when he had a spare hour to climb up into the hills. There he would observe the steaming water churn and spew from the bowels of the earth. The thick bushes sprouting from rugged terrain surrounding the pools gave him cover while he sat on the smoothest large rock he could find to muse over his life in this little town. The tantalizing warmth of the water's vapors would lull him into reveries. *I am glad to have my brother and his wife here, but I need to make my own my life. Rosalia will arrive some day and be my wife. I will look into those lovely blue eyes and smooth her pretty blonde hair every day. We will have children to fill our days and tend to us when we grow old. But until then, I must save my American dollars to rebuild my house, or I must forfeit the land. Someday, maybe sooner than later, I'll be able to set up my own kosher butcher business.* He tilted his head to the left and then over the right shoulder, feeling the crackling and release of stiffness there.

He buried his frustration of having to build his own lodging anew in the labor itself. Mastering the tools and implements, cutting and smoothing the wood, fitting dovetail joints, hammering the long steel nails, filled him with pleasure. He would scan the depth and breadth of his very own land, imagining Rosalia there cleaning, cooking, sharing his bed. He made a clamor in the woods hewing logs, setting them with pitch, and hinging doors and windows.

As before the war, fellow Jewish congregants who had a free Sunday afternoon graciously lent him a hand. They sweated side by side in rough work clothes, and over time Carl became more closely acquainted with them. He discovered that this was the standard for everybody, Jew or gentile, who made his home in Hot Springs. As a community, they bolstered one another however they could. Hard feelings, grudges, slights, and misunderstandings were put aside when a new Jewish immigrant arrived in town and began to build a home. Even though he had already weathered six years in America, most of it had been in New Orleans hiding from the bloody chaos of the war between the states, he was still relatively new in Hot Springs. Much to his surprise, some white Christian town folk showed up on his land to help as well.

The cabin was more than halfway finished, Carl estimated one day near the end of autumn as cool temperatures set in. Its oak plank walls, which Carl had felled, hauled, planed, notched, and placed with the clever use of long steel chains, rose one story to meet the angled roof. Despite his manly bravado, he couldn't have accomplished any of it without the tutelage of Horace, Geoffrey and Billy, all skilled carpenters. Although they had started out lending a hand for free, they soon asked Carl for hourly pay. Carl had no choice but to scrimp and save his small earnings from his work at Gersman's Dry Goods and handed over much of it to them. He was determined to finish the structure inside and out before Rosalia arrived in town.

The roof itself was a masterpiece, Carl reflected with smug satisfaction. He had elected to employ corrugated tin sheets rather than the commonly installed wood shake shingles that he caught sight of all over town. So many homes had burned to the ground during the war, he figured that a material unassailable by fire would be safer even in peace time. The winters here, Samuel had informed him, were not as severe as those in Europe, and so he wasn't concerned about tin pest rust setting in on the roof. Even if rust developed, he could replace the sheets one at a time as needed with modest cost. He had priced the imported slate tile roofs at Humphrey's Building Supplies, but they were unaffordable for him. A shame, for although he did not want his house to sport the same slate roofs as the houses his hometown, Rosalia might have liked being reminded of the Old Country. The corrugated tin roof gave his new home a shiny, silvery top hat. The sheen wouldn't last as it weathered, but for now it was impressive.

The structure still awaited Carl's gradually improving building skills: birch kitchen shelves and cabinets, sturdy front and back steps leading to porches, and of course the outhouse in back. The windows and doors were in place, but they needed to be trimmed with sills and jambs. Rosalia will sew the curtains for the windows, Carl mused, his neck warming as he thought of her. Although Samuel and Gussie constantly begged Carl to stay with them, he was now sleeping on a small horsehair mattress on the floorboards in the unfinished house to give them their privacy, using the nearby woods for a toilet.

"If this is going to be the kitchen, where will you put the stove and stovepipe?" asked a cheery, small, wiry blond-whiskered helper named Horace Fletcher. He was of mixed Irish and English descent, a boastful sort of fellow. He liked to show off his war injuries from the 1862 battle of Shiloh in Tennessee.

"Shiloh? Ach, that is Hebrew language for place of peace."

"T'wern't nothin' lahk that. T'were a place of evil where the Goddurned Yanks cut down most of our troops, includin' our commmandin' General Johnston. Ah'm lucky ta be alive!"

Carl couldn't keep his eyes off of Horace's leather boots. They were unique, pale tan leather decorated with red and black diamond-shaped patterns. Horace stood with hands askew, gazing around the roughed-in empty room,

"The stove goes over here," Carl answered in his service-able but still heavily accented English. He pointed a narrow, roughened finger. "In northeast corner."

"Naw. I have a much better idea, my Hebrew friend, " Horace grinned. "How about you put it closer to the door leading to the bedroom? That way your wife can go quickly from one house chore to the other. Haw!"

Two men hauling in a pile of oak planks set down the load in the middle of the kitchen and snorted their appreciation of the idea, while Carl blushed. He liked these fellows, good-hearted and generous of spirit, with their calloused hands and bawdy humor. He suspected that the freedom of this new country glowed within them just as the oppression of the Prussian tyrant lay dark and somber in the hearts of those he had left behind. The difference between the two countries never ceased to astonish Carl.

"Ah say we take a wee rest about now, " Horace sighed. He sat down carefully on a flat board that lay on top of the pile of planks, and two other husky carpenters followed suit. They pulled out leather canteens filled with water, and Horace added a splash of scotch from a tin flask to his canteen.

"I have no wife yet, same as you gentlemen," Carl smiled sadly and took a sorrowful swig of scotch from Horace's proffered flask. "But soon my bride will be here from Germany, may Adonai protect her travels."

"Well, okay, maybe the pickin's is slim here in town, and you gotta wait fer this so-called bride from Germany. We'll believe that when we see it." smirked Billy Hermann, waggling thick eyebrows over his dark mahogany eyes set close together like two beads. "After all, we're in the edge of nowhere, middle of the forest. But there's ways to pacify a man's needs, ain't there, Mr. Ratchins?"

Geoffrey Ratchins nodded in agreement, black whiskers waving sideways to indicate a broad grin underneath them.

"Sure is a way. We call it the Rooming House."

"What is this. The room in house?"

"No, no, buddy, the Rooming House. It's a place, shall we say, that will satisfy your manly dreams. Leastways it fulfills mine. What you say, Billy?"

Carl suddenly realized what they were talking about. He remembered that Abner had mentioned it was one of the few buildings left undamaged. There were brothels in the old country, but they were kept secret and were illicit. He had never been to one, but secretly, he had always been curious about them and longed to go.

"But, but…these are breaking the law in Prussia," Carl stammered. "Not here?"

"Oh, they're against the law in this town, Carl, and that's why we kinda ride on over there late at night in the dark, when everyone's asleep, includin' the sheriff and his deputy. Although Deputy Paige does his share of visitation same as us. I tell you what," Ratchins burped loudly, and wiped his sweaty palms on the front of his brown plaid shirt. He stood up and loomed over Carl a good foot and a half, being one of the tallest men that Carl had ever seen. "We - Bill, Horace and me - are going to take you over to the Rooming House for an evenin' you will never forget, I can assure you. Make sure to bring money."

Two nights later, on a Saturday when the half moon was bathing the town and hills in white light that glimmered on rooftops and lit up the tallest trees, Carl's three new friends rode on horseback to fetch him. The autumn air was sharpening its teeth on the landscape, biting at the men's faces with a hint of ice and sleet to come.

They rode slowly, wending along a narrow deer path that Carl didn't think he ever would have noticed. His three escorts seemed to know it well as they maneuvered their horses around dark, squat bushes and tree stumps. They were heading south, away from the heart of town and into the outskirts. Billy was whistling a tune that Carl wasn't familiar with. The piercing notes drifted into the underbrush and beyond. The shadows danced in front of Carl's eyes as branches shuffled in the intermittent night breeze that blew loose leaves around scattershot. He almost couldn't believe that he was out here in the nighttime forest with three fellows he didn't know very well, heading to one of those forbidden places he never imagined that he would enter except in his dreams. His stomach churned and a heaviness suddenly weighed upon his brow, bringing him on the verge of a headache.

He recalled his first and only experience with a woman named Magda, an older woman with light brown, wavy hair and shiny brown eyes to match. They met while waiting for the steamship to weigh anchor in the port of Hamburg. Their liaison lasted the length of the trip across the Atlantic, as she sneaked him into her first-class cabin from his miserable seat in steerage. Carl knew it couldn't continue beyond the ocean voyage, as he was already betrothed to Rosalia. The memories of that sweet time were soured with tremendous guilt. Nevertheless, his thoughts of Magda aroused Carl and heightened his desire to have a woman in his arms again. He licked his lips nervously and peered ahead at the men leading him. Were they experiencing the same lustful thoughts and urges? They were all inebriated from Horace's ever-present tin flask of whiskey.

They rode for several miles along the deer path until it met up with a large road perpendicular to it, where the forest had been cleared. The full moon was starting to descend into the eastern sky, still bright but growing dimmer. Not far down the road a golden light was visible, gleaming through the tree branches. The men rode toward it and came to a two-story clapboard structure nestled in a dell and lit up on all sides with lanterns hanging from poles. They swung down from their horses and tied them to nearby trees. Geoffrey took the stairs two at a time until he came to the front door and knocked loudly with his fist on the polished maple front door. Silence hung in the air for a few minutes as they waited, and suddenly the door smoothly swung open.

"Welcome to you, gentlemen," a feminine voice crooned. "Come in and sit down a little bit. Would you like a drink?"

Carl followed his three friends into the foyer of a large, two-story Victorian house. Even in the dark of night he could discern gingerbread patterns decorating the eaves. It was the grandest structure he had ever seen outside of New York City. Certainly, nobody he knew in Oppein lived in such a place.

A woman with thick, jet black hair captured in a pearl comb atop her head, curls poking out and lapping at her forehead and cheeks. Heavy makeup on her face and hands could not hide her age from Carl, which he guessed to be forty or fifty years. Her lips were stained crimson. He hadn't seen that very often and found it unusually appealing. She ushered the men into a sitting room on the left side of a long, shadowy hallway. There were several doors on either side of the hallway, and a polished oak staircase to the second story. Carl had never been in such a house before, and he gaped with surprise and admiration. He and his companions removed their wide-brimmed hats and sank into a gold-tasseled green velvet sofa.

"My name is Missy," cooed the woman to Carl as she handed him a tumbler filled with a ruddy substance. "Brandy for you, sir? It'll go on the bill later, of course."

She crossed the room and raised a silver-handled bell sitting on a glossy black upright piano, walked to the front of the hallway and rang it four times, pausing deliberately between rings. The men heard footsteps coming down the hallway.

"Only four," Missy called down the hall. "Maybelle, you can go back in, I don't need you this time. That's a good girl."

Four young women entered the sitting room, but the men could smell their lemon and rose perfume even before they presented themselves in the flesh. Two were wearing low-cut gowns made of a thin, gauzy fabric. The third prostitute was in a heavy cotton nightgown that fell just above her hips and revealed a strip of light fabric for underwear. The last girl into the parlor had on a quilted robe, emerald like her eyes, that she hadn't bothered to close. She was wearing no underclothing.

"Girls, turn around and show whatcha got," ordered Missy. They obediently swung in slow circles, lifting their gowns, smiling and winking at the men. Carl couldn't stop staring at them. All very young to be doing this. Despite his misgivings about their tender age, his passions were aroused and ran like hot currents into his loins. He longed to stroke the satin skin of a woman, feel her curves under his thick hands. One of the girls, almost as tall as Carl and with long, stick-straight hair so pale gold it was almost white, came toward him and sat on his lap.

"Y'all wanna come along with me, honey? What's yer name? I'm Betsy."

Carl stared at her for a moment, studying the wide-set icy blue eyes and the tiny dot of pupil dead center in each, the rich beauty of those eyes filling his mind with an insinuating intoxication.

"My name is Carl." He could think of nothing else to say.

"Oh, yer from a different country, aren'tcha? That's excitin'. Ah'll show ya how we do it in the United States of 'Merica. Come on."

She slid sinuously onto Carl's lap, which caused the sheer fabric she was wearing to lift up around her thigh. He knew she had done this deliberately to excite him, and it had its effect. They went down the hall hand-in-hand as she chattered gaily to him about the various options at their disposal. Would he like a special jessamine-scented cream?

Does the gentleman want to be on the bottom? Her whiskey-tinged breath floated across his face and inflamed him even more. Three doors closed behind him and he mused fuzzily that Geoffrey, Horace and Billy had already gone into bedrooms with their whores. His companion motioned him into her quarters, a small but cozily decorated room, made intimate with brocaded tapestries that hung along two walls, and a gas lamp on a table casting a soft, low ochre light.

Carl wanted to ask the girl how old she was, but at the same time he feared that knowing her young age would place a hindrance on his anticipated pleasure. Her youthful face and expression hinted at early teen years. When she slipped off her almost transparent gown, the taut skin and slight musculature confirmed to Carl that she couldn't be more than fifteen. He felt a lustful guilt, wanting to take this nymphet into his arms and knowing at the same time it was wrong for more than one reason. His sexual locomotive overcame all these thoughts, and quickly he was upon her in the blankets and sheets of the bed, scattering several small pillows to the edges. She drew him between her legs, and he reached his hands upward to grab each of her budding breasts, then sank into her with a full erection. She made soft panting noises punctuated with loud moans. His orgasm overtook him with a tremendous roar of pleasure. He relaxed on top of her.

"Sweetie-pie, y'all please lie right here next to me," Betsy gasped. Carl knew he was crushing her underneath his husky, solid frame and rolled to one side. She took a deep breath and reached to the side table for a small whiskey glass. She sat up and sipped gingerly at it.

"Carl honey, you kin pay Missy on the way out. Fifteen dollars."

He reddened as remorse rankled his mind, and gazed one more time at her smooth, youthful waist and stomach, slender shapely legs, the inviting vee at her crotch, the enticing breasts. She noticed and asked perkily,

"Do you want to have another go, honey? Only ten for a second time." Carl shook his head, dressed as quickly as he could and returned down the dark hallway to the broad, bright expanse of the parlor. He took fifteen dollars out of his small leather money bag and handed it to Missy. Suddenly, out of the corner of his eye he noticed another man standing nearby. Would this be Betsy's next customer? The idea of it aroused him.

"Carl, I'm pleased to introduce you to the owner of the Rooming House, Walter J. Nibley. Mr. Nibley, this here's Carl,"

The two men eyed each other, taking in one another's appearance for a minute or two. Walter Nibley was taller than Carl by half a foot, with broad shoulders and a paunch. A short, brown mustache and well-trimmed beard surrounded wide, thin lips that parted into a sinister smile and revealed a gold front tooth upward and two missing teeth along his lower jaw. Carl looked around quickly for his three companions in vain.

"You a Jew?" Walter J. Nibley asked Carl loudly, rubbing his left eye while talking, plagued by a tic in it. He was dressed in an expensive suit, and Carl noticed with a start that a gun holster hung around his waist, the ivory gun handle poking out conspicuously. Nibley smoothed his light brown, heavily pomaded hair with a large, thick hand.

"Yes, Mr. Nibley. I am Jewish, I come from Germany."

"Well, long as ya pay, I don't care. But just a warning, there's folks here who don't abide the Jews. After all, y'all killed Christ."

"Don't go threatening our payin' customers, Walter!" Missy's wide-set hazel eyes narrowed in warning. Then in a warmer tone she continued, "This is Mr. Carl's first time here. Please do visit us again soon, sir." She smiled prettily at Carl and batted heavily painted eyelashes. He swallowed hard and attempted to smile at her, but it turned into a slight scowl.

Carl hurried out the door and into the now very dark night, as the half-moon had deserted the landscape. Jeffrey, Horace and Bill were waiting, already mounted on their horses and smiling broadly.

"Didja tip her, Charlie?" asked Horace.

"Tip? What is this?"

"Oh, git back in there and give little Betsy a dollah or two, damn you!"

Carl did as he was told, mounted his sorry old nag awkwardly, and then they all clopped back along the obscure deer path. The three men peeled off in another direction when they neared his cabin. He led Vashti into the little lean-to he had built for her, went inside, and curled up on the kitchen floor without bothering to remove his clothing in the blanket Gussie had knitted and gifted him.

The next morning Carl awoke groggily and splashed his face with water in a bowl he had scooped from the hot springs yesterday. It had become icy cold overnight and did the job of waking him up. The light of sunrise was already strong, telling him that he had slept late. Not surprising, given his debauchery of the night before. He walked outside to breathe in the fragrant, fresh air of the woods, then went to feed Vashti. There on the floor of the lean-to lay Vashti, eyes half-open, mouth frozen in an equine grimace, legs stiff and outstretched on the rough floorboards.

11

Dora caught sight of Sara Dovkin hovering at the front gate, observing the merry beer-drinking and toasting, chatting punctuated by bursts and guffaws of laughter, children chasing one another around fathers' trousered legs and mothers' chintz or woolen skirts. She couldn't help but notice Sara's narrowed black eyes and thick black eyebrows as she watched Rosalia, surrounded by her siblings and Anna-leya Steinberger in a corner of the garden. Relatives had gathered to wish Rosalia a good and safe journey now that the War between the States had ended in April of 1865, over a year ago. The Wolfsons had struggled to save money for her passage to America for many months, and with small donations here and there from others, had been able to purchase the second-class ticket so that she would not have to travel alone in steerage, which they knew from others who had done it was not safe for a young woman. Not in attendance were Uncle Benjamin, Aunt Naomi, and Daniel, the consequence of a rift between the two families.

Isaac stood by the dining table he had carried into the garden, chatting with the men. He passed around steins of beer donated by his boss for the celebration, and they proceeded to toast. Isaac started the rounds.

"Here's to your kind and generous hearts, helping our family to raise the money for Rosalia's journey. We are grateful for this mitzvah from our relatives and dear friends."

The steins glinted in the bright June sunlight as they were raised aloft and the men shouted. From across the garden, the women smiled and raised their own steins.

"A toast to Carl Gersman and Rosalia Wolfson, soon to be bride and groom!" cried out Rabbi Schecter. The steins sailed upward again. The women echoed the Rabbi's words with their own toast, calling as one, "Mazel tov! Congratulations!"

Sara flung open the gate, stomping past a group of excited aunts discussing Rosalia's wedding in America. Tight-lipped, she headed directly for Dora.

"Well, you have made a fine family gathering here for your daughter, now that she will be leaving Germany," Sara Dovkin began.

"Please have some kasha with chicken and beer or apple cider, Sara," Dora offered congenially, sensing the wrath concealed behind Sara's stiff smile.

"I will do no such thing. I will not celebrate the future marriage of such a daughter as yours. She is a girl of questionable morals and bad behavior. She does us a favor by leaving town. The town is well rid of her."

As she spoke, her voice gained volume, until the last two sentences literally echoed off the porch wall and flew to the corners of the garden like swarms of bees stinging the ears of the celebrants. A sudden hush fell upon everyone, and as one their eyes turned up to the porch where the women stood glaring at each other like two hooded crows. Bitter invective thrust its way into Dora's mind, and she longed to fling it at her wretched neighbor, but she managed to reign it in. Still, the glint of vindictive triumph in Sara's eyes and the twisted moue on her face were galling.

"Sara, we all know how you have suffered. But this does not give you the right to speak badly of others and bring the evil eye. My daughter is a decent girl, and she's going away. Why are you trying to ruin our farewell celebration?"

"Decent girl? Hah!" sneered Sara. "All the town knows she is loose and improper. Is her future husband aware of this? Ach, I saw with my own eyes, she kissed Herr Hamstadt, ja, the bookstore owner. Disgraceful!" Her wrinkled cheeks bulged and reddened, giving her the countenance of a dried apple.

People began murmuring indistinctly to one another and to themselves until a piercing voice cut through the patter.

"That is a lie! I did not kiss Herr Hamstadt, he kissed me by surprise, and I did not like that one bit. And you are an evil snoop! I hate you and I am so glad that I will never see you again!" Rosalia was hurrying toward the woman as she spoke, her eyes narrowed in fury and fists balled at her side.

"Oy, here comes the little tigress. Watch out," Aunt Eva muttered to Dora, who glared back at her.

Sara Dovkin was beginning to edge her way backward toward the front gate. Dora took a step toward her neighbor and said softly, "Sara, you are a good woman, but given to too much belief in gossip and the dishonest and exaggerated stories that circulate about everybody. Go home. And you, young lady,…" Dora grabbed Rosalia firmly by the arm as the girl rushed toward Frau Dovkin, fist raised to strike, "will control yourself and sit down."

The tiny iron latch clicked on the gate as Sara Dovkin slammed it behind her and hurried away. Dora felt mortified by the unexpected dressing down her neighbor had delivered in front of family and friends. She knew that Sara had done the damage that she had intended. Strangely, though, now Dora felt her first glimmer of relief and happiness at her eldest daughter's departure. Her leaving would be a good thing and give her a future. Like a falling star in a black sky, Sara had inadvertently done her a *mitzvah*, a good deed.

The days following Rosalia's farewell gathering were filled with hurried preparations for her leave-taking. Isaac had written to their friends the Meyers, who had emigrated a few months ago from Gliewitz to New Orleans and received an answer several weeks ago. They would be delighted to escort the Wolfsons' eldest daughter to Hot Springs after she disembarked at the Port of New Orleans in mid-July, as they were planning to move there anyway. Dora stitched jewelry into the lining of a blanket, a tiny ruby pendant on a gold chain that had been given to her by her mother. She sliced and dried plums, apricots, and apples in strips that Rosalia could take on her journey to eat on the train. She cracked and added walnuts and almonds to the fruit. Rosalia, Edith and Annaleya helped Dora, all four of them sewing Rosalia's trousseau, working needles furiously to complete everything in time for her departure. Annaleya sniffed and wiped her eyes at intervals.

"How will I bear it when you go? Who will go insect-hunting with me and help me with my English lessons? And listen to my silly secrets?"

"You must get your husband to bring you to America," Rosalia pronounced as if it were a done deed. "Then we can be happy housewives and raise our children together. Our husbands will become good friends, too," she waxed rhapsodic, spinning a daydream. "We will own farms next to one another and ride horses to each other's fields. We will be the most beautiful girls in Arkansas, and we will sew the most elegant gowns to wear to balls and dances."

"Yes, and you can teach our children English. You are so wonderful at the language, Rosela, I don't know how you learn it so quickly. And we will go to look at the hot springs and maybe put our feet in the magical hot water that Carl has written us about. And we will grow old like sisters together."

Dora smiled at their juvenile chatter, wondering how much of what they said would ever come true.

"I hate to spoil your sweet visions of the future, but who knows if there are balls and dances in Hot Springs? We read from Carl's letters to you that it is full of forests and wild animals roaming near the town. And really, who will pay for your fine ball gowns? Not your husbands."

"I don't need the gowns and balls," Rosalia answered quickly. "That's just what Annaleya and I imagine for fun. I want to be a teacher, to teach girls so they can read and write and learn history." Her cheeks flushed a deep pink and she bent over her needlework, fiercely stabbing the white broadcloth and yanking the blue thread.

The day of her departure arrived unseasonably hot for a late August day, and the sun was fiercely gilding buildings, streets, and tree branches as it rose mercilessly overhead. Isaac had already sent a letter to Carl that his daughter would be on her way to America in July. Isaac's dray, normally stacked with beer barrels from the brewery, was now piled with the entire Wolfson family, along with an oak traveling trunk, a hat box, and a large linen bag. These would be Rosalia's only possessions once she arrived in the new land. Anything else she needed, Dora and Isaac reassured their daughter, would be provided by her betrothed as was proper.

There was barely enough room for them all in the small conveyance, so they jostled and leaned left and right as the old black gelding stepped gingerly along the main street, Wilhelmstrasse, westward out of town and toward the train station. Even Henry and Jake were allowed to travel along, as it might be the last time they saw their sister. Henry, being the oldest son, seized the honor of perching on top of the travelling trunk.

The port city of Hamburg was a long train ride away. Along the way was Oppein, where both cousin Avram and Carl Gersman's parents lived. Isaac had already sent word ahead to them with an itinerant salesman from the Schmidt Brewery, which was now operating at half-volume from a different building, requesting to meet them and stay overnight.

Rosalia was attired in her one good dress, a light cornflower blue gown embroidered at the bodice which slid around her petite waist and then flared at the hips in a cascade of taffeta. On her dark gold curls sat a stylish French chapeau, a gift from Great Aunt Eva. It was a deeper hue, like the sky at twilight, almost matching her eyes, with a thin veil that stopped at her lovely, full bottom lip. Keeping the veil flush on the sides were two matching pearl hatpins, a gift from her father for her wedding day since he would not be in attendance for the momentous event, he reminded her sadly.

"Rosela, I am sending you out into the world with a special gift," Isaac had told her the night before when he handed her the pins wrapped in a soft cotton cloth.

"A gift, Papa?" Rosalia had taunted him with dancing eyes, only a trace of liquid in the corners giving her away. "Please do be careful not to make me cry."

"There will be dangers ahead, I suspect, and you are travelling alone. We are entrusting you to the ship and the ship's captain, but we do not know if they will care about you as we do and will make every effort to protect you. So you must protect yourself. Do not forget that you have these hatpins. They are thick, and they are sharp. I pray to Adonai you will never have to use them to protect yourself, but if you must, do not hesitate."

He pressed his lips on the small bundle and then placed them into his tiny daughter's hand and kissed her forehead. She opened the cloth and studied the shiny metal spikes topped with slightly elongated, iridescent white pearls.

The dray was nearing the edge of town and the homes were spaced further and further apart, with fields and forests flanking the road. The musky mixed scent of earth, livestock, and sweet blooming wildflowers that edged the road hung heavy in the heat, and Rosalia breathed it in liberally for what she believed must surely be the last time. She swiveled her neck to gaze at the town disappearing in the distance, and with a start glimpsed crimson flames licking skyward among the buildings. Black smoke spiraled upward into a dirty cloud and hovered over Gleiwitz. She could not help but cry out.

"Are you calling for your boyfriends?" teased Henry. "Too late for that now!"

"Shush, you lump of dirt," Isaac scolded. "Roselah, what is wrong? Are you feeling ill?"

The stunned girl could hardly speak, she was so riveted and horrified by the sight of Gliewitz burning. She turned to her father, then back again to the town along with everybody on the dray. The flames and smoke were gone.

"Gliewitz was on fire," murmured Rosalia. She took a great breath in. "But not anymore. It must have been my imagination but seemed so real."

"I don't see any fire!" yelled the brothers in chorus.

"Mama, Rosalia's having another vision," Edith stated importantly. She turned to her sister beside her on the narrow wagon bench. "I advise you, don't tell Mr. Carl Gersman anything about these crazy sightings you have, or he may not marry you. He'll say you're insane and that's a good reason to break off the engagement. Then where will you be, all alone thousands of kilometers away from us?"

They all fell silent as the road passed underneath and drew them closer to the train station. When they arrived, Isaac escorted his oldest daughter, his oldest child, to her seat, made sure she had her ticket for both the train and the ship passage, and kissed her farewell.

"Do not talk to anybody, particularly any men. I know that will make for a lonely journey, but it is far more important that it be a safe one. We will write to one another, yes?"

Rosalia couldn't speak. She nodded numbly and raised her hand to her chapeau, touching the hatpins her father had gifted her. He smiled through tears approvingly and said,

"You are travelling alone and must protect yourself. Don't be afraid to use them."

12

Samuel Gersman's store was tucked into a side street off downtown Central Avenue. It was a low-slung wood frame building couched between two dramatic outcroppings of pale novaculite, a rock peculiar to Arkansas that Carl always marveled at. Samuel sold dry goods to the townsfolk, miners still hoping to strike it rich in the West, and the occasional visitor from points east. Since Carl's partner, Avram Steiner, had died, a business associate in New York, a cousin on his father's side, procured many goods and shipped them to Samuel for a cut of the profit. He managed to find very desirable items, such as Irish linens, Whitechapel needles, India teas, and silk thread. Samuel was a clever salesman, friendly, helpful and informative. He knew what to order for the townspeople and how much of it and made a fairly decent living. Carl admired his brother's entrepreneurial vigor and bullish work ethic and tried to emulate it. However, the demands of building a house to live in with his bride-to-be drew him away from the store more than he wanted.

Samuel was preparing the store for a day of customers one morning in early June when Carl came striding in, his face exuding excitement. He grabbed his brother's shoulders over the display counter and smiled broadly.

"She is coming! I got a letter from Rosalia's parents. She is on the steamship and will be here next month. I will be a married man very soon."

Samuel grinned back at Carl, nodding his head as if it were on a spring.

"I hope she is pretty and can cook. Then you will be blessed. Well, she may be on her way, but I could still use a hand putting out the wheat flour and corn meal."

"First of all," Carl began, jutting out his chin, "I happen to know she is very pretty. I have met her already. She was much younger, yes, but anyone could tell she was a beauty and would only get more beautiful. As for cooking, I am a lucky man if she learned from her mother."

"That's nice. Come and earn your living, little brother."

Samuel waved him to a back corner of the store where boxes filled with various dry goods stood. Carl ripped open the box planks or pried them apart with a hammer claw. He did not mind working for his brother, but he looked forward to the day he would have his own kosher butchering business. The two men worked silently for the rest of the day, counting inventory, arranging Irish linens, towels, beeswax for making candles, dyes, soap and dozens of other items on the shelves. The store was busier than ever these past few months. Everybody in town was involved in some way in reconstructing what had burned down during the war years, even the womenfolk. For that, they would need tools, work gloves, brooms, nails, lanterns. And of course, the need for dry goods was universal and ongoing.

Late in the afternoon, when the warmth of the day was gathering intensity and the sunlight slanted in through the half-shuttered southern windows of Gersman's Dry Goods, Horace Fletcher came limping with a cane across the oak floor planks. His strands of thin blonde hair were plastered back with a pomade, and his shirt was stained dark with sweat under his armpits. Even with the limp and hunched over, he towered over Carl.

"Howdy, " he called out before he reached the small, cluttered counter where Carl stood staring at him. "Where's Sam?"

"He is behind the store unloading supplies. What happened to you? Why are you walking like that?"

"This is called 'a limp', Carl my good pal. I'm limping because my rotten sonofabitch no good horse stepped on my foot when I was saddlin' him up. He's a new one, and high-spirited."

"Limp," Carl repeated. "New word. Sorry this happen. Happened," he corrected himself. This English language was sometimes similar to the German and Yiddish tongues, and other times as alien as the very bottom of the sea. "My horse died. I think old age."

"Aw heck, that's a damned shame about yer horse. I come to buy some tobacco, rolling papers, flour, tallow. Fetch me that, will ya, Carl?"

As Carl put together Horace's order, he couldn't keep the news to himself.

"Rosalia is coming on the boat! We will marry soon."

"Well, dang, Carl, this is good news. Better not let her find out what you been up to." Horace winked and his slight, long frame shook with suppressed laughter.

"Please, Horace, do not tell her about that place. I ask you from my heart."

Carl was horrified at the thought of their secret outing becoming known to his wife-to-be, spreading to the Jewish community and then to the entire town. He, Horace and the others were making regular weekend visits to Missy's Rooming House. Despite his religious observances and desire for marriage, Carl could not keep from indulging in his sexual appetites, unsatisfied for so long before now.

"Oh, don't you worry, friend. We will keep that buried in the root cellar until we go to our graves."

Carl's twisted stomach relaxed with relief. Still, there was self-loathing mixed in and a certain distrust as he realized that his standing in the Jewish community and with his future wife rested on the discretion of this man. Horace handed him a dollar. Carl had finally gotten used to the touch of the dollar, so different in look and feel from the Marks they used in Europe. He rubbed the bill between his thumb and middle finger. They came in only one color, dull green, with words in English and Latin clustered beneath strange symbols. And the coins, so confusing at first. Now he could distinguish one from another and their values, but they gave him difficulty when he first had arrived in New York on the way to Arkansas.

Just before Horace departed, the front entrance creaked slightly, and a little girl, skin dark as a moonless night, slipped inside and skipped to the counter. She smiled shyly at Carl and reached into a pocket of her homespun tan cotton dress, which floated, patched and oversized, around her small frame. Her spindly legs showed from the shins down, two little pieces of ebony. Her hair was pulled tightly into two pigtails above her ears, each wrapped in a little bow of white yarn. Carl smiled warmly at her and said,

"Good afternoon, Lucy. I am happy see you. What do you want today?"

She smiled back in delight. "A little candy, please, sir, and Mama need two yard of calico."

Carl laughed and said, "Lucy! Mama say first get candy, then cotton? I give you one candy free, don't tell nobody."

Suddenly Horace, who had stopped in his tracks when the child entered, grabbed the girl by the elbow and shoved her against the counter.

'What you are doing, Horace?" Carl asked, astonished. "You do this to little girl?"

"What're you doing, letting darkies in here? This here's a store for whites, no darkies allowed in unless they slaves fetching for masters, and there's no more of that, thanks to the damned war. So let 'em stay out and buy f'um each other." He scowled angrily, the skin of his pale face reddening, blonde eyebrows, creating a wake of furrows in his forehead. Despite his temporary incapacity, he raised his cane in the air and brought it down in a hard smack on the child's back. She screamed in pain and fell on the floor. Horace staggered backward and stabilized himself quickly with the cane, shaking in rage. Carl rushed around the counter to lift the weeping girl up and comfort her.

"What, you crazy? This store, this store…" Carl stammered, "is for all color of people, not only white. How you can do this? Hurt the little girl?"

Samuel hurried in from the back lot of the store, looking around worriedly.

"What is all this commotion, brother?"

"You ain't gonna see me in here no more, Jew boys!" Horace yelled, veins throbbing visibly at his temple and neck. "Not if you think we whites're gonna do business same place as our own former slaves! Folks're gonna hear about this!"

He pushed out the door with his cane as quickly as he could, slamming the oak door so that it jumped in its frame and rustled unsteadily for a few seconds. The brothers listened silently to the sobbing child, and then Carl picked her up in his muscled arms, thickened with the daily, monotonous chopping and sanding of wood.

"Tell your Mama sorry, pardon please," Carl whispered in her ear, mortified. How could he and Samuel ever make it up to her or her family? "You come this store anytime." He pressed a small, hard cinnamon candy ball into her cupped right hand, then placed her carefully on the floor.

"I walk with you home," Carl insisted. "Make certain Horace don't hurt you again."

"Strange, all this," Samuel said to his brother in German. "The *shvartzes* have been patronizing my store since before the Civil War. When they were slaves, they came to fetch goods for the plantations. And during the war, well, you know we weren't even in town because it was so dangerous here. And now that we're all back here and resuming our livelihoods, a white gentile throws a fit a week when they see a shvartze buying our goods. But it still takes me by surprise.

Things could get very ugly, brother, and we need to tread lightly to protect ourselves."

"I don't know exactly what you mean by 'tread lightly', Samuel, but if that means we throw the *shvartzes* out of our store, I say no. This is not right. Don't forget, our ancestors were slaves. Surely Hashem wouldn't want us to treat badly these people finally free from bondage."

Without waiting for a response, Carl swung out the door with Lucy's tiny dark hand resting in his beefy pale one, and together they walked to her mother's house. Lucy wasn't crying anymore, but she still winced with pain every few minutes. As they walked, Carl began to reflect on the conversation he had had with Horace before Lucy walked in. With a start he realized that Horace had leverage over him because of their visits together to the Rooming House. Horace could ruin him in front of Rosalia and the entire Jewish community. Geoffrey and Billy could do the same. He had lived in Hot Springs less than a year after the war ended, but he was already in a true predicament. And he had nobody to blame but himself.

13

The three wizened, elderly, chocolate-skinned sisters entered Samuel's Dry Goods store on an early Monday morning at 9:30, as they had been doing since before Carl began working there. They always sidled in one at a time, murmuring to one another in their floral cotton day dresses and modest straw hats. The rough pine door would creak closed behind them and then slam abruptly. *Must build a new door soon,* Carl would say to himself as he did every day for the past seven months that he had been working for his brother. Meanwhile, he must give his attention to the three shvartze ladies. Their dark skin fascinated him, and he wished to touch it even though he knew that could never happen. He wanted to see if their skin felt like his own or his mother's skin. Turning to the women, he smiled broadly.

"Marie, Violetta, Betta Jean, good morning. I see you three, I know it is Monday! You want the usual?"

Violetta Biggs, the most talkative of the three, said, "The usual, Mr. Gersman. Pound a flowah, half pound a sugah, pound a conemeal. We outta bakin' powdah, so half cuppa dat. An' taday les have us some gun powdah too. Five ounce oughttah do."

Marie and Betta Jean were fingering the fabrics lying on a table in the center of the store and commenting softly to one another.

"Shore….pretty…." came to Carl's ears. Sometimes he had difficulty comprehending the speech of the darker-skinned Americans. It was not exactly the same speech as he heard from the white inhabitants of Hot Springs. The words were the same, he knew, but some of them sounded different. It was getting easier to understand as time went on.

He turned to his task and began filling bags with the requested dry goods. Sometimes people in this town paid with money, but other times they came with items to trade, just like in Oppein. Samuel had instructed Carl to accept the trades with discretion; it kept inventory moving and people coming in, which attracted even more customers. In the long run, even though many of the exchanges did not equal in value what Samuel's Dry Goods sold them, it still worked out. Today the three sisters had brought a large burlap sack full of fresh vegetables and fruit from their garden.

Carl was engrossed in serving the three sisters when he heard the door creak and slam again. Heavy boot steps thudded on the oak planks of the floor. Carl turned around to face the customer, bags of flour and sugar in his hand for the sisters. The narrow, ivory face of Reverend Isaiah Upton scowled at him above a flannel brown shirt buttoned up his neck to the top button.

"Hello to you, sir," said Carl. "Please, I will help you soon, first let me give the ladies this. Ladies, all this plus gunpowder is one dollar and thirty-two cents. I am happy you pay in onions, spinach, tomatoes, apples. Good deal."

Carl smiled and took the bulging burlap sack from Violetta, who then joined her siblings at the fabric table, eyes cast down. The three were quiet and still. Only their fingers moved slowly across the cottons and linens.

Reverend Upton fingered his thin white mustache. His right hand fluttered at his throat nervously. Then he swung the fluttering hand outward toward Carl and pointed with a bony finger.

"Sinner! Come to my Baptist Church and be saved."

Carl sighed and the sisters began edging toward the door behind Reverend Upton.

"No more of this again, Isaiah," said Carl. "You want to buy something? I sell you. If you don't want something at store, then time for you to go."

The sisters rolled their eyes upward as Isaiah twisted his head around to look at them.

"What is this evil here? You allow the darkies into your place of business alongside the pure white people? Jesus, save us all! They have their own stores. They must keep to themselves so as not to taint us. Shame, children of Cain. Leave this establishment at once."

"No, no, no, the ladies stay. Do not come in here and say what to do with customers. This my business, my brother's business. You want to throw out the customer? Go away then, I don't sell you nothing." Carl's face turned a deep rose shade, his eyes narrowed and the chestnut-hued eyebrows above clapped together.

Suddenly Isaiah lunged toward Carl and swept his outstretched arm in a violent thrust to knock several sacks of flour and sugar from a nearby shelf to the floor. Sugar granules danced across the floor like a snow flurry and one flour sack lay open, puffing white dust upward and across the store.

Carl was well aware that none of the white Christian businesses in Hot Springs allowed the Negroes and in some cases, Jewish people, to enter and do business. In fact, some stores and restaurants had the sign "No dogs or Jews allowed." He and Samuel welcomed the newly freed *shvartzes* into their store. The Germans made no apologies, even though some gentiles refused to patronize them as punishment for it. They weren't all that much different than the Germans and other Europeans they had left behind, at least not in this way.

"You *meshuggah*, crazy man. You pay for flour and sugar on floor." He began to shout at Isaiah in German, sprinkling it with choice Yiddish insults.

"Submit thyself to Jesus," intoned Isaiah. "You may not curse me in Satan's language. I am protected by the holiness of Christ." He huddled his hands together under his chin and intoned, "Lord Jesus, please bring this wayward sheep back into the fold so that he may repent of his sins and belong to you. This Jew will surely go to hell and burn in eternal damnation if you do not open his eyes to the truth."

Carl understood little of the prayer. Where was the sheep? What did a sheep have to do with this altercation? He knew when someone was trying to pressure him, though.

"The ladies, they stay and shop here! You, *shmuck*, go and shop at white only store. I don't care." He glanced around the store to locate his three shoppers but stared at empty space where the three had stood just moments before. Violetta,

Betta Jean and Marie had taken off like startled partridges flushed from a bush.

"Why you bother me?" Carl asked Isaiah. "I don't bother you. You make good customers go away."

Reverend Upton leaned over the counter and put his face close to Carl's. Carl could smell his stale breath soured with whiskey and wrinkled his nose in repugnance.

Softly, Upton said, "I know you are an Israelite, and the Israelites killed our Lord Jesus Christ. So you are condemned to hell right there, sir. If I can save your soul, that would be something powerful glorious. Powerful glorious in the eyes of our Lord. Only He can forgive and save ye."

Carl's entire face reddened like the setting sun. Who did this *alter kacker,* this old fart, think he was, already drunk in the morning and creating a ruckus in the store?

"You stay out of this store," Carl yelled in a rage. "Go home your family, I don't want you in here no more. You make trouble, and I don't care your religion. Have my own, that is good enough."

The two of them stood squared off with hands on hips, face to flustered face, scowling with equal ire and righteousness. The abrupt silence was like a metal fence between them, unbreachable. Reverend Upton suddenly broke the silence with a frustrated guttural, "Agghh, you Jews are all alike, so proud and born for Satan's flames."

He swung around, his coattails making a low whoosh, and stalked out of Samuel's Dry Goods. Carl leaned heavily against the splintered counter and wiped sweat off his neck and forehead. It was even dripping down his nose, making a tiny splash on the tin money box that the brothers used for transactions. Slowly and carefully, he filled three bags, one with flour, one with sugar, one with cornmeal, and tied them tightly at the top to keep them from spilling. He stepped into the storage room where they kept the gunpowder and filled a small sack. He swept the spilled grains into a dustpan and dumped them in the trash can, then spent some time cleaning the floor.

He locked the door to Samuel's Dry Goods, pocketed the key in his pants, and headed out into the bright daylight of Central Avenue. He kept walking, his mouth set in a determined line, until he reached the home of the three sisters. He had walked past their home many times in his strolls around Hot Springs, and always got restrained but friendly waves from at least one of the sisters if they happened to be gardening in their front yard. They kept a tidy, small residence in a poor neighborhood where only Negro people lived, on the outskirts of town, and gardened every possible inch of dirt around it. A neatly trimmed path made of steppingstones ran through the garden from the front yard along the side of the house and into the little backyard. He walked up to the front door and knocked softly. After several minutes had passed, he knocked again, a little louder. Violetta's face appeared in a crack in the door, and then when she saw who it was, she opened the door wider. Mournfully she gazed at Carl, shaking her head. Carl handed her the bags from the store and said,

"This is gift to you. I don't want no pay for it. Sorry this terrible thing happen in the store."

Violetta smiled sweetly at him as Marie and Betta Jean gathered behind her.

"You a decent man, Mr. Carl," Violetta said. "We's not afraid to come back to yo' store. Just not when dat mean white reverend is in it. We see him, we's gonna leave and wait fo' him ta go."

"I tell him already don't come back, never, never," Carl emphasized hotly.

"Oh deah, dat might be trouble fo' us, sugah. Da white folk don't lahk ta be tol' what to do. We jes' have ta look out fo' him and stay out da way."

"Don't worry. He is a stupid man. You make nice food with flour and sugar and cornmeal. Maybe nice roast chicken. Have fine dinner. I will see you again at store," As Carl left the sisters' little yard and started back to the store, he heard Violetta shut her door firmly and lock it behind her.

Samuel was waiting for his brother, tapping his foot impatiently as Carl walked meekly into the store. Carl always opened the store at eight o'clock every morning and kept busy tidying up the dry goods and merchandise, adding more to the shelves when necessary, organizing dollars and coins in the money box, dusting and sweeping, and waiting on customers. Samuel would join him later in the day as business picked up and stayed later than Carl to close the store and count the daily take. Never before had Carl locked up and abandoned the store in the middle of the day.

"What the hell is going on here?" Samuel swore at him, his deep-set brown eyes blazing like heated pennies. "Where did you go?"

Carl related the story of Reverend Upton to his brother, and they both declared war on the man. They agreed that he would never be allowed into their store or on either of their properties for any reason. They resumed their work duties at the store, but Samuel insisted that Carl leave an hour early, business being slow that day. He could relax and rejuvenate his spirit. Carl hugged his brother, grateful for a little extra time off, and left quickly.

He thought first of going back to his house, still very roughly framed in and not quite closed to the elements. He headed that way, then suddenly directed his steps instead toward the center of town, where the hot springs pooled and steamed. Before reaching the main thoroughfare, he heard a low growl. It seemed to come from a building on the corner, but as he stepped up his pace to a trot, alarmed, he realized it originated from the midst of a nearby walnut orchard. A black bear as large as a buggy emerged from the orchard and shambled through the dead leaves. Carl ran, glancing nervously over his shoulder every few moments, but the creature had retreated deeper into the woods.

As he strode southward down Central Avenue toward the springs, he marveled at the beauty of this strip of civilization fringed like a holy man's waist with dense forest and sanctified by the mystifying ponds. Central Avenue lay like a dry riverbed at the bottom of a canyon, the foothills of the Ouachita Mountains rising on either side behind rows of stores, inns, and saloons. The hills were forested with short-leaf pines, green ash, and blackgum trees. They thinned out as the slope incline lessened, and it was here, between the tree line and the street, that the boiling waters tumbled up and out of the maw of the Earth in several openings, then dipped below the ground again. Heated beyond human tolerance by the Earth's tremendous pressure deep below, they could only be approached cautiously. To fall in was certain death. Along Central Avenue the boiling effluence emerged and cooled as Hot Springs Creek.

Carl mulled over what he had seen in his months of living in this little town on the brink of American wilderness. He couldn't help but notice young and old men missing limbs or blind in one or both eyes, a preponderance of widows, and more orphans than one would imagine in a town of this size. Not so easily observed were the emotional scars. Carl could only sense the silent anguish that lurked in the townspeople's eyes. They had all lost someone, been attacked, terrorized, or run out of town. Some had fought with one another bitterly over the issue of slavery, so bitterly that family members, friends and neighbors were now completely alienated. During the months that Carl was building his new home, he had heard snatches of conversation about estranged loved ones and neighbors, sad asides, angry comments about the status of the newly freed slaves. It seemed to him that the luckless dark-skinned folks had gone from the frying pan into the fire, an expression he recently learned from Samuel.

Carl's building helpers had confided some ugly thoughts about the free darkies, the voting darkies, the ex-slave who had the gall to run for office. *Why, some of them even own land in the North,* wheezed Horace, gin-tainted breath blowing past Carl's nostrils. They would taunt him good-naturedly for being an "Israelite", but even as he smiled tolerantly at their ignorant gibes about the Jewish religion and people, he knew that they regarded him as a threat because he was different. This behavior and dislike of Jews reminded him what he had suffered in the old country.

He sighed deeply, ruminating on all of this, as he eased his long legs onto a rough plank of pine timber that served as a bench at the edge of one of the pools, referred to as corn holes by the residents in town, that had captured and cooled underground water to a tolerable temperature. The steam rose above him seductively and into the air like a white-hot finger.

A shadow fell across his legs and the rustle and jangle of clothing startled him out of his reverie. Looking up, Carl saw a ruddy, unsmiling face, manly despite the long dark hair that hung in a braid casually draped over a beaded leather-clad shoulder.

"The hot springs are happy for your visit. I see the smoke curling toward you. May I sit here?" he asked and without waiting, sat on the bench beside Carl. He stretched out his arm and extended lean, tan-colored fingers, which Carl shook politely.

"Hello, I am Carl Gersman. You are an Indian?"

"My English name is Thomas, the name my white Pa gave me. I am a member of the Quapaw tribe of people. My Quapaw name is Waddite, from my mother. It has a meaning, 'crosses the stream'. Your English is not so perfect. Mine is better. What language did you learn as a child? You do not sound like the other white men."

"Ah, that is not easy for to explain. The language of my father and mother is German, and I come from country of Germany."

The deep-eyed, serious fellow pulled a beautifully woven piece of fabric out of a large leather pouch slung over his shoulder. In the shadow of a buckeye tree, the brilliant green, vermillion and mustard hues of the textile almost leaped out at them. He smiled at Carl and his unusual gray eyes had a spark in them.

"I made this. For twenty cents you can give your woman a gift. I'm giving you a good price. I like you."

Carl smiled at the Quapaw man wistfully.

"You, my new friend, are good salesman. My 'woman' is coming from far away, she is not here still." He hesitated. "But I think, maybe yes, I buy this for her as marriage gift."

He pulled out his own small leather pouch and extracted two silver dimes, rubbing them between his fingers like tender leaves. Coins here were still slightly alien to him, so different in appearance from the hefty silver Vereinsthaler coins he used in Oppein. The two men made the exchange, and the Quapaw then sat beside Carl, his lanky, leather-dressed legs sprawling outward as he leaned his elbows on top of them and hunched in toward the warm pool of water a mere foot or so below the bench. As the steaming vapors rose up from the flowing creek, he bent his face forward and breathed in deeply, exhaling with a slight sighing sound. He sat up erect and square-shouldered, took Carl's hand briefly, and gave it a gentle shake.

He shifted his broad shoulder slightly to turn and face Carl directly.

"You are friendlier than other white people here. They will not sit next to a Quapaw or half-Quapaw like myself. They will not make pleasant conversation with us, but they take our goods or our money. And not just those who live here. Also wealthy visitors with illnesses who come to soak in the springs and be cured. Prospectors passing through on their way to the West. None of them like the Quapaw people, the Choctaws or the Cherokees."

"Nice to meet you, Thomas. I can call you Waddite instead? Do I say it correct, yes? Ach, good. I like the sound of it. Pardon, I think you are half-breed Indian my brother tell me about. You live here in Hot Springs?"

"I travel between my white father's home here and the reservation where my mother lives. The Quapaw tribe hasn't lived here for many years. This place you call Hot Springs was for thousands of years a hunting land for my ancestors. Here they killed the deer, rabbits, bears, many kinds of animals in these woods, for food and furs, and traded with the Choctaw people too. And sometimes they relaxed in the warm creek pools. Nobody owned those soaking waters, a strange notion of the white people. We shared it as it is a gift to all from Mother Earth. My mother, her mother and father, all the tribes, were free to go where they pleased. But then to keep the settlers from fighting over the springs, the Indians claimed it and sold it to the American government in 1830. Some of my tribespeople travel to Hot Springs occasionally to do business. Mr. Hamilton on Fountain Street is happy to buy our woven rugs, dolls and baskets made by the women and girls of our tribe. And a few other people and stores also buy our goods. The white leaders make us live in Oklahoma on land not beautiful like this, and not good for hunting. They call that land "Indian Reservation". We call that land the end of the Trail of Tears."

"Mr. Waddite, thank you for history lesson. I am grateful. My people, the Jews, are tribe people too. My people come from twelve tribes, ten lost in desert in land far away from here, across the Atlantic Ocean. Only two tribes survive now. So we are same that way."

Waddite's thick, dark eyebrows rose sharply as he swung around to face Carl. "You, with white skin, come from a tribe? That news surely will be interesting to the other Quapaws. I will tell them about that. What is the name of your tribe?"

Before Carl could answer, a harsh voice rang out from behind the two men.

"What the hey.… A white man sittin' with a redskin? Since when do you socialize with these no-good murderin' sons o' bitches? Git up and git outta here, Indian boy!"

A parchment-white hand tightly grabbed hold of Waddite's upper arm and yanked hard. He slipped backward off the pine bench awkwardly, then leaped up and pulled off the still-grasping hand. He swung around to face his aggressor, rising to an impressive height over him. The two men began to shout at each other angrily, cheeks turning red with fury, eyes narrowed, fists shaking. Carl could only catch some of the phrases: "dirty redskin", "think you are?", "was our land", "not your business". Before they could come to blows, he stood up and waved frenetically at the two quarreling men.

"Excuse, *excuse!*" He had to shout to distract them in his direction. "Sir, please stop. Not necessary to fight. Why you so angry? I am not true white Christian man, sir. I am a Jew. So it is fine I sit and talk with Indian man."

The intruder, a rangy, clean-shaven man with wide-set eyes and ears that stuck out from his head like pink flaps from under a round, black Homberg hat, stared at Carl in surprise. "Well, I'll be … a Jew and an Injun. What is this town coming to? Nothing but riffraff who don't know their place. Well, I know there is some Jews in town but you ain't welcome here neither. Go on and keep each other company, you two dirty pig butts. Just stay out of my shop or I'll throw ya out by the seat of yer pants. I won't be selling you any of my shoes or boots or repair any o' your'n."

He backed up a few steps gazing at Carl's face, then at Waddite's, turned and stumbled off across the hillside, his lean frame lumbering under a dirty tan apron that flapped around his thighs.

When he had disappeared over the incline, Waddite turned to Carl and grinned.

"That was Arthur MacDougal, the town cobbler. He is always in foul tempers, a discontented man. Everybody in Hot Springs knows this about him. Pay him no mind."

Carl scratched his chin through his bushy beard in wonder. This country overflowed with freedom, he heard when he lived in Oppein, but now that he was in America, he saw the freedom was tainted with hatred for the *shvartzes,*

Indians, Jews, apparently anybody who was not a white Christian. It reminded him of Prussian society, rampant with notions of superiority and inferiority. White Christian aristocrats in Europe could tread all over anybody of a lesser status, could even kill a Jew or a Roma with impunity. Still, there were no aristocrats here in America. Carl wondered if the shopkeeper could shoot him dead and then not go to jail because he killed someone who was not a white Christian. He would have to ask Samuel about that.

The two men lowered themselves back onto the bench above the warm pool. Waddite reached into his leather pouch and then stretched out his arm to pass a small leather flask of alcohol to Carl.

"You made a friend of me today, Carl. I know that Jews live here in Hot Springs, but until today I knew nothing about them. Now I find out that fewer of your tribes survived than the Indians. I hope to learn more."

Carl turned the flask over in his hand, then sniffed and studied the dark liquid inside. It emitted an earthy, alcoholic odor that Carl couldn't recognize.

"What is this drink, Waddite? Make me drunk?"

Waddite laughed heartily, nodding his head up and down.

"Only if you drink too much. This is corn whiskey. The Cherokee invented it, and the white people stole their recipe. There are hidden stills and hidden Cherokee making and selling it. It will ease your time waiting for your woman to travel here and be your wife. Or save it for your wedding day."

"If you want to learn more about Jewish people, come to my wedding ceremony. I invite you. Bring your father and mother."

Waddite grinned broadly. "That, my friend, would be like corralling wolves and bears in a pen and asking them to get along. And with that savage notion, I must bid you goodbye. My Quapaw friends are waiting for me on Central Avenue. Today I travel to Oklahoma to visit my mother."

They shook hands solemnly and smiled at one another. Waddite trudged down the hill and disappeared behind a row of buckeyes. Carl was troubled by the shopkeeper's outburst, but delighted at meeting Waddite, and his mind was aswirl with thoughts. Strangely, he felt a mantle of contentment settle upon his mood as he peacefully watched the unstoppable heated spring tumble down a nearby hillside in its bed. It emerged from a small, rocky eave, flowed several hundred feet, and tucked back underground at another culvert.

All that heat and vapor, Carl mused as the noise of the water rumbled in his ears. He turned and gazed behind him at seven or eight long, low bathhouses tucked into the hillside, in various stages of resurrection after being torched by the Bushwhackers during the war. One of them was free, a government-built edifice, but the fancier ones were privately owned, and the proprietors collected entrance fees. Well-heeled visitors and gold and silver prospectors on their way west were keeping those private bathhouses in business. It seemed to Carl that despite the devastation of the war that had just ended, this was a promising town in which to prosper.

He stood up when his toes began to shrivel from the delightfully warm water, briefly stretched his arms up to the sky, and started moving slowly downhill. Once again, a low, fierce growl assaulted his ears and caused him to swing around and scour the white pines a short distance behind him. There was the black bear, baring yellowish teeth the size of his butcher knife. Was it following him? Carl didn't wait around to find out.

14

The tall, elegantly suited gentleman waited patiently as the line of passengers boarded the great steamship about to set sail across the Atlantic from New York's harbor to Europe. He nodded pleasantly to the other voyagers, tipping his brown silk topper, smiled politely at the ladies, and helped to lift a heavy bag or awkward bundle here and there. Even now, years after he had been shuffled off to an orphanage and then an uncaring home as a servant, grimy and thin from malnutrition, he was forced to reflect on just how far he had come in life. Yes, he was quite a long way removed from the misery of his childhood.

Young Roland Longman's luck had arrived in the form of a mentor, a ham-handed, stout bartender named James Sears, who took him under his wing and tutored him in the gallantries of social behavior. When he wasn't bartending, Jimmy, as he was known by friends and locals, was procuring women for a burgeoning brothel trade tucked deeply into the recesses of a rough and tumble New York City neighborhood. The take was good, and risk was minimal. He was protected by a couple of city cops as long as he parted with a small percentage of his earnings, and circumstances improved when he stumbled across Longman, poor as a cobbler's apprentice, possessing few skills, and trolling desperately for work. He wandered into Sears's bar, a roughened boy looking for a job.

Sears noticed Longman's fine features, his square jaw, deep set green eyes and shock of burnished hair. These were assets in his trade that would lure the ladies into a web of false promises until they were too entangled and tainted to flee.

However, the lad behaved like a farmer's son in a field and needed polishing. Roland Longman was eager for any kind of trade he could find and all too gladly went along with James Sears' lessons in civil manners and even more, in the finer points of discreet seduction. Sears had observed a spectrum of these techniques in his bar as well as the after-hours parties he put on at home. He even financed a course of German classes for Roland so that he could use some basic phrases with the German immigrant women.

These reflections on his past kept Longman calm and unhurried, along with the realization that there was plenty of time to pass on the voyage. This was his fourth "commerce journey", as Jimmy referred to it with a salacious wink. He felt more confident than ever that he could succeed as he had done before in enticing one or two young female passengers to trust him. He targeted only those who appeared to be just past childhood and not yet in their twenties, were traveling alone and were of modest means, judging by their dress, speech and most importantly, their location in steerage. As a first-class traveler, he had access to the entire ship, whereas the steerage passengers were limited to only the bottom deck. By creating an 'accidental' mishap in that miserable traveling section of the ship, he would apologize profusely and begin the introduction. Very tentatively he would find out the target's name, age, background, destination, and then proceed on to her problems and complaints. Gingerly, delicately, he would allow her to reveal her struggles and conflicts, offering no advice but a great deal of sympathy and complete understanding. When motivated, he even invented a sister with a similar complaint to compare symptoms and outcomes and engender even more signs of compassion.

To satisfy her curiosity about himself, Longman would fabricate the background of a merchant family on the East Coast, a father who sent him abroad once a year to sweeten the European contacts they did business with. He learned to hang back for stretches of time on the three to four-week voyage to prevent an impression of over eagerness. He would enter steerage on various pretexts and catch the eye of his intended victim. Their interactions would be intermittent and brief, but he would linger slightly longer each time. Longman timed them, glancing at his gold-fobbed watch as the conversation went on. Then he would break it off with an apologetic excuse. Business required his attention to some matter in his stateroom, so deeply sorry to rush off like this. Perhaps they could continue this fascinating discourse on another day?

The day of his embarkation finally arrived in late April. The huge transatlantic steamship creaked in its berth, small waves slapping at its shiny metal hull. A diving seagull's piercing shriek as it skimmed the air currents above the harbor brought Longman out of his reverie. He breathed in the soft, brine-tinged zephyr ruffling his hair and stepped briskly into the sturdy rowboat heading for the vessel anchored in deeper waters, a small leather valise in his gloved left hand. This journey would take him to Hamburg, and after a week or so of curious exploration and enjoyment of libations and cuisine at the local taverns, he would steam back across the enormous Atlantic Ocean to the port of New Orleans, and finally northwest to Hot Springs, Arkansas. He had business associates in both of those fine, excellently decadent towns.

The steamship's anchor was hoisted, and the vessel slowly chugged westward. Roland observed the crowd of folks waving their goodbyes to their loved ones. They became smaller and more forlorn as the rowboats distanced themselves from the land and headed to the U.S.S. *Eolus* with their precious cargo of voyagers. He had no one in this life to wish him safe journey and did not want to be reminded of that. No matter how fiercely he convinced himself it wasn't important, the pinching loneliness of a lack of family life fought its way to the surface, angering him and suddenly he felt like a little boy. He quickly clenched his fists and teeth, deliberately focusing on the thought of women: sweet, soft, vulnerable, profitable. He had serious business to attend to, and it must not be compromised by the folly of self-pity over worthless memories.

James Sears had given Roland enough financing to purchase passage on the steamer and several sets of gentleman's clothing. The travel expenses would be deducted from Roland's earnings, but the clothes were a gift from his mentor. They were of fine cut and quality and would last for a long time. Any replacement clothing would be at Roland's expense. Two husky stewards hauled his personal effects in two large trunks, leading him to his first-class cabin.

He entered and gazed around admiringly at the polished walnut wainscotting along the walls, the beveled mirror over a fine birdseye maple bureau. Then there was the bed, sturdy and wide, which made him smile. He pressed a coin into each steward's hand and waved them out of the cabin. Once he was alone, he sat on the bed and tilted his head to listen. The bed was quiet, he was pleased to note. Fine feather filling in the mattress. No crackling or groaning of wooden posts. It was quiet and smooth.

He arose from it and went over to the mirror, studying his reflection. Then he carefully trimmed his handlebar mustache and beard and combed his thick, wavy auburn hair back into a neat curve at the nape of his neck. Searching through his valise, he located the pomade bottle he had packed there, pulled it out, and applied it assiduously to his hair, adding shine and fragrance. He flung open his trunks and immediately began to smoothe out and hang up his clothing on hooks in the small armoire next to the bed. His appearance was a crucial part of the lure, and he was obligated to tend to its every aspect before leaving his room to engage the other passengers.

After a half hour or so of organizing and preening, he emerged and made his way down the narrow corridor to a small flight of metal stairs that led up to the deck of the *Eolus*. He glanced at the disappearing strip of land that was New York Harbor, and then began to survey the passengers, silently evaluating, assessing, sharpening his senses for the passage home, when his true work would begin.

15

The city of Hamburg washed over Rosalia like a wave of noises, odors and sights. She had never seen a large city. Even in these early morning streets of charcoal and purple shadows, strains of violin music floated from one open apartment window, the pungent aroma of frying oil from another.

She made her way from the train to a cab on the street waiting for a fare. The mare made her way pluckily over the cobblestones, and Rosalia bumped up and down on a leather upholstered seat, her first time in such a fancy conveyance. Her eyes widened with every turn of the street as she gazed at the shops and well-dressed inhabitants of the town strolling or bustling in every direction. She soaked in the women's fashionable silk, brocade or wool cloth dresses with their bustles and sophisticated, feathered hats. She suddenly became aware that her own attire appeared shabby and outmoded in comparison and suffered a pang of shame. It only lasted a moment, however; she reminded herself that, with the generosity of family and her own hard work, she had managed to acquire a ticket in second-class and not steerage.

The train ride, also her first, had been tiring and tedious, and she was relieved to be off the snorting, smoking, rattling metal beast. Fortunately, much of the travel had been at night, so she had slept some of the way. She tried unsuccessfully to push away the fresh memories of Mama, Papa and Edith crying, the boys sad to see her go without realizing how permanent it was. She had sobbed along with them and wished fervently that she could take them all with her.

Other conveyances surrounded the cab as they made their way to the harbor. Some were simple drays like Papa's, and others far more expensive and elaborate, pulled by sleek, muscular coursers. A few of the buggies peeled off to the left or right, and a dozen or so continued alongside or ahead of the cab until they reached the water's edge where small dark gray skiffs awaited to row the passengers to the steamship bobbing in the blue distance. Here the cobblestones stopped, and the horses were stepping on dirt roads. Well-dressed gentlemen helped both delicate and robust ladies from fancy carriages, and valets and footmen unloaded cedar travelling chests and boxes. The reinsman climbed down from his box and helped Rosalia with her trunk and hat box.

Rosalia's heart began to bang against her ribs, and she could hardly catch her breath. The ship that would be her home for the next three weeks would be taking her to the port of New Orleans, Louisiana. It loomed like a bobbing white, nameless animal on a vast greyish-jade sea that never ended. The words "U.S.S. Eolus" were painted in huge black letters across its white prow, barely visible in the distance. Suddenly she did not want to leave her hometown. Strangers would surround her, and who knows what they would do? Or perhaps worse, she would be completely alone and have nobody to converse with, and nothing to distract her from her frightened thoughts and doubts.

She imagined her father's arms around her. His familiar dark beard brushed her forehead as he leaned over her and murmured, "You will be fine, daughter, Hashem will protect you." This soothed her a little, but still she had the jitters running up and down her spine, as if the little grasshoppers she and Annaleya hunted for had found their way there and were leaping from one bone to the next.

The passengers gathered near the water's edge lapping below the roadway. The water looked like a deadly, bottomless pool to Rosalia as she lowered herself into a skiff. Two rugged crewmen towed her trunk behind her, and she clutched her hatbox by its handle and her light baggage close as if they were another set of limbs growing from her body. She could not stop from glancing behind her at the city buildings and roads as the skiff floated and nodded on the waves while other passengers boarded it.

A Torah story came to her, the one Mama told her many times about Lot and his wife leaving the evil city of Sodom. They were instructed by angels not to look back, but Lot's wife did and turned into a pillar of salt. Now she was doing the same thing and suddenly comprehended why Lot's wife turned around for a last look. She was leaving all that she was familiar with for a strange place called the United States of America and disembarking at the port of New Orleans.

She recognized the word Orleans vaguely from a place in France just south of Paris. She had studied some European geography from a book she found at Herr Hamstadt's bookstore and remembered its placement on a colorful map. But this New Orleans was far from there. From that city she would ride overland to a state named Arkansas, which simply terrified her at this moment. Her grasp of English did not prepare her for the word "Arkansas". This name didn't seem to be an English word. What language was it from? Her mind was whirling with fragments of thoughts and questions, leaping like a terrified rabbit from one to another.

She was grateful for the distraction from her whirling mind as she looked up at the rows of warehouse buildings lining the Elbe River, rusty, brick red, stalwart though weathered. The river led to the North Sea, stretching in front of her, salty, icy and lethal. Rabbi Schultz instructed at a recent Shabbos service she had attended that God created the oceans as a blessing, so she reminded herself of that if only for comfort.

The steamer grew to gigantic dimensions as they drew near until Rosalia was tilting her head back to see the side of it. The sloshing oars slowed and then stopped as the rowing seamen positioned the craft for the pulley that would haul it to ship's deck level. Rosalia moaned softly as the skiff tipped left to right, weighted down with twenty or so riders and their baggage. Then she was handing her passage ticket to a small fellow in a striped suit and military cap and stepping onto the planked flooring of the steamship.

The men hauling Rosalia's trunk nodded at her to follow them to her room down a narrow corridor lined with doors. A sudden wave of gratitude washed through her when she was escorted to a private, second-class cabin. She had heard enough about steerage to recognize how lucky she was. A private room at the mid-level deck would protect her, a lone traveler, even though she would have to share the toilet facilities with strangers.

She entered a small but brightly white-washed room with a small bed, a carved oak nightstand with a porcelain basin perched on top, and a floor of dark wooden boards. The crewmen dropped her trunk in a corner and stood in the doorway, motionless. Rosalia realized that they were waiting for a tip, so she dug two coins from a little cotton bag she had tied to her wrist and handed one to each, at which point they scurried away.

Completely alone for the first time in days, she reveled in the stillness and calm. She sat briefly on the bed, noting its softness, plump pillow and thick blanket, nothing like the hard board and thin covers she shared with Edith. This pleased and cheered her, and she hung onto that feeling like a lifeboat in a raging current.

Then she hurried back out into the corridor and with a few misguided steps down the wrong hallway gradually found her way to the outside deck. She leaned on the gleaming steel rail to wave at the tiny dots lining the riverbank that were bidding goodbye to their departing relatives and friends. Even though her family was not among them, she pretended they were in the crowd waving too. The ship shuddered as a loud, deep blast bellowed, announcing its departure. Rosalia felt light-headed as she watched the rowing skiffs separate from the side of the majestic ship. She could feel the blood slipping away from her face and suddenly became dizzy. She grabbed the railing tightly and swayed backward.

A voice at her ear startled her. "Ma'am, you are safe with me." A deep, warm voice, maybe a little too warm. A warning formed in her mind against it. Then a firm, large hand gripped her elbow. She twisted her neck around to see who was behind her, still woozy. A handsome male countenance smiled down at her, chestnut brown hair waving across his forehead and carefully pomaded behind the ears. An expensive felt fedora perched atop the chestnut waves. A well-trimmed handlebar mustache adorned the grinning upper lip, the chin was smooth-shaven, and the nose was straight and finely shaped. The neck was trimmed by the satiny grosgrain lapels of a smooth brown wool jacket.

Rosalia pulled her elbow away from the grasp of the man's hand and turned around slowly. The ship's motion made her even dizzier, and she heard the distant spanking sound of waves against its hull. Before her stood a well-dressed gentleman with a gold cane and a broad smile. He couldn't be more than twenty-something years old, Rosalia thought. My age. And he is a gentile. The warning voice became louder in her mind. Still, his apparent interest in her well-being gave her spirits an involuntary boost. She couldn't stop the feeling of warmth that infused her at the interest and concern from another person among this ship full of strangers.

"Let me help you to a seat, Madam," the man spoke to her again. He placed both hands on each elbow and she allowed him to guide her to a nearby deck chair. When they were both seated, he said,

"Please forgive me for being so bold and forward. I couldn't help noticing that you looked ill and unsteady. May I have the pleasure of your acquaintance? My name is Roland Longman."

Rosalia shivered involuntarily with a combination of delight and apprehension. An American! She had never met one before. She peered shyly at his meticulous appearance, well-arranged hair, tidy and expensive suit and gold-tipped cane. She was certain that he wasn't Jewish.

"Rosalia Wolfson, sir," she answered shyly. He leaned closer toward her to hear the faint words she murmured.

"Please tell me, if you will be so kind, as my curiosity is peaked," remarked the gentleman. "Why is a lovely young lady such as yourself travelling alone to America? Leaving, no doubt, a fine family behind."

His voice, so deep and refined, worked like a sedative on Rosalia's overwrought nerves. She was accustomed to the loud, brash calls of her kinsmen and townsfolk, or the harsh, clipped tones of the German gentiles of Gliewitz. And here was an opportunity to practice her mastery of English with a true speaker of the tongue.

"I am engaged to be married to a gentleman in America," she said with an embarrassed smile. He noted her German accent and responded in kind.

"Ah, is a very fortunate fellow expecting you in New Orleans? I am filled with envy."

Rosalia's cheeks reddened at the implied compliment. Then she realized with some surprise that he had spoken to her in her own language. She responded in English, however,

"I go from there to Hot Springs, Arkansas with family friends. He lives there, not New Orleans."

A glint in Longman's eye caught Rosalia's attention, a glint that had not been there a moment before. From somewhere unknown an invisible breath of dread and warning brushed her insides like a dark hand waving her away from the edge of a precipice. Had she told this stranger too much about herself? Perhaps, but she would conceal her misgivings and continue to chat pleasantly with him, to while away these difficult hours as the ship pushed out to sea and away from all that she knew. But she would be cautious to reveal little else about herself. She was relieved when he continued the conversation in English.

"What a striking coincidence. I am familiar with Hot Springs. A very good friend of mine lives there, and from time to time I visit him. Perhaps one day I will happen upon you and your future husband while I am in the town. It is a small place, so that is not unlikely."

"Perhaps, yes, that does…will happen," Rosalia stumbled a bit ungracefully on the foreign language. She didn't know what 'striking coincidence' meant, but the rest of it was very clear. Suddenly Longman rose, his tailcoats flapping behind him in the light breeze that was dancing across the deck.

"It has been a pleasure, Miss Wolfson. A lovely name."

She suppressed a gasp. He remembered her name.

"I have matters to attend to as I am on this passage for business. However, I look forward to seeing you again for a stroll on the deck. Then we may continue this fascinating discussion." With a slight bow and warm smile, he turned and headed toward the white metal stairs that led to the upper decks of the wealthy and elite passengers.

Rosalia was once again a solitary traveler, surrounded by couples and families. She seemed to be the only traveler in second class with no relative, servant or companion. She listened carefully to the languages being spoken, and made out German, some German dialects, Dutch, English, French and several other languages which she couldn't identify. Reclining on the deck chair, breathing in the alien salt-tinged air and trying to recover her senses after the shock of departure, she thought a great deal about the American, Roland Longman.

16

Two weeks into the ocean passage, the Eolus weathered a squall as it neared New Orleans, and many of the passengers were hunkered down in their cabins or huddled together in steerage. Some of them sought solace in one another's arms, and others, more afflicted by the lashing waves, insisted on solitude at the ship's railing where they could lose their breakfasts into the sea without making a total spectacle of themselves. Crewmen were rushing from one deck to another, clanging up and down metal stairs to search for damage and begin repairs. The entire vessel was dripping with ocean water, but the noonday sun emerged from swirling, weirdly shaped receding clouds and worked its evaporating magic on the puddles and droplets.

During the chaos of the brief but raucous storm, Roland Longman scurried down a flight of steps that led from the main deck to steerage. First Class travelers were allowed almost anywhere on the ship, whereas the passengers in steerage were stuck in the hold. The rank odor of that section of the ship was wafting up the metal staircase. He peered into the area and saw the lower-class voyagers sitting on long benches along the walls, kerchiefs and rags pressed to their nostrils. Usually the portholes near the ceiling of the room were left open for ventilation, but in a storm they were shut and locked tightly by the crew to keep steerage from flooding. Typical well-bred and monied passengers never ventured there, but steerage held Longman's treasury of impoverished young ladies traveling unescorted. He would single one out and lure her away from the crowd and into his cabin, like the proverbial spider and luckless fly.

As the steamship rolled from port to starboard and back again, Longman gazed around at the people packed elbow to elbow like pint glasses on a bar shelf. Now used to occasional storms at sea, he clung to a pipe running alongside the rough ochre wall where he stood and studied the women, one by one. *That one, married. Next one, also with her husband. Redheaded lady, traveling with her children, no good. There's a beauty, auburn-haired, thin green shawl, distant look in her blue eyes. She is probably on board alone.*

He watched her briefly and looked away; it was unwise to get caught staring. Already his formal, rich attire had captured the lower-class denizens' attention and a few of them were whispering to one another and giving him sideways glances despite the storm's lashing. He ignored them and continued to surreptitiously study the auburn beauty. *The lass is alone, that is certain. There is nobody comforting her now when the ship's bouncing about like a pebble in a tornado.*

Longman knew from his casual conversations with the voyagers in steerage that they were leaving their countries for a variety of unsavory or tragic reasons. Some were in tremendous debt due to gambling and drinking, and the New World was their escape from creditors who pursued them. Some left for the freedoms not available in their country of origin. Many had family in America who had scraped together the price of passage to bring loved ones to live with them. However, the rare girls traveling alone, Longman knew, were often fallen women with tainted reputations. Their prospects for marriage were hopeless, and that left precious little future for a poor woman in Europe unless they were lucky enough to hire on with the landed gentry. They were perfect for his purposes, and easier than he could have ever imagined snatching away in the midst of a crowd.

As the hapless passengers tried desperately to stay seated on armless and backless benches, the ship swung violently and even seemed to spin around. Conversation was difficult due to the shrieking wind, unremitting slap of rain and creaking of the entire boat. Longman took advantage of the rocking motions to sidle his way next to the woman in the green shawl. He spoke loudly into her left ear,

"Kind lady, will you come to the upper deck and assist me with my elderly aunt? We set forth with her maid, but she took gravely ill and we are looking for someone to replace her. My aunt is fragile and now feeling sickly in this storm. We will compensate you well."

The girl stared at him and said nothing. Then she looked away, blushing. It suddenly dawned on him that she didn't understand English. He would try his limited but serviceable German. He found it almost comical as he tried once again to speak in her left ear over the roar and commotion of the storm and lunging vessel. She slipped away from him along with the entire row of people seated alongside her on the bench as the ship tilted to port. Communication was challeng- ing, but Roland had discovered that a storm brought much more response from a woman than normal, as she was usually frightened and therefore needy of comfort and support. He was practiced at ignoring the glares and sideways glances of the passengers in steerage, as he knew that would make little or no difference to his success. Persistence, a plea for assistance and a genteel impression were his greatest weapons. Mustering his best German accent, he repeated his request in German, adding,

"Madam, my aunt is awaiting me and I cannot tarry much longer here. Please say you will accompany me to assist her in her distraught state. You will find conditions in first class much more desirable than these. Aunt Augusta is most likeable, and you two will get along excellently, I am sure."

A slight nod of the head from the girl sent a thrill of elation through Longman's chest and down to his groin. From this point on she would be in his hands. He looked forward to the shock and horror on the girl's face when she discovered his true intent. That moment filled him with a sadistic pleasure that he never tired of. Nevertheless, she remained firmly on the bench and didn't move towards him. He had to continue to cultivate her trust.

"Madam, my apologies for poor manners. I am Mr. Roland Longman of Allen and Longman Associates. We are attorneys-at-law in the United States. May I have the pleasure of your acquaintance?"

"I am Greta Schuler." A crashing wave obscured her voice, and Longman gave her a quizzical look. "Greta Schuler!" she repeated loudly over the din of splashing water and other voices in steerage. Perfect. A young German girl, traveling alone.

A moment of calm in the wind gave Longman the few seconds he needed to offer his arm – ever so shyly – for her to grab hold of. She did so, and together they tipped back and forth to the metal staircase and scrambled crazily up to the rain and gusts outside. Longman took the opportunity to press his body against hers, excusing himself profusely all the while for the unfortunate weather that forced them to collide as they made their way toward his cabin. He relished Greta's wide-eyed look when they arrived at his upper-class cabin door. Although the ship was still plunging around in the waves, the effect was less severe on the fourth level. She eyed the door jamb and knob gleaming with polished brass trim, and hesitated for a moment, twisting slightly as if to leave. Longman knocked gently at the door, feigning concern for Aunt Augusta within. While Greta stared at the door, Longman slipped a small key from his front coat pocket into the palm of his right hand.

"Auntie, are you all right? I have company and help for you. You will be very pleased."

He paused for several seconds and then rapped more sharply.

"Auntie? Please answer me. Are you in bed?"

More silence, and then finally, "Aunt Augusta! We must enter with or without your permission as now you worry me. If you cannot respond, I must look in on you immediately."

Longman gave Greta an innocent shrug and knitted his eyebrows as if greatly concerned. He moved quickly behind her, placed one hand on the small of her back and turned the brass doorknob with his other, ushering her firmly inside. Then he closed the door firmly behind them, turning around to lock it with the tiny key in his palm. The "click" of the lock turning made Greta start. Gazing around the cabin room, spacious in comparison to the crush of people in steerage, she sought in vain for Aunt Augusta's presence. Then she glanced back at the cabin door. Longman savored the look of fear that gathered in her large, clear green eyes as it dawned on her that she might be in a predicament. The dark reddish-brown eyelashes fluttered slightly like miniature flags.

"Perhaps Auntie is in the bath," Longman mused, prolonging the deceit. He strode over to the bathroom door and peered in. "Oh, hello, Aunt Augusta. Allow me to present you to Greta Schuler."

Greta breathed out noisily through her nostrils, a breath that Longman knew she was holding for longer than natural. She walked over to the bathroom door, and looked in. No Aunt Augusta. Turning to face Longman, she gave him a puzzled look.

"Ach, where she is, sir? Where is your aunt?"

Silently Longman clenched his right fist and thrust it hard into her abdomen. With a noisy gasp, Greta fell to the floor, clutching at the lush carpeting in agony. He knew better than to mark her face.

While she was still trying to regain her breath, Longman spoke to her.

"You are a beautiful girl, and now you are mine. No questions asked. I expect total obedience, Greta."

She stared back at him with eyes now narrowed and squinting. He loved the confusion that he knew he engendered. It thrilled him to watch the fright and intimidation begin to work its mystical wonders upon her will. He bent down and tore off her green shawl, then grabbed the hem of her pretty but simple beige travelling dress, both hands on either side, and threw it up as high as he could, almost covering her chin. She was able to struggle now, so he pressed his large hand upon her chest and worked with the other to rip off the bloomers underneath. Her soft-looking thighs and mound of auburn pubic hair beckoned, particularly as the wild motion of the steamship rolled her hips from side to side. He straddled her, pulled his pants down and found himself profoundly excited. He raped her with abandoned savagery as she began to shriek. Lying tightly atop her, he shoved a handkerchief into her mouth, a tool that he always kept in his upper jacket pocket for these moments. It would be unwise for cabin neighbors to hear anything. Once he had climaxed, he allowed his weight to crush her underneath. Despite the handkerchief gagging her mouth, she was able to sob noiselessly. Longman saw the pain in her contorted face and tightly shut eyes and smiled with satisfaction. She had been a virgin and would be easy to dominate. Once in a while he made a mistake and snagged a tart, a target much more difficult to control. Greta, however, was now no longer pure and would be well aware of her worthlessness.

He lifted himself off the trembling girl and grabbed the rope he kept in his bottom desk drawer, just a foot away from both of them. As she tried to sit up on the floor, he flipped her over onto her stomach and roughly tied her hands behind her back, expertly knotting the rope. He picked her up – such a light one! – and dropped her onto his bed. He pulled a chain from under the bed and hooked one end around her neck and the other end down and around a leg of the bed.

"This is your place for the rest of the journey. I will bring you everything you need. The more you cooperate, my now-ruined lady, the easier it will be for you. If you need to use the toilet, I will take you."

She was shaking from head to toe and struggling. He would leave her alone for a while; solitude always gentled them. He cleaned himself up and changed his pants. Then he slipped out into the hallway, locked the cabin door, and headed down to the dining room to get some food and libation for the girl. The poor bastards in steerage ate and drank little and of amazingly poor quality. He knew that refined refreshments, far superior to the cheap herring and porridge she was eating from a communal bucket, would win her cooperation more easily than anything else.

Longman dawdled in the dining room, flashing his wide smile at the ladies and tipping his hat. The kitchen server brought him two apples, two rolls and a pork pie left over from yesterday's lunch service, along with a fork, knife and napkin, all on a tray. It was still early in the day, between breakfast and lunch, and the squall was moving on. The dark storm clouds lifted and the dining room brass and silver finishes suddenly gleamed with a hint of daylight. The ship's rolling movements stopped as it plowed ahead into the Atlantic waters. Cautious passengers peered from their cabins, smiling with relief. He descended carefully with the tray of food down a flight of stairs to the second-class deck.

After two turns around the deck, Longman spied a tiny figure, short of stature with blonde hair peeking out from under a bonnet. Rosalia Wolfson! He had just partaken of glorious sex with a woman, but this one commanded his full attention. Dare he lure her into his cabin along with Greta? He had never captured two women in one voyage, but this doll-like beauty was so tempting. It would be a risk, and he needed to think it over before embarking on such a task. They had dined at his first-class table together several times during the journey, and he had gained her trust, but only a little. She was notably cautious. However, his thoughts became a tangle and he found himself intensely desiring to have contact with her.

She hadn't seen him yet, so he would move past her to make it seem as if crossing her path were merely fortuitous and not deliberate. Gazing in the opposite direction, Longman crept up behind her, then walked in front of her a few feet and waited for her to recognize him, but either she didn't or she was too modest to acknowledge a man she was only recently acquainted with. He turned and feigned surprise, tipping his fedora to her.

"Miss Wolfson. What a pleasure. How are you faring after this dreadful storm? I hope you avoided the upset stomach that so many others suffered."

She smiled at him slightly, lowering her very round, deep set blue eyes just a little.

"My stomach is fine now, the ship is not, how you say? Moving this way, that way……."

"Rocking," Longman provided the word helpfully.

"Yes, not rocking now, I feel much better. But I am not eating breakfast and now a little food is good idea, yes? You are taking food to your room?"

He realized that he was holding the tray in front of himself and immediately lowered it onto a nearby table.

"I was not well either," he lied, "and desired to be alone when I tried a few bites of food. But perhaps with your pleasant company, I will be more encouraged to eat." He sat in a deck lounge chair and motioned for Rosalia to take a seat next to him. She hesitated, then took a seat across from Longman. Her care to preserve her dignity flamed his desire for her. Nevertheless, his business-minded thoughts were warning him to keep to the trade, which meant not becoming emotionally enticed by a woman. As he wrestled internally with his feelings for Rosalia and his desire to carry out the primary commercial purpose of his presence on the ship, he managed a cheery smile.

"Please, Miss Wolfson, tell me about your family and home life. Keep me distracted from this seasickness the storm visited upon me, and I will be forever grateful."

Rosalia looked directly into his eyes, which made his cheeks flush, and shrugged her shoulders.

"Not very much to tell you. I have two brothers and one sister. My father works in beer factory. My hometown name is Gliewitz. I am from Prussia, state of Germany."

She stopped talking abruptly as the waiter came to their

table to ask if they had decided what to order for lunch. Longman realized that Rosalia was keeping her information brief and general. She was guarded. He had never abducted a woman from the second-class level before, only from steerage. Could he be so bold as to attempt this? Back and forth he seesawed with the positives and negatives of the prospect. The fact that she was traveling alone and was not in the upper-class ranks of passengers was the deciding factor for him. She was vulnerable enough to be a target. Although he would love to keep her for his own pleasures, he knew that her petite figure and blonde hair would bring a lucrative price.

He listened to her intently as she described the German town of her origin. He offered a few false descriptions of his own family and ersatz profession. He had learned to speak slowly and carefully to these refugee women whose English was less than perfect.

"My older brother inherited the estate from our father, and I got nothing. I never got along with my brother. We were always fighting. So when my father died, I went away to university and became a lawyer."

She dabbed at her mouth with a linen napkin and looked down at her plate. Longman studied her intently, weighing whether what he observed was a demure young lady or a shamed woman run out of town. The latter would be ideal, of course, but either way he was determined to have this petite blonde jewel with the interesting face.

"Why must you travel so far to marry a man?" he asked her. "Surely there are fine gentlemen in – what is the town? – Gliewitz? They would be happy to have you for their wife, I have no doubt. Is this man so special that you will take a ship across the Atlantic Ocean for him?"

"Mine parents and his parents arrange our marriage," she explained.

He had spoken with ladies in first class who were traveling for the same reason. They were consistently traveling with female escorts, maids and such; certainly not alone as she was. He could sense that she was not going to open up about her real reason for leaving Gliewitz, traveling by herself, to wed an unknown gentleman in America.

"Is your intended and future husband a very important man in Hot Springs? Such a lovely, elegant woman as yourself deserves to marry a mayor or a successful businessman." Flattery worked well in steerage. It ought to have the same effect with the next ticket level up. Longman just caught a hint of dark pink appear in her cheeks.

"Ach, no. He is not important at all. Immigrant, same as me. We are Jewish immigrants. You see, the Germans do not treat us well in Prussia."

This was wonderful news. It meant that if Miss Rosalia Wolfson went missing, nobody of significance or power would be alarmed. They were merely poor Jewish immigrants seeking their fortunes in America. With great restraint Longman kept himself from laughing out loud. Instead, he tipped his fur-lined fedora, rose slowly and deliberately, bid her good day and sauntered back to his cabin with only a few bites of food and a half glass of wine for his captive.

17

Rosalia didn't see the dapper Mr. Longman for over a week. Since second-class voyagers were not allowed on the first-class level, she had no recourse but to occupy herself with embroidery and English studies from the text and German-English dictionary she had brought aboard.

To take her mind off the mild seasickness that plagued her, Rosalia strolled on the deck that wrapped around the ship at her cabin's level. She could hear the loud thrum and splash of the paddles flanking the massive vessel. She loved to look upon them as they rolled noisily into and out of the ocean waters like a sea creature with multiple fins. She was filled with wonder at the force of the paddle wheel's energy as they thrust the ship forward with their mighty motion. She was also curious about the other sections of the ship, but very uncertain as to the rules of conduct. Which areas were open to the public, and which were banned? She hadn't seen any posted signage yet.

As she strolled along the deck of the majestic ship, she glanced sideways at the married couples passing her arm-in-arm. She became aware of the gentlemen in their silk or straw hats, morning coats with sack suits underneath, stealing furtive peeks at her. She brushed a stray blonde tress back that had escaped her modest gray cotton bonnet and flown across her face in the sea wind and tried to stand slightly straighter and taller as she stepped along the deck planks. Some of the women were sizing her up as well, and she tried to imagine how she appeared in her pale blue taffeta dress. Her mother had sewn matching blue bows at the hem but no furbelows or ruffles like the other women's more fashionable dresses had. It was assuredly the most beautiful attire she owned, and she was grateful to both her mother and her sister for the extraordinary effort they had made to help her get it finished in time for her departure. She had deliberately chosen the color to reflect the blue of her eyes.

A shadow fell across her line of vision as she glanced down at her high button boots to avoid tripping over a coil of rope carelessly left on the deck. She lifted her head and saw Roland Longman walking beside her. He didn't seem to have seen her yet, as his head hung to his chin and his eyes were fixed on a document that he intently perused. Rosalia waited impatiently for him to recognize her and bid her good day. He must be concentrating on some sort of business affair. How to attract his attention? She longed for company and conversation. After a few minutes, she gathered her nerve and cleared her throat loudly, adding a feeble cough. Longman jerked his head up from the paper and looked in her direction. Rosalia felt a warmth climb up her neck to her cheeks when his eyes met hers and his lips curved upward into a hint of a smile.

"Who do we have here? Miss Wolfson, a pleasure to see you out and feeling better than the other day, one would imagine? Or have you developed a cough?"

"No, Mr. Longman," she responded quickly. "I am much better. I am eating a little bit now."

"Excellent news. Perhaps you will join me in the first-class dining room tonight?"

"Thank you to invite me, sir. I am eating in my room for now. The cabin stewards bring me a plate of food and glass of watered beer. I cannot drink or eat much because I have a bit of ocean stomach." She moved her hands to imitate little wavelets.

Longman laughed and placed his gloved hand on his own stomach.

"That is called 'seasickness' in English. And may I say, you appear in plenty better condition than the majority of wayfarers on the U.S.S. *Eolus.* I commend you on your sea legs."

Rosalia knew that he was complimenting her somehow, which made her flush with pleasure. But what were see legs?

"Excuse me, please, sir. I do not know this expression. Can you explain?"

"When you get your sea legs, you can walk more easily as the ship moves up and down on the waves. You look quite comfortable strolling on the deck. What is your destination today, dear young lady?"

"I am looking for, what you say in English? Those things that make much noise that we hear now and turn over in the water to move boat forward."

Rosalia gestured with her arms, rolling one over the other in a rotating motion. Longman laughed again.

"Those are the paddle blades, Miss Wolfson. How enchanting that you have a curiosity about you and an eagerness to see something new. Well, good fortune lies at your pretty brown boots, for I know of a perfect place from which to view the paddles. Will you take a stroll with me to do just that?"

"Yes, thank you very much, sir. I will go with you where I can see the paddles, and I will use my sea legs." Rosalia rolled the new words around in her mouth and mind, determined not to forget them.

Delighted but trying to conceal her enthusiasm, she allowed him to move along at her side. Now she had a walking companion, and she no longer glanced at the promenading couples taking the air but gazed straight ahead with her chin up and a slight smile. Longman guided her up a flight of stairs, down a hallway, up yet another flight of stairs, and to the doorway of a structure with many windows. Above it spanned a wooden bridge where the ship's helmsman stood and steered through the frothing dark green water.

"This is the pilot house, Miss Wolfson. From here the helmsman steers the boat and can see quite far into the distance, and into many sections of the boat as well."

He tapped lightly on the weather-worn, splintery door and within a minute one of the crewmen opened it. The seaman's eyes widened when they took in the diminutive, well-dressed lady standing by the side of the gentleman who had knocked.

"Well, will you look what the waves fetched up to me today? Come in, come in, madam. Ye want ter take a look 'round? Tis a feast fer yer bonnie blue eyes! Ensign Hastings here at yer service."

The pair entered, and Longman placed his left hand gently but firmly at the small of Rosalia's back, just above the bustle. To steady her, she reassured herself. Within the pilot house, the extremely wide and high windows provided a tremendous view of the ocean surrounding them. From each direction, Rosalia was able to study carefully the lay of the ship, captain's quarters, the smokestack, the colossal paddle wheels flanking the ship on both sides. Ensign Hastings pointed out where crew quarters were and where passengers' quarters lay. Rosalia swept her vision from "stern to aft", as Ensign Hastings described it. The overall massiveness of the ship caused her to shiver inwardly as it swayed and slapped against the oncoming waves like a gigantic, lumbering beast.

"You are riding on the best in the fleet. 'Twas a Union Navy ship in the Civil War, just a year ago. Then got decommissioned, and now she's strictly commercial."

Roland and Rosalia gazed silently at the horizon together for several minutes. Although she knew that she was promised to another man, she was nonetheless warmed by the presence of this man beside her in the midst of unknown surroundings and threatening ocean depths. His gentle demeanor and sweet smile calmed her and summoned to her memory the steady love of her father. In unison they turned and exited the pilot house, both thanking Ensign Hastings politely. As they started down the slippery steel steps to the next ship's level, Longman leaned his head slightly down toward Rosalia's.

"I would be most honored to sit next to you tonight at dinner, if propriety and your constitution allow me the pleasure."

"I would be pleased to join you, Mr. Longman. But I will eat and drink very little."

Longman patted back a chestnut lock of hair that was pulled from out of his derby by a puff of wind. "What is your room number? This time I will come by at five o'clock to fetch you."

Rosalia hesitated, then informed him, "Room twenty-four. Thank you kindly for a tour of ship, Mr. Longman."

They parted ways, Longman heading to another flight of stairs that would take him to his luxury quarters, Rosalia down another level to her more modest ones.

The day passed slowly for Rosalia as she looked forward to the evening meal with a handsome male companion. She would be spared the lonely dining that she spent mostly in her room, fearing to venture out among the finely appareled couples that dominated the second-class dining room. She was aware that most of her other fellow immigrants were choking down a dismal, thin stew poured from a common bucket into the one cup each traveler was allowed for the entire journey. This she had learned from Mr. Longman, who, so he told her, went down there every other day to donate better quality food that he purchased from the kitchen. A philanthropist as well as a gentleman. Where are his faults?

At a few minutes after five o'clock, Rosalia heard a short rap at her cabin door. She smoothed the front of her blue taffeta dress and adjusted her blue silk bonnet, tying it under her chin. Then she remembered the hatpins that her father had given her before they had put her on the train for Hamburg. Another rap at the door.

"Have a little patience!" Rosalia called toward the door. "I am almost ready."

She reached into the pocket of her traveling coat and pulled them out. They were twice as long as her index finger, longer than necessary to secure a bonnet. Why two, she wondered? One hatpin is usually plenty to secure a bonnet, and with the ribbon tied under her neck, the hat would maintain itself against the sea breezes. Perhaps Papa wanted her to have an extra in case she lost one. She staked the bonnet firmly to her hair with one of the metal spikes, careful not to poke her scalp, and then slipped the other one a few inches beneath the first.

She slowly opened the door. Roland Longman stood before her, filling the door frame with his own. He had donned a heavy navy-blue suit with gold tassels on the shoulders, giving the impression of a maritime officer. He wore a felt Homburg hat, which Rosalia recognized the style of from her hometown. Longman extended his arm, and Rosalia hesitated. Jewish women did not allow men other than family members to touch them. However, she did not want to go against the customs of the Christians on the ship and become obvious as a Jew. Guiltily, timidly, she placed her tiny, white-gloved hand on his forearm as she had seen the gentile women do, and they proceeded to the dining room. She prayed silently to Hashem for forgiveness.

The dining room appeared to her like a whole new world of elegance. Chandeliers with shimmering candles hung from ornately carved medallions on the ceiling. Oak wainscotting covered the walls. Waiters bustled about in black and white uniforms with linen towels over their forearms and platters of food and drinks balanced on their outstretched hands. Large round tables covered with white linen tablecloths filled the room.

There were four other couples at the dining table that Longman had arranged for them to occupy. The chatter at the table was challenging for Rosalia. Expressions, subtle jokes and idioms in English flew by her ears as she attempted to grasp at those words and phrases that she already knew and cobble together some meaning. Two of the couples had children that had already eaten with their nurse maids earlier and were in their rooms playing games and settling down for the night. One gentleman was the dean of a university in Massachusetts, which piqued Rosalia's interest immediately. She craved the knowledge that professors imparted to boys and withheld from the girls. Rage took her by surprise and made her stomach spasm. Why wasn't she born a male? The unfairness of it prompted her to speak even though she was trying to be quiet and only listen.

"Are women allowed in your university, Professor Dearbourne?"

The professor raised his thin eyebrows high into a wrinkled forehead. "Heavens, no! All men, of course, as is proper. The girls go to a different college if they so choose.

Many of the girls do not finish, as they get married and then, well, there you are. Women and professions do not mix."

Rosalia's face flushed pink as she said angrily, "This is because the men do not permit it. Men get married also. So then they should stop their professions just as do the women."

The entire table of diners were riveted upon Rosalia. Roland Longman sighed and shook his head. At the same time, he could not stop a wave of admiration from welling up in him. This girl had spirit! He was beginning to develop a fondness for her, something he considered dangerous and undesirable to his ultimate aims.

After a few seconds of silence, the men laughed to one another about the preposterousness of women attending college, finishing and developing an earnest career the way men did. After all, they huffed, the women get pregnant and then who will take care of the children? The men? More laughter ensued, which lifted everyone's spirit. It seemed that Rosalia's protestation had provided lively amusement for the group.

When the final dessert plates had been cleared and wine glasses removed by the gloved waiters, a small band of instrumentalists played piano, violin and cello. Several couples stood and danced to the music. After two songs, the ship's captain stopped the entertainment to announce to the crowd,

"We will be arriving in New Orleans tomorrow in the late afternoon. It has been an honor to transport you across the Atlantic Ocean in this fine steamer. She is one of the best of our commercial fleet."

"Tomorrow?" breathed Rosalia to Roland. "I don't believe! I think we never disembark this boat."

"Are you excited about seeing your new land?"

"Yes, very much. I am thinking….." At that moment Rosalia was remembering Carl, his large, deep brown and gold eyes and soft, full mouth. She would be his wife very soon, and then the babies would come. What chance was there for her to become educated? Her ambivalence appeared to Longman as a flirtation and gave him the opportunity to invite her for a dance. But this was simply too much for Rosalia to tolerate. She had allowed his arm to touch her hand, but dancing with the opposite sex was strictly forbidden and considered grounds for ruination of a Jewish woman's reputation. Not that her own was salvagable back home, she thought with bitterness. But she would do her best to be honorable and respectable now that she had departed Gliewitz and the trail of memories that she wanted to escape.

"No, thank you very much. No, I cannot dance with you. I am promised to another man in marriage."

"I understand," Longman now addressed her softly. "Miss Wolfson, I have a wedding gift for you and your future husband. What is his name, your betrothed?"

"Carl. Carl Gersman."

"Fine name, Carl Gersman. I have a gift for you and Carl that I would like to give you now. It is in my cabin, and so I ask that you indulge me and come with me to take it out of my trunk for you. Tomorrow, I will not see you as I will be settling various business deals with a certain associate on the ship. It will take most of the day, and then I must pack and put many things in order before I disembark. So please, come along for just one short moment so that I may bestow it upon you. You may remain in the corridor while I go in and retrieve it."

Rosalia's eyes widened in surprise.

"How you have a wedding present for us? You did not even know until now about my marriage for the future."

Longman hesitated briefly, then answered smoothly,

"I always carry several precious items onboard when I travel. If a business associate is going to marry, or perhaps his son or daughter, I am prepared. In this case, it is you. And in exchange for our delightful conversations and pleasant time spent together, please indulge me. You certainly deserve a wedding gift, coming from so far and traveling so bravely to a new country."

Rosalia nodded her head, and the two of them left the dining room. The tinkling of glasses and clicking sounds of plates and forks being cleared away faded as they exited onto the deck and headed down a long, echoing corridor to Longman's room. The oak boards creaked under their treading boots. At the door of Longman's cabin, they halted as he drew the door key out of his front trouser pocket and inserted it into the keyhole. Before he turned the lock, he stared over his shoulder at her and said,

"Not many people know this, but my Aunt Augusta is traveling with me this time, and she has remained in the cabin quite ill from seasickness. I have told her about you, and she wishes to meet you. Would you be so kind as to peek in and say hello to her? She would be most grateful, and I know that it would help her spirits."

"Of course, Herr Longman. Excuse me, Mr. Longman. I had no idea your aunt was with you. Poor lady."

Longman looked up and down the corridor, which was empty, and swung the door open. He leaned in, blocking Rosalia's view of the room, and called softly,

"Aunt Augusta. Are you awake, dear? The fine lady I have been telling you about is here to give her regards personally."

There was only silence, although Rosalia thought she heard a muffled rustling, as of fabric or blankets moving. Longman stepped aside to allow Rosalia to move into the door frame. She leaned her head forward and said,

"Hello? Are you feeling well?"

Suddenly she was shoved firmly inside the room, so hard that she lost her balance and fell upon the carpeting. Longman shut the door quickly behind himself, looming over her with a sly smile that seemed to transform him into a stranger. Frightened, she attempted to stand, but Longman leaned down and pinned her to the floor. She glanced around the room, frantic to flee, and that was when her eyes lit upon Greta. With horror she took in the form of the woman trussed in ropes, hands tied behind her back and a white cotton cloth in her mouth, upon the bed in the corner. The woman's eyes were wide and wild, and met Rosalia's with a lightning-like gleam, then closed.

"What is going on here?" Rosalia cried out. "Who is she? Let me up!"

Fury began building in her calves and feet, propelling her to strain against Longman, to no avail. He was much stronger and larger than she was, and had her easily in hand.

"This is where your story alters, my dear, Rosalia. You are now my property and my prize. It is a shame that I've grown fond of you, but you will bring a huge price when I deliver you to your fate. Tomorrow you will leave the ship with me, and tonight we will celebrate in my cabin."

As he spoke, he lowered his face next to Rosalia's, breathing into her ear. She caught a whiff of alcohol.

"How can you do this?" she screamed at him in rage. "Other passengers have seen me, talked to me. They will wonder where I am! You are a *mamzer*, a monster!"

She felt his brawny hand tugging at the front of her gown, pulling and jerking, and realized that he intended to tear it off. The memory of her cousin Daniel throwing her day dress over her head so many years ago danced to the surface of her thoughts and fueled her anger even more. As she opened her mouth to scream, Longman released her briefly and pulled a white cotton cloth out of his vest pocket, exactly like the one Rosalia had spotted in the bound woman's mouth. In a split second, the cloth was in her own mouth and she began to despair. Then she remembered her father's words. *Do not go anywhere without your bonnet and hatpin.* She managed to reach her left hand behind her neck and jerk the hatpin out of her bonnet. She quickly plunged it fully into Longman's throat stretched open above her. Just as the gown gave way and ripped down to her bodice, revealing her white under slip and corset, he dropped her abruptly with both hands and gagged. Blood seeped out of the wound and dripped onto Rosalia's face and chest. Longman rolled off of her, gasping audibly as the blood gathered momentum and flowed even more. She leaped up, pulled the cloth out of her mouth and ran to the door, flung it open and was free.

Rosalia ran down the corridor alternately sobbing and swearing in German and Yiddish. She headed crazily around corners and into passageways that she didn't recognize. The entire surroundings began to take on a sinister appearance, unrecognizable and alien. She looked for stairs going down to her deck level and finding them, grasped the railing with one hand and held her torn dress against her chest with the other. She headed down the metal steps, the sound of her footsteps echoing like little hammers in her ears, making her temples throb. At that moment, Ensign Hastings was climbing up the same staircase. He stopped abruptly to view the sight of Rosalia, sobbing, blood dripping down the side of her left cheek, bonnet half off, and gown held up only by her gloved left hand pressing the torn blue taffeta material against her bosom. She barely saw him, half-blinded by tears. He gazed at her in wonder.

"Miss Wolfson, whatever is going on? Did you fall? We must get you to the ship infirmary at once."

He tried to take her elbow in his arm, but she cringed away from him. He led her down two flights of stairs to an area that Rosalia had not been to before. The sign "Infirmary" was painted in black on a wall next to a doorway, and in they went. Rosalia was unable to speak as her throat was constricted and her mind unable to form a single word. She couldn't give any explanation for the circumstances Ensign Hastings had found her in. Several minutes passed in silence as Rosalia alternately gulped air and then emitted short, piercing screams. She grabbed at the piece of taffeta hanging down in front and tried pressing it back into one piece. In her mind, Longman's leering visage loomed and then retreated repeatedly until Rosalia thought she would go insane. To break the spell of the ugly vision, she finally spoke aloud to Hastings.

"Roland Longman attack me in his cabin! He tear my dress, look!" She released the blue fabric to reveal the rips as well as the spots of blood that had dripped onto it from Longman's injury. "And other lady is already in his room, he tie her hands and feet. He place the cotton in her mouth same as me, so nobody can hear her call for help. But I escape! She is still in his room."

Hastings' pale gray eyes widened and then narrowed as he listened attentively to what Rosalia was saying. When she stopped talking, he shook his head slowly and squared up his shoulders. Relief flooded through her tortured thoughts and memory flashes of what had just happened. Now somebody knew the story and would stop this terrible man from pursuing her and hurting other women.

"I'll have the crew go to Mr. Longman's room immediately and search it for the lady you speak of. Meantime, we'll ask 'im fer his version of the story. This sort of thing cannot go on in a respectable steamer such as ours."

He left Rosalia with a nurse, a fair-haired, heavy-set woman with a cold washcloth and bandages in one hand and a bottle of smelling salts in the other.

18

Gussie gave birth to a son in March of 1866, and the Rabbi blessed him with the name David at the baby-naming ceremony. Carl was filled with delight and amusement watching the infant grow and thrive in his parents' tender care. It was the nighttime whimpering and crying that didn't enchant him.

After dinner with Samuel and Gussie, Carl would walk the mile and a half back to his house in the woods or ride his new mule Strudel if he had her with him. Most nights he was too exhausted to mull over his solitary existence and fell sound asleep as soon as he changed into his tattered linen night dress and lay down on the little horsehair mattress. It was only on Saturday nights, when he was refreshed from Shabbos, the holy day of rest, that he yearned for a woman to wrap his arms around and express his passion with.

He spent Saturday mornings attending services in Rabbi Schecter's sitting parlor, and afternoons napping. This left him some energy to spare when darkness fell and he was in his partially built house, and that is when the temptation of Missy's brothel beckoned to him. He would pull together as much currency as he could from his meager earnings, unable to afford the pleasure of prostituted sex more than once a month. Off he would go on his clandestine mission, with or without Horace, Geoffrey or Billy, requesting Betsy's favors but settling for Angie or Charlotte if she was busy with another customer. Always the following morning he would pray to Hashem for forgiveness, heart heavy with regret.

Late September brought the Jews of Hot Springs together for the high holy days. Carl had the opportunity to address the congregation and formally thank many of the men who had helped him construct his residence and the women who had brought food and drink over to them as they labored in the forest clearing. After Yom Kippur services concluded, the Jews had atoned for their sins, and the sun ducked behind the horizon, the congregation broke their sunset to sunset fast and feasted on brook trout, bagels, the ceremonial braided challah bread and pickles and kosher wine from the Rabbi's own small vineyard. As they were assuaging the growling pain in their stomachs after twenty-four hours of food deprivation, Rabbi Schecter announced to the crowd, tiptoe-ing to be seen above the shoulders and heads of those around him,

"Please lift a glass of wine in prayer and celebration for our newest member of the community, Carl Gersman. He is going to be our kosher butcher, amen! No longer will I provide the butchering, only the blessings. This will free more time to tend to your spiritual needs."

"Amen!" came collectively from the crowd as everybody said the blessing and drank.

"There is more to feel blessed about," he continued. "Carl is bringing a bride from Germany, arranged by their parents. She will be here next spring."

Carl's fellow congregants applauded him and whacked him good-naturedly on the back and shoulder as they toasted this good news that most of them had already heard about. Samuel also received some friendly cuffing and congratulatory handshakes. The women smiled delightedly from their section of the parlor cum synagogue, whispering and commenting among themselves and kissing Gussie's cheeks.

The next morning, when the light of the sun was just a gray streak behind the hills, Carl arose early, dressed and ate in his new little kitchen at the sanded and polished dinner table he had built, a bit shaky on its four legs and needing some adjustment, mounted Strudel and directed the little mule towards the section of town where the *shvartzes* lived. He wanted to find a way to save his earnings and replace Horace and the others with workers who would be happy to trade services for cuts of meat. Perhaps a few Negro men could be tempted, as they didn't seem to be doing well. Jobs were scarce and nobody was offering them one. Their little ones were thin and raggedy and seemed hungry all the time.

He rode the mule to the home of the three sisters who shopped at Gersman's Dry Goods. They might know a man who needed work. He found their rough little residence easily enough because he had delivered quinine to them not long ago when all three were sick with the influenza. He dismounted from Strudel, tied her to a fence post, and made his way through the weedy, narrow path that led to the sisters' splintered abode.

Marie answered his knock and stepped back in surprise. Then, after briefly squinting her eyes, she queried tentatively,

"Mr. Gersman? What bring y'all round heah early in da mohnin'?"

"Hello, Marie," Carl greeted her with a broad smile. He saw that she had put on a little weight since the illness, a good sign. Her gray curls were bundled up in an orange and indigo scarf, and she wore a red-stained white apron over a dark, thin day dress.

"I hope I did not wake you. Pardon if I did."

Marie shook her head no, gray curls bouncing.

"Perhaps you can help me. I want to give work to a Negro man. I need help to finish building my house. You know a man needs work?"

Now Violetta and Betta Jean were standing behind Marie, listening in. Marie was nodding and looking thoughtful. The women chatted excitedly among themselves, and then Violetta said to Carl,

"We have a nephew with buildin' skills. He be glad to work fuh y'all, Mr. Gersman. He live five oah so block f'um heah, on Maple Street, numbah six oh foah. Jes' tell him his aunties sent y'all."

"Thank you, thank you very much. I am grateful. When I marry, please you all come to wedding?"

All three women grinned at Carl simultaneously. Betta Jean spoke this time.

"Folk don't take it well foah dah Negro people and white people mixin' and socializin' but thank ye anyway. An' congratulation', Mr. Gersman."

Carl tipped his straw hat and mounted Strudel for the second time that morning. As he clomped along on the dusky gray mule toward Maple Street, he puzzled over the phenomenon of the *shvartzes,* the dark-skinned people in America. He was aware – everybody was – that their parents and grandparents and great-grandparents had been dragged against their will over to America from Africa starting in the 1600's. They had been bought and sold like merchandise and treated in many cases worse than the livestock. An actual war that tore up the country, and which he had lived through, had been fought to free them. Now that they had their liberty, they could go where they wanted, find jobs for pay, educate their children, stay together as families, and the men could vote.

He learned through friendly conversation over beers in town that many of the Negroes were leaving the South and heading to the North of this immense country for employment and better living conditions. Why were any *shvartzes* still living in Hot Springs, or anywhere else in the South for that matter? He saw that they were treated horribly and spurned by white society as if they were vermin. They were threatened with violence, probably more often than he knew.

Before he could ponder any more over this quandary, he was at the front door of a tiny shack on Maple Street, Number 604. As he dismounted the mule, a lean young man emerged from the tumbledown hut and stared up at Carl silently, defiantly. His front right tooth was missing, skin dark as night, ebony ears perched almost perpendicular to his head. Carl could just catch the sound of a baby giggling inside.

"May I hep you, suh?"

"I am Carl, Carl Gersman. I work at Gersman's Dry Goods Store on Whittington Avenue."

The man did not respond, but eyed him warily, arms held behind his back, stance wide but shoulders hunched over. Carl continued, "Your aunties send me to you."

Now he had the man's full gaze, a look of curiosity.

"How you know mah aunts?"

"Give me minute, I explain. Your aunts, three sisters, yes? Shop at my store. I go to them, ask they maybe know a man wants to work for me. They send me to you."

"What kinda work?" Suspicious glance beneath his thin black eyebrows.

"I am building house in forest off Whittington Avenue. Need to dig well for water, build outhouse and woodshed. I can't pay you money, but I can trade labor for good cuts of meat. Good quality beef, lamb, chicken."

"Meat, huh? Shoah sound good ta me, heps me put food on the table foah mah fambly. When do I start?"

"Come with me. You have horse or mule?"

"Nah, suh."

"Strudel is small and young. She can't take two riders. So we all walk to house together. My name is Carl. What is your name?"

"My name Benjamin. Please, suh, lemme tell mah wife where ah'm goin.'"

He hurried back into the hovel. Through the battered doorway Carl could observe Benjamin dandling his infant on his knee for a few seconds while he chatted with his wife. His voice, rich and resonant, floated across the air like a musical instrument, entrancing to Carl even though he couldn't make out the words. Soon Benjamin was out the door again and strolling with Carl and the little mule under the wan morning sunlight toward Whittington Avenue.

The two men spent the better part of the day splitting logs, planing them smooth, and setting up blocks of oak on level, cleared ground where the outhouse and woodshed were to go. Carl reveled in the smell of freshly cut wood, the feel of tools in his hands. He loved watching shape and structure reveal itself in his busy hands. He also realized that sharing the smell and feel of wood and tools made the experience even sweeter. Benjamin hadn't brought along a crumb of food with him, and his dark, widely arched eyebrows jumped with surprise when Carl offered to share a piece of Gussie's cornbread and a chunk of goat cheese with him late in the afternoon. They ate quietly, side by side on the back porch steps of the house, until Carl asked him through mouthfuls of food,

"I have question for you. Why do you stay here after war? Many Negro people go north to find job, I hear."

Benjamin looked down solemnly at the ground between his feet, slowly shook his head, and then glanced over at Carl. His eyes had turned as sorrowful as a dying doe's.

"We was livin' in Mississippi. Mah wife's mothah and sistah were sold some years ago. We do not know the plantation.

Now we's lookin' foah dem, and she won't go nowheah until we finds 'em. Problem is, we don't know who bought dem back den. So when Ah kin, Ah goes tah diff'rent towns a'lookin' and a'askin'. Dah white folk don't hep us – please don't take no offense, Mr. Carl – so Ah kin only ast other coloreds dat was once slaves. So fah, no luck."

"What happen to your family, Benjamin?"

"Mah Mama gone North wid her new husband. Mah Pappy kilt in de wah. Jest me an' missus an' de baby now." Spoken matter-of-factly.

They resumed work until darkness threatened to overtake them. Carl gave Benjamin a canvas bag filled with several large hunks of goat meat and two chickens he had erred in kosher butchering that were perfectly good for a gentile. Benjamin hefted the bag gently with the slightest flicker of a smile at the corners of his mouth and nodded his head at Carl.

"Most grateful, suh."

"I like you, Benjamin. You are good worker. Come back tomorrow. We will start to dig the well. Can you find this place? You can? Good. And please, be careful. Very careful."

"What you mean?"

"I saw something very bad, long time ago. Before the war. I know what can happen to Negro in the woods."

A shock of recognition flashed in Benjamin's round black button eyes. He nodded, lowered his head and jogged quickly with his bagged payment of meats down the path that Carl had raked from the front porch steps and through the buckeyes and apple trees, and then disappeared.

19

It was the end of June, 1866, and Carl had finally completed the building of his new house, thereby partially fulfilling the Homesteading Act. He still had to work the land for four and a half more years before the five acres the government had provisionally gifted him was officially his own. In Rabbi Schecter's sitting parlor, Carl, Sam, Gussie, and their friends and neighbors celebrated the new home that he and his bride would reside in. After prayers, a speech by Rabbi Schechter, and blessings over the wine and bread, they walked the several miles over to Carl's new house to place a mezuzah on the doorpost. Carl had carved and painted a 4-inch casing out of birch wood and Rabbi Schecter had inserted the tiny scroll of parchment containing the required two biblical passages from Deuteronomy. As Carl hammered the tiny religious icon into the upper right jamb of the door frame, memories flooded in of the mezuzah on his parents' door sill that he had grown up with and kissed many times via fingertips as he entered his childhood home, now thousands of miles away. He could hear Samuel sniffling softly behind him.

Carl felt lucky to find a woman who would cross the Atlantic Ocean alone and enter a foreign country to marry him. The congregation consisted of mostly men, a handful of married women, three boys and not a single, marriageable girl. There were a dozen young girls who would be eligible to wed in a few years, and a few girl babies. They had all been born in Hot Springs. Jewish women immigrating to America were far and few between before the war, and there was plenty of complaining among the menfolk about the scarcity of them. Now that the time of reconstruction was here in the Southern states, more women were coming to Hot Springs, drawn by the reputation of the magical springs themselves. Things were changing as marriable men were starting to make a good living in the new country.

He knew that the steamship carrying Rosalia to New Orleans was due into port the first week of July, and his excitement tinged everything he did, saw, smelled, felt with a delicious edge. Surrounded by the Jews of his newly adopted town, he recalled how uncomfortable he had felt when he first arrived, and how much more at home he was now, seven years later. Every day he smelled the allspice shrubs, shortleaf pines and witch hazel trees in the morning air and heard the rustling of ground birds scurrying through the bushes. The scents and sounds of his new environment were now familiar.

On the Thursday before Saturday Shabbat service, Carl awoke groggily and hung his head over a cold beef sausage and a tin cup of milk from his newly acquired she-goat. He had visited the brothel in the woods the night before despite swearing to himself that he would forego the immoral pleasure of it forever, now that Rosalia was on her way to him. Most times he went with Horace, Geoffrey and Billy, but last night he had found his way alone to Missy's. On his low but respectable salary of five dollars a week from the store, this was an extravagant indulgence, and he was having difficulty paying for basic supplies. He vowed to himself again to eschew The Rooming House forever.

He arrived early at Gersman's Dry Goods. A glimmer of sunlight was fanning out through the trees and gilding the hillsides. The intensity of the light hinted at hot weather to come that day. Carl rolled up his sleeves in anticipation and set to work opening boxes of merchandise that had arrived the night before. He arranged laundry soap, Irish linens, canvas bags filled with wheat flour or sugar, long and short-handled shovels in their proper places around the store, checking the inventory lists carefully as Samuel had instructed him.

This was the time of day he enjoyed the most, savoring the serenity of solitude. All too soon townspeople would be knocking the rusty screen aside and surging through the rickety door to make their purchases. The customers that intrigued Carl the most were the gold miners making their way west to strike it rich. They provided a hearty if inconsistent profit for the store as they replaced broken tools and added new ones on their way to the frontier. Carl wondered what kinds of adventures would befall each one, travelling far through a wilderness teeming with predatory animals and unknown perils. Would they find any more gold in California or silver in Nevada and become wealthy? Would they fail and go hungry? Would they be taken by surprise by the huge bear called 'grizzly' and end their lives under its dagger-sharp claws?

His thoughts in the quiet of the morning were abruptly interrupted by the quick creak of the screen and rasp of the door as it swung open. The face of the Indian he had met at the hot springs appeared with the strange, gray eyes, then his light bronze neck and shoulders, a long black braid draped over one. *Injun,* Carl corrected himself silently. That's how they pronounce it, the Americans.

"Waddite!" Carl exclaimed. "You find my brother's store. Come in and look." He beamed at the fellow. "The colors of the skin, they are many in this town. Is it like that all over America?

"You remembered my Quapaw name, newcomer. I am impressed. Most white people do not even want to hear it spoken. Are you done with the house that you and your bride will live in? Did you start up your butcher shop?"

This man could be a good friend. He brushed away a small tear that caught him by surprise. A long time had passed since he had seen his friends in Oppein, and he just now realized how much he missed them.

"House is all finished! We have celebration tonight, maybe you join us. I will start butcher shop soon."

The old front door creaked, and a tall, slightly hunched man slipped into the store quietly. His nasal half-snort, half-laugh punctured the air just then, and he said to Carl in a thin, sardonic voice,

"Carl, you still goin' on about yer imaginary lady friend from Germany? And ya think ya kin fool this Injun about that? Whaddaya say, Mr. Quapaw lover? Real or ain't real? 'Cause I got a greenback ridin' on it that she ain't real. "

Carl beamed widely at Horace Fletcher standing there in his patched, thin work pants and shirt, blonde hair hanging past his shoulders in lank tresses.

"My Rosalia, she is very real, Mr. Horace, sir, and if you are betting money about her, then good! I win the money. It will be wedding present from you. Now, something here you want to buy today?"

"Actually, Carl mah Jewish partner in crime, I came to sell you something."

Horace pulled a rifle out of the knapsack he was toting and rested it against a wall. Carl had seen many of them in town and hanging on racks in people's homes, even in the homes of his Jewish acquaintances. Samuel had a rifle and a small gun he called a 'thirty-eight', which he had informed his brother referred to the size of the weapon. Carl had become accustomed to the daily sharp reports of gunshots echoing through the forest and hills surrounding Hot Springs. It was merely folks getting dinner, his brother had informed him. Hares, partridges, coons, opossums and a myriad of other animals abounded in the Hot Springs region and were easy hunting.

"Looky here, Carl," wheedled Horace, turning the rifle over in his long-fingered, rough hands. "This here is a fine piece o' weaponry, and it's high time you owned a rifle. 'Specially if yer goin' ta provide meat for the little woman to prepare for mealtime. You need the rifle, and I need the money. Was a time I didn't need to sell nothin' fer money when I had some acreage and slaves to pick the cotton. But those days are over, and we gotta do what we can to survive. Five dollars for this beaut, what do ya say?"

The rifle had an ominous allure, with a polished honey-hued walnut handle and a gleaming iron barrel. Carl imagined himself downing one of those gigantic black bears he'd caught sight of through the trees. Or shooting a venomous snake like the one he'd almost stepped on camouflaged in a pile of dead leaves behind his house. Life here surrounded by the dense forest truly butted up against the brink of death. However, he would not be using the rifle to kill deer for venison, as it was forbidden by kashrut laws of kosher butchering. The animal's suffering must be minimized as much as possible by means of a well-placed throat-slash with the sharpest possible of knives.

"I like this rifle and want to buy. Only problem," Carl winced in embarrassment, "I don't know how to shoot." In the old country, Jews were prohibited from owning firearms or any other type of weapon besides knives for cutting meat. Even swords were banned from their hands unless they joined the Prussian army.

Horace's dour countenance immediately swept upward into a delighted smile.

"Well, well, you Hebrews surprise me all the time. No shootin' skills at all? Easy, big fella, I can teach ya on yer new Winchester. After ya purchase it from me for an excellent price. I will give y'all a good deal!"

At that moment Samuel emerged from the back storage room, wiping his grimy hands on a tan cotton apron tied around his waist. When he spotted the rifle being brandished by Horace Fletcher in front of Carl and the Indian man Waddite, he shouted,

"Don't shoot that thing in here, you fool. Put it down!"

Carl quickly explained the proposed sale, and his brother looked relieved. In German, Samuel explained to Carl,

"I thought we were going to have trouble. This fellow Horace, he's a troublemaker. But it is long past time for you to have a rifle to defend yourself, little brother. I know, I know, we were not allowed to in Germany. But this is another country with different rules and more freedom. Allow me to examine it more closely for flaws, crooked barrel, bad handle. I know enough about rifles now to spot something like that."

Horace passed the Winchester over to Samuel, who raised it to eye level and turned it this way and that. After a few minutes, Samuel approved the Winchester with a nod of his head. He asked Horace,

"How much are you asking my brother for this?"

In response, Carl pulled a crisp five-dollar bill out of his pocket and handed it to Horace. That represented an entire day's work. Horace pocketed the bill and slowly placed the rifle in Carl's hands. They made arrangements for a shooting lesson the following day. Horace plucked a bag of flour, a bag of sugar, and a garden hoe from the shelves, and paid for them with his freshly earned currency. Waddite had been observing all of this silently from a corner of the store stacked high with frying pans and tea kettles. When he stepped forward to examine Carl's new acquisition, Horace squinted at him and scowled.

"Well, well, here's the town half breed. You'll let anybody in here, won't ya? Even half Injun, they're all cheats and crooks."

Carl and Samuel sighed simultaneously as if on cue. They had heard this familiar accusation before, in the old country. It was one of the standard descriptions of the Jewish people by the gentiles, who labeled them as pilferers to justify their own barbarous treatment of them. The corners of Waddite's mouth turned up into the slightest of smiles. His solemn dark walnut eyes met Carl's, and at that instant Carl knew that the two of them shared an inexorable link to the unavoidable experience of hate and judgment by others. Horace, sensing something other than hearty agreement coming from the Gersmans, muttered darkly,

"Well, ya can't trust nobody these days. It's a sorry thing, slaves walkin' free, Jews and Redskins all over Hot Springs. What's the town comin' to?"

He continued muttering to himself as he exited the store, pulling in frustration on a beard that sprang sparsely from his chin like strands of hay.

The daylight falling through Gersman's Dry Goods front window finally grew dim, and the heat abated slightly. Samuel and Carl closed the store early, as usual, for Friday Shabbos services. They tidied the shelves, picked up items that had been scattered or had fallen because of careless customers, took daily inventory, counted the bills and coins in the till, swept the floor and rolled down the brown canvas shade that would cover the wide window for the night. Carl turned the Open sign to Closed that stood between the pane and shade.

They removed their aprons and headed for home to freshen up for the religious service and celebration that evening.

Gussie was in a dither in the sitting room, twisting around to check the bone buttons in her only dressy gown. Samuel had bought the silk fabric, ruffles and buttons for her as a delayed wedding gift after the war ended and textiles became available again. She laced up her dark leather boots carefully, making sure each eyelet caught the string. Covering her raven hair with a lacy white linen cloth, she called to the men,

"I am ready to go. Samuel. Come help me with the baby."

The brothers emerged from Samuel and Gussie's bedroom where they had been decking themselves out with the best clothing in Samuel's wardrobe. Carl was donning a white shirt, gray corduroy vest and trousers that he had borrowed from Samuel, as he still owned nothing but work clothes.

"Come, little David," Carl swung his nephew into the air and rubbed his tiny nose with his own adult one. The infant began to mewl, then howled loudly. "Oh, you don't like your Uncle Carl? What did I do wrong?"

Gussie lifted the baby carefully from Carl's arms and went directly into the bedroom with him.

"Baby's hungry, Gussie must nurse him," Samuel explained. By now, Carl didn't need the explanation. When Gussie and David were ready, they struck out on Whittington Avenue, and in a half hour or so all four of them were walking on Central Avenue toward the synagogue. The streets were lit only by the last rays of sunset, and mauve shadows stretched eerily across the road. They hurried their pace to arrive for the ceremonial candle lighting that would transform an ordinary Friday into Shabbos. Other Jews were walking quickly as well in the same direction, the men dressed in their distinct silk black top hats and long, dark coats like a brood of ravens flocking in the street. The women walked behind together in simple, cotton white dresses, with multi-colored scarves draped across their hair and tied under their chins. The Christian townsfolk had become accustomed to this end-of-the-week black and white-bedecked march of the Hebrews. Sometimes the congregants had to dodge an apple core wrapped in a rag or ear of rotten corn thrown at them by mischievous juveniles out to amuse themselves.

The Gersmans entered the modest, oak-planked home of the Rabbi that served as the temple for the Jewish residents of Hot Springs. Carl and Samuel joined the men on the right side of the bimah, near the front. Gussie sat with the women on the left side of the temple, all of them blocked from the men's view by a long cattle gate covered by canvas and several royal blue and white tablecloths draped over the canvas. Gussie chose the last row of benches because she might have to take the baby outside to nurse if he became hungry and started wailing.

As Carl settled in and greeted new acquaintances, he gazed around at the simplicity of the room, such a stark contrast to the more ornate synagogue his family had attended in Prussia. The bimah, a small stage for Rabbi Schechter to address the crowd, was adorned with only a bouquet of wildflowers in a small pewter vase that the rabbi had traveled with from the Old Country. A square pine table with two brass candlesticks holding stubby white Shabbos candles stood below the bimah. Rabbi Schechter's wife Sadie lit the candles, and the orange and gold flames pierced the darkening room like miniature stars. The men and women spoke the ages-old Hebrew blessing over the candles to welcome the holy day of rest. Prayers were spoken, whispered or muttered, filling the air with that peculiar lack of synchronicity that marks a Jewish service. Rabbi Schechter removed the Torah from its ark with great reverence and ceremony and started reading from it at the bimah.

Five minutes into the reading, David opened his tiny eyelids and began to squirm, then whine like a half-full teakettle. He took a deep breath in preparation to wail loudly, like a wave retreating to gather strength and smash itself against the shore. When Gussie heard him suck in air, she rose quickly and walked with the swaddled babe in her arms out the front entrance. Carl grinned and stuck a forefinger in each ear, nudging his brother so that he would see. Sure enough, the baby's loud cries pierced the air and briefly interrupted the Rabbi's reading of the Torah. He smiled benignly and said something about the blessing of the growing Jewish community, albeit growing noisily, and continued to read. David's crying grew distant and then there was silence again.

Suddenly there was another scream, high-pitched but easily recognizable as a woman's. Samuel and Carl instantly knew it was Gussie. They jumped up as one from their bench and moved quickly, jostling knees and stepping on toes in their haste. Other noises reached their ears while they were attempting to extricate themselves from the benches and reach her. The sounds of horses neighing and snorting, hoofs stamping the ground, and the shouts of loud, deep male voices came to their ears. Now the entire congregation stood with faces washed in fear. Everyone moved out of the benches and rushed in a crowded jumble toward the small front door behind Carl and Samuel. Rabbi Schechter called,

"Do not push, be *menschen,* civilized people."

Only those nearest to him heard his admonishment, as the din grew even louder. Another sound added itself to the cacophony, a sputtering, crackling and hissing. Several of the women began weeping.

By now, Carl and Samuel had squeezed past most of the crowd and almost fell out of the doorway due to the swell of the crowd pushing forward. As they righted themselves, they stared in utter shock at six men swathed in bright red, purple and yellow blankets and bearing lit torches flickering brightly against the dark sky.

The oddly-dressed men began circling the congregants on their mounts. One man appeared to have the horns of a steer rising from his shoulders. Another had a cow skull tied around his waist. In the black night, their bizarre adornment glowed eerily, lit by the torches they held aloft.

Suddenly one of them tossed his torch at Rabbi Schecter's front porch, then another did the same. The dry, rough planks rapidly caught fire and spread across the front of the structure. The riders rode their mounts close to the congre-gants who were running down the street and away from the conflagration. Clouds of dust kicked up by the horses' hooves swirled in their faces and dirtied their clothing.

Carl could hear shouting in the din of the fire and clopping of hooves. Suddenly, he heard more clearly what the riders were calling out.

"Dirty Jews, get out of this town and go back to where ya came from!"

"Christ-killers! Y'all ain't never gonna vote here.

"We'll shoot n' hang ever' one o' ya!"

"I'll show y'all, tryin' ta take our land!"

Carl winced at the hostile messages. Despite his lack of fluency in English, he understood exactly what they meant. As they danced their horses in circles around his fellow congregants, looming over them in menacing anonymity, Carl thought he saw Prussian army uniforms under the blankets. Then the blankets fell away and there were the arrogant, sneering faces of King Wilhelm's men, sabers in their clenched hands. He stared in disbelief, rubbing his eyes with his fists.

"What're you gapin' at, ya ugly ape? "

"Yeah, are ya volunteerin' ta hang on the nearest tree?"

Carl thought he recognized one of the voices but couldn't say who it could be. Without knowing why, he glanced downward at the boots being worn by the familiar voice, probably because it was the only part of him that wasn't covered. With a shock he recognized the bright crimson leather and black pattern of a boot he had seen somewhere before. Samuel appeared at his side, grabbed his arm and pulled him along, running with the rest of the crowd. Gussie and the baby were not with him.

"Where is she?" Carl shouted in his ear.

"I can't find her. Help me look for her! I hope she is on her way home."

The panicked crowd surged into Central Street, but not before several of them had cast glances behind them and raised a cry together.

"The rebbe's house is on fire! It's burning!"

The crackling of the flames had intensified, and Carl glanced back to see the roof of the beloved edifice flickering red, dark smoke rising and visible in the glow of the fire.

Now people were running in all directions, some through the woods and others down the street with only a waxing gibbous moon and a streetlamp to light their way. Samuel and Carl continued to move forward, looking for Gussie and David. They had brought along a small lantern but hadn't had time to light it in the commotion. They ducked into a small cul-de-sac, and with shaking fingers Samuel lit the lantern and held it high, gazing around in all directions. The muffled sounds of hurled epithets, clomping horse hooves, and snapping flames surrounded them like threatening thunder. Those sounds were pierced by yells and shouts, and then clanging bells as a fire truck pulled by a sturdy mule lumbered down the street laden with men holding buckets. Samuel began to weep.

"Don't worry," Carl consoled his brother. "We will find

Gussie and the baby soon. They ran away when they saw the men covered in blankets riding up to the synagogue. She is probably home already."

People were rushing by them, dark blurs in the night, in the opposite direction. One man called to them,

"My friend, you're goin' the wrong way. The fire's this way! We need all hands to put it out!"

Carl called back,

"We have to find my brother's wife and baby!"

His words were lost in the night air as they ran into downtown Hot Springs and through Main Street. It appeared that every resident in town was roused and armed with buckets and rushing towards the fire, which was filling the air with its brash burning odor. Alarm bells were ringing in the distance. Church bells from a nearby steeple added their own pealing tones. The brothers continued through town and headed north on Whittington Avenue, searching for Gussie in every shadow, behind bushes, hedges, trees, in alleyways.

When they finally arrived home, Samuel sprinted to the front door, flung it open and hollered his wife's name. Silence and emptiness greeted them. The men ran into the bedrooms, the root cellar, and even banged on the privy and roamed the little garden and grounds surrounding the house, but Gussie was not to be found. They stared at each other in horror.

"We have to go back," Samuel said, then broke anew into weeping. Carl felt a painful sob rise in his throat but knew that he had to suppress his own tears for the sake of his brother. One of them must be a steady pillar in this crisis.

"Come, Sam," Carl whispered. "Back we go. We will find her and David and bring them home."

This time they saddled up Samuel's horse and Strudel, even though it was forbidden on Shabbos, and rode them into town and across Central Avenue again. Despite the exhaustion that had overtaken them both, they rode their mounts forcefully. They began to ask any stray person that they passed on the street if they had seen a young woman dressed in white with a babe in arms. All they got in return were gruff shakes of the head from the men and polite no sirs from the few women who were out and rushing to the fire, their faces glowing eerily in the pale lights of their lanterns.

As they approached the rebbe's home for the second time that day, Carl and Samuel began to breathe in hot smoke. They coughed and ducked their heads, eyes tearing. Both of their animals were snorting nervously and rearing. When they got there, they saw men passing buckets of water to throw onto the flames. The fire had spread and was laddering up the branches of trees and over to other rooftops of neighboring houses. The intense blaze brightened the landscape in all directions. The brothers could see that Gussie was not there. Samuel began gasping frantically. Carl grabbed his shoulder and exclaimed,

"We must ask everybody where the crazy men on horses went. They might have her. Let's go!"

Carl could hardly believe this was happening, but he forced his fright down into his churning, sickened gut like a rabid beast that must be contained. The two men spotted

Rabbi Schechter in the middle of the bucket brigade, passing the water-filled pails madly. They rushed over to him and together explained that Gussie had been outside with the baby when the attackers came, and now she could not be located. His sweating brow buckled with concern.

"She is not in my house. I know because I checked all the rooms before I left."

Rabbi Schechter's front porch and entry were completely burned and the exterior of the building was charred, but most of the fire was out now. His neighbors were pouring water on smoldering embers. The fire truck was still there, but all of its tankards were empty now.

In the darkness a horse clip-clopped behind him and stopped, and a familiar voice spoke behind Carl.

"I will find your wife, your sister-in-law. One of the men who attacked your people took her, and I think I know where. They have done this before to the colored people in town. Follow me. I know the Ouachita Mountains like the inside of my mother's *hogan,* her house. Pray to your God, as I will pray to mine, that she and the little one are safe."

Carl turned and looked into Waddite's narrowed and determined gray eyes glinting in the light of the lantern he held.

20

R oland Longman sat on the bed stunned and in pain from the wound in his neck. He grabbed a kerchief and held it tightly to stem the flow of blood that was seeping down his neck and towards his chest, staining ruby the inside of his snowy ruffled shirt. Greta Schuler lay next to him, whimpering and squinting as she attempted vainly to loosen the rope bonds digging into her wrists. He only allowed one minute or so to pass before he leapt up to embark upon what he called his 'distress plan'. He had had to employ it once before on a British steamer to avoid exposure and capture, and it had played out well. He lifted Greta off the bed and lowered her into his cedar traveling trunk, covering her with a thick tan and dusty rose quilted blanket. He had prepared the trunk long ago with discreet airholes along the sides so that he could spirit away a captive female without her suffocating in it. She lay cradled in his clothing and shoes, muffled and tied. The last he saw of her before he closed the trunk lid were her terrified green eyes gazing up at him.

When two crewmen banged on Roland Longman's cabin door, he was dabbing at his throat with a plush cotton towel that he'd grabbed from his bathroom and applying pressure to the wound. Dark red bloodspots dripped a trail across the carpet. The hatpin had sunk in deeply, leaving him in excruciating pain. Fortunately, it had missed the neck artery. He knew explanations would be demanded for the violent attack upon him by a lady. He gathered his wits and thoughts together as best he could despite his downright agony. What a mad vixen the little Israelite was! He was astonished at her quick counter-attack and escape from what he had determined would be her destiny as a brothel slave. He scolded himself immediately for taking a chance with a female not voyaging in steerage. He had already hidden Greta out of sight, so he called out,

"One minute, please, sirs. Give me a moment."

Collecting himself and wincing as he moved across the room, he opened the door a crack,

"Why are you pounding on my door, swabbies?"

"I am Ensign Hastings, sir. You have been accused of insulting and assaulting a gentlewoman aboard ship. The captain wishes to speak with you immediately."

"I look forward to such a conversation, given that 'tis I have been attacked, not the lady, which word I use questionably."

Longman joined the crewmen in the corridor and the three strode together to the captain's quarters. Keeping a relaxed expression on his countenance, he nonetheless realized that he would have to think quickly upon the moment to explain his actions. He grumbled inwardly at the great waste of time this trip was going to cost him.

The captain's quarters consisted of a spacious but spartan suite on the highest level of the ship with a panoramic view of the horizon. Small white clouds scudded below immense long trails of lacier ones, the pale sapphire firmament showing through here and there. It was a dazzling sight that Longman couldn't help but admire despite his preoccupation with his pain and the accusations to come. He seated himself at a straight-backed, armless wooden chair pulled up to a wide oak table covered with maps. Captain Wilkins of the U.S.S. *Eolus* glared down at him from a loftier cushioned armchair at the opposite end of the table.

"Indecent behavior toward the womenfolk is intolerable on my ship, sir. My crew is, as we speak, tending to a young lady, a Miss Rosalia Wolfson, who appears to be in a state of excitation beyond all normalcy, her gown and corset ripped apart in the front. She accuses you, Mr. Longman, of luring her into your cabin and thereupon attacking her brutally. As if this were not enough, she also claims you harbor within your rooms another woman, unidentified as yet, bound, gagged, and veritably helpless. Crew members are searching your rooms as we speak. Can you explain any of this? And quickly, man, as I have a ship full of passengers who must not become aroused by rumors of misbehavior and violence aboard."

Longman leaned forward, engaging the eye of Captain Wilkins with his own. The captain's white handlebar mustache quivered. Longman noted the tics in the captain's face and steeled himself for tough oratory combat. He would need to dig deeply into his treasure trove of falsehoods to protect his reputation.

"This so-called "lady" you refer to, she is no lady. Firstly, she is a Jewess, and thereby no Christian gentlelady. Secondly, the tale she tells you is false, and in fact is the reverse of what she says. The girl has a loose reputation, which I happen to know from sources I shall not reveal for purpose of decorum. She fulfilled this reputation today by following me to my room, entering thereupon, and raining upon me kisses and caresses, murmuring love coos into my ear. Suddenly she demanded money of me, which if I withhold, she threatened to accuse me of untoward behavior. Indignantly I denied her request for legal tender, and she next ripped her own dress down the front, to my great astonishment. Then she pulled a hatpin out of her bonnet and stabbed me in the throat in great ire, as you can see here." Longman stopped his story to lift the towel gingerly from the wound in his neck and reveal it to Captain Wilkins, who gasped in dismay.

"She is an evil Jezebel to be reckoned with. Insane or crafty, who is to say? But lock her up you must, to protect the other passengers from her machinations."

Captain Wilkins wiped his brow and shook his head slowly, eyeing Longman silently for a minute. Finally he responded,

"And what about her report of a woman bound and gagged in your cabin? What of that?"

"More lies by milady Jezebel," snapped Longman indignantly. "This is a most preposterous lie. You may search every inch, every centimeter indeed, of my rooms and you will find no captive. Why on God's good earth would I do such a thing?" He almost believed his own words, he delivered them with such force and confidence.

Captain Wilkins continued to rub his brow, appearing deep in thought for a time. He spoke now,

"This casts the incident in a whole new light. We must address Miss Wolfson once more and present her with your accusations as well. For the time being, I ask that you remain in your quarters and take supper there tonight. It will be brought to you. Please forgive the restriction, but as captain I must err upon the side of caution."

"How dare you? You condemn me to my room after all I have spoken, in truth, about this extraordinarily devious female? Why must I be punished? Surely, she is the one who should be confined, not in her quarters, but in the brig as a common criminal!"

Secretly Longman was relieved to spend the next few hours in his room as the ship weighed anchor and passengers debarked. His timing couldn't be more perfect, as now he could escape to shore. The less that he was observed and remarked upon by crew and passengers, the better. Even more, he could not afford to reveal the injury to his neck and the pain he was suffering in public without attracting the wrong kind of attention.

"Mr. Longman, I regret the restriction. However, you must see that there are two sides to this story, and I cannot make judgment easily here. We must take a tally of the passengers to assure that nobody is missing. Until then, please be patient. This is a serious incident, and we must proceed carefully. Miss Wolfson will also be confined to her quarters at this time. But prior to secluding yourself in quarters, kindly visit the infirmary for attention to that nasty wound."

Longman had no intention of presenting himself to the infirmary. He pretended disgust, bunching his eyebrows together tightly. Then he ushered Captain Wilkins out of his cabin and closed the door to them, still clutching the towel to his bloody throat. His only thoughts at this moment were of the girl in his possession and how he would smuggle her off the ship.

"Do not fret, Greta," he said in a commanding tone, "you will not die in there. You are worth a great deal to me."

He rushed out of the cabin and down the hallway, searching until he found two Negro stewards that would carry the trunk immediately down the ship's ramp to the dock. After paying them handsomely for the service, he promised them twice that amount if they would secure a hansom cab, load the trunk into it and await his arrival. He must pay extra for the private hansom so that no other riders would join him. The two darkies did his bidding, and when they were gone with the trunk, he pulled out of his travel bags a blonde wig and black beret and donned them. A loud banging at the door and the voice of a crewman stopped him abruptly.

"Mr. Longman! Mr. Roland Longman! You are hereby commanded to remain in your room until the captain arrives to speak with you! I will be guarding the door with a weapon until then!"

Longman slid his long-handled dagger from its scabbard and flung the cabin door open hard, knocking the guard aside. He leapt upon him with all of his bodily weight, and caused the crewman to stagger and then fall. He plunged the knife deep into the hapless man's throat, then jumped off him and backed up so that the blood streaming to the floor wouldn't stain his shoes or pants. Nobody would hear this death, he thought smugly. No gunshot. Then he grabbed his travel bags already filled with his toiletries and smaller essentials, as he had been preparing to disembark soon anyway, and dashed along the halls of the ship.

Down the metal stairs he clanged, and then another flight of them to steerage, where he mingled with the line of lower-class passengers lined up and waiting for the first- and second-class passengers to come ashore before them. Keeping the swell of panic rising in his chest at bay, he mumbled apologies in a cockney accent that he knew well from his childhood as he scored this way and that through the crowd to get ahead. The angry scowls of exasperated, foul-smelling voyagers did not discourage him from rudely pressing forward. When he reached the front of the steerage line, he ducked brazenly under the rope holding them back and flew down the ship's ramp onto the dock.

Behind him, he heard a commotion and knew instantly that the guard had been discovered and the crew was looking for him. He immediately slowed down and strolled casually, trusting in the blonde wig and beret to fool them, which it did. He did not allow himself the joyous realization of successful escape until he had located the two Negro stewards standing dutifully beside a hired hansom with the trunk inside taking up the entire floor of the conveyance. Handing the waiting men the generous sum of fifty cents each, he hopped into the buggy and ordered the driver to take him to the French Quarter of New Orleans. The money he had paid the servants to get the trunk off the ship was well worth it and would be repaid many times over when he sold Greta to the brothel in New Orleans.

Captain Wilkins left the helm to the dependable Ensign Hastings. He was conferring with Chief Mate Rogers about the tragic incident involving Miss Rosalia Wolfson and Mr. Roland Longman. So far neither of them had backed down on their respective versions of what had transpired. An ordinary seaman had searched Longman's cabin for a hostage while Longman was being interrogated, and had found nobody. The Chief Steward compared the ship's bill of lading with passengers aboard and indeed, one female passenger had come up missing: a Miss Greta Schuler of Hamburg, Germany. She was in steerage, traveling alone. This was grave cause for concern for Captain Wilkins. They were responsible for the transport of every passenger on board, no matter their station in life or placement on the vessel.

The people in steerage were questioned, but nobody seemed to remember a red-haired young lady traveling alone except for one man. He claimed to have observed someone fitting that description leaving steerage in the company of a well-dressed gentleman. Upon hearing this, the captain and crew became increasingly suspicious of Mr. Longman and less inclined to place Miss Wolfson in the wrong.

Adding to their suspicion of Mr. Longman was the appearance of Miss Wolfson, an unlikely aggressor at maybe four and a half feet tall in her boots and and weighing little more than a sparrow. However, without proof they could neither arrest Roland Longman nor lock him in the brig. In the meantime, ship's crew were hunting high and low for the missing Miss Schuler.

Captain Wilkins heard a vigilant seaman in the crow's nest call through a bullhorn, "Port of New Orleans ahoy!" He feared that they would dock in port with still no knowledge of the missing passenger. Nor would there be resolution of the violence that had occurred in Mr. Longman's cabin.

Wilkins had captained many voyages across the sea from Europe to the United States and back again and had gained some insight and sensitivity toward the characters of people from so much exposure to them. He relied on that intuition now, and it raised the hairs on the back of his neck when he spoke with Longman.

The young woman seemed vulnerable and innocent, perhaps her only fault being gullible enough to fall into the web of a conniving seducer. When he spoke with her, she was moaning, not about herself, but over the missing woman she claimed to have seen. She was sure, and swore to God Himself in Heaven, that the poor woman could only have come to a bad end at the hands of the treacherous Longman. She suspected that Longman had thrown the woman overboard. She sobbed loudly, devastated to think that she was the cause of the woman's demise. Wilkins assured her repeatedly that she was not to be blamed for such a fiendish action, if it had occurred at all. As tough and thick-skinned as he had to be to command the crew of a large ocean-going steamer, his heart softened at the sight of a weeping woman.

Nonetheless, both she and that fake dandy Longman must be confined to their rooms until the ship weighed anchor off the port of New Orleans. Unfortunately, the two of them would have to remain in their quarters on the vessel until Wilkins and the crew could locate the missing Greta Schuler.

Wilkins gazed ahead at the port of New Orleans growing larger, like a widening beige band stretching behind a strip of aquamarine water. Quickly the skyline became more distinct as the ship drew nearer and transformed into two- and three-story government buildings, warehouses, shops and saloons. Rowboats tugged at their ropes along the shore. Magnolia trees further in the distance dancing lightly like green-haired pixies.

It was time to steer the vessel into the mouth of the Mississippi River and alongside the deep-water wharf of the Port of New Orleans. Then his load of passengers would disappear into the Cajun heat and spice of New Orleans. The ship shuddered slightly and slowed considerably as it made its way into the Mississippi Delta and north toward the massive wharves of New Orleans. Captain Wilkins steered the ship into a berth, then hurried to the helm and grabbed the bullhorn.

"Time to drop anchor, mates." His voice reverberated against the hard surfaces of the steamer. Several crewmen scrambled to the boarding deck and there they hoisted and lowered the huge metal weight into the murky waters of the

Mississippi River. It was the only port in the United States with deep waters for the largest of ships, which saved them the interim step of lowering passengers and cargo into skiffs and smaller boats at a distance and rowing them to the landing. Several hours of unloading passengers, trunks, baggage and cargo passed, as Captain Wilkins paced restlessly and studied each person's face as they disembarked. He was anxious to put an end to the incident between the scoundrel Longman and the distraught Miss Wolfson. Even more worrisome, the missing passenger Greta Schuler still had not been located.

Third Mate George Billings, a gangly, tanned, jet-black haired and mustachioed fellow, had been assigned the task of checking each passenger's name on the list of lading. He noted the name "Schuler, Greta", between "Scarborough, Eleonora" and "Schultz, Joseph". As each passenger went down starboard, Hastings crossed their name off. Finally, the last passenger wobbled down the loading ramp, and Greta Schuler's name remained uncrossed. Billings strode quickly over to Captain Wilkins.

"Cap'n, take a look at this. Greta Schuler, name on the passenger list, did not appear nor go down to the wharf. We sure enough have a puzzle here now, eh? Seems as though lady with the tore dress warn't spinnin' a yarn after all."

"Now that my ship is unloading passengers, gather three seamen to go room to room, cabin to cabin, including all the lavatories, both men's and women's, and find Miss Schuler. Neither Roland Longman nor Rosalia Wolfson may debark until she is accounted for!"

He spat this last sentence out, furious that a possible scandal could darken the otherwise beatific voyage he had just commanded across the Atlantic Ocean. If it turned out to be murder of a passenger by another, his record as a sea captain could be stained with scandal. He closed his eyes, attempting to regain his composure. If this was the case, Mr. Longman must be brought to justice.

Third Mate Billings gathered three ordinary seamen, and they sprinted along the upper deck and clattered down the metal stairs, each one taking on a ship level to hunt for the missing passenger. Ensign Hastings hurried off the steps from the upper deck to join them. Another hour and a half passed, achingly slow for Captain Wilkins, until at last the four shipmates presented themselves before him at the helm. In the meantime, he fretted, passengers were scurrying about gathering their belongings and had already started to disembark from the *Eolus*.

"Report, Ensign," Captain Wilkins spoke crisply to Hastings, who stood stiffly before him saluting and impeccably uniformed. Wilkins found himself slightly light-headed and clutched at the bottom of the large wooden steering wheel that had guided his ship and had been a silent companion for many years.

"Sir, Miss Greta Schuler is nowhere to be found on this vessel. We have searched every room, all the lavatories for both gentlemen and ladies, lockers, galley, sleeping quarters, steerage, boiler room and fo'c'sle,"

"Then we must arrest Roland Longman and hand him to the Port of New Orleans Authorities. There is enough suspicion to warrant a proper investigation by the law. We shall go to his quarters at once."

Captain Wilkins and the four sailors traced their steps back to Longman's quarters.

"Where is the guard?" he cried out.

The door of Longman's cabin stood ajar. Seaman Charles McGregor lay face down on the floor. The seamen and Ensign Hastings gathered around their crewmate and rolled him over.

"He's gone," murmured Ensign Hastings, hanging his head and then looking up with tearing eyes at Captain Wilkins. "The wretch cut his throat!"

Wilkins could see the crimson blood that had pooled under the late Seaman McGregor and spread on the front of his white uniform. In a rage, he flung open the door of Roland Longman's room, drawing his own firearm, a long-barreled .30 caliber pistol. Staring back at him was his own reflection in the silver-framed mirror over the basin. The cabin was empty, as well as the lavatory. Roland Longman had fled the ship.

21

Gussie had just finished nursing David when the horseback riders came thundering toward the synagogue. They carried burning torches, which lit up the strange, colorful capes flapping around their shoulders and the deer antlers that they wore on their heads. She could smell the burning torch oil as they approached. Their eyes glinted in the firelight and filled her heart with dread. They slowed down as they neared her and the baby. She glanced behind her and noticed the flames of their torches reflecting on the tilted, silver-plated mezuzah that adorned Rabbi Schecter's doorpost.

One of the horsemen seemed to be the leader. He waved the three others into a circle just a few yards from where Gussie sat with David in her arms. She began to quake, first her shoulders and arms, then her knees, until she almost dropped the baby onto the ground. She heard the leader call out gruffly,

"We have our target, men! Dirty Jew Christ-killers in our town, stealing our land!"

"Say, friend, lookee behind you. One of 'em's sittin' right thar with a babe in arms," called out one of the men. He swung his mount around and loomed over Gussie. Her frightened face shone in the torchlight.

"Perfect time to give them ugly Jew bastards some trouble."

He dismounted with some difficulty, the cape wrapping around his legs and tangling slightly in the stirrups. Gussie was already backing up and heading toward the synagogue, but it was too late. The man grabbed her roughly by the waist and yanked her away from the house. Husky arms and beefy hands thrust outward from under the capes to grasp Gussie's entire body and shove her upward onto the leader's shuffling brown and white Appaloosa. She screamed in fright as the leader hopped up in front of her. She could smell a strong liquor, whiskey or gin, on his breath despite the fact that he faced away from her. The odor seemed to leak from his skin.

"Send those Christ-killers ta hell, boys!" he called out and wheeled the horse around to gallop south out of town. Gussie clutched David so tightly to her chest she thought she would smother him. She was forced to cling to the cape of the horseman seated before her so that she wouldn't fall off and kill herself and David. They rode hard for what seemed like hours in the darkness. Her terrified heart thumped like a creature with a life of its own. She feared more for the baby than for herself during that endless ride into the menacing darkness.

Five other horsemen came up behind them from out of nowhere, it seemed, and they rode together for a while longer. They finally stopped and dismounted, and two of them pulled Gussie roughly out of the saddle and onto the ground. In the hellish flame of the leader's torch, Gussie could only see the road before her. The men wended their way along a rocky hillside, one man pulling her by the arm until they came to the entrance of a cave. It gaped at Gussie like an unholy golem's demonic mouth. The flickering torches created sinister shadows flickering around its outside circumference. One of the men dragged her into this cavern, spitting chaw and laughing. The baby was now grunting and mewling, and she knew that any second now those noises would turn into frantic, hungry wails. The men left her and David on the dank dirt floor of the cave in inky solitude and vanished. David opened wide his tiny, sweet red lips and howled like a little beast.

Time passed slowly, an odd sensation for Gussie, as she never had a moment during the day when she wasn't working or tending to the babe. She nursed David, and the silence pressed around them with only his pleasure-filled infant grunts and suckling sounds filling the air. Once a bat loosened its grip on the cavern ceiling and swooped over her head, startling her. David finally fell asleep and she removed him from her breast, swaddled him in her shawl and shuddered like a trapped insect.

She worried about Samuel and Carl missing her and searching to no avail. How could they possibly find her, dumped here like a sack of potatoes in a root cellar? She was disoriented and unsure of where this cave lay in relation to the town of Hot Springs. Then other, uglier thoughts pushed their way to the surface, thoughts she did not welcome but harried her mind in this solitary stone jail. She trembled at the prospect of the hateful horsemen returning to the cave. Would they kill her and David? Would they rape her first? Could there possibly be a black bear hibernating deep in the bosom of the cave who would awake and, discovering the intruders, tear them to bits? Tears that she had held back while nursing David now flowed freely down her cheeks and over her chin, plopping copiously into her lap and and onto her shawl covering David. Would they starve to death here? Or could she escape, wandering among the hills and woods until she found Hot Springs again? Instead, she began to focus on the baby, playing with his diminutive fingers, counting his toes for him in a sing-song lullaby, brushing off leaves and twigs that had fallen into his fluff of brown hair as they rode through the woods.

She mused that she had seen more than she wanted to in the war-ravaged town of Hot Springs. An unwilling witness, she had stumbled upon the black-skinned Americans enduring whippings and humiliations,. They took place at the ends of small streets, behind hedges and fences, against the sides of buildings blocked by the magnificent sheer granite walls that jutted oddly into downtown. In Germany, the Kaiser's soldiers fomented the same subterranean tidepool of hatred and violence as in this odd American town, blistering as the springs themselves. The Civil War had ended not long ago, and the darkies, as the gentiles called them sometimes, were now free by constitutional law. Then why did it seem not to be so?

The dawning rays of the morning sun slowly sifted into the cave's entrance. She could dimly discern a swarm of bats hanging from the cave's ceiling and shivered. They were almost the same color as the cave walls themselves and blended in cleverly. The cave smelled dank and earthy, not altogether an unpleasant odor, but a smell that made her agonizingly aware that she was in a place where she didn't belong. David's diaper began to get soggier, and she fretted that he would soon dirty it and she would have no way to change it for a fresh one. She would just have to empty the excrement, wipe it off the best she could, and reuse it on his poor, wet bottom. Her stomach began to growl for food, and her mouth was dry with thirst.

As the dawn lightened the walls of the cave, she heard the larks and wrens begin to trill their lilting melodies in the tree canopies. Woodpeckers dug into pine trunks with their hammering beaks as the morning sun awoke them. The bats were mostly silent, but occasionally one or two would chirp their cryptic messages to one another. Then another noise, very distant, reached her ears, and with every minute, a faint thumping of hooves on the ground grew louder. If her abductors were returning, she would make a run for the forest and head toward what she hoped was town.

Gussie stumbled to the inner edge of the cave clutching David to her bosom and fearfully peered into the growing light of day. She glimpsed three bobbing horses' heads, then their graceful necks, next their galloping front legs and withers. They moved quickly toward her, gaining on a hill and then riding down it carrying three men. From afar she could tell the men were wearing normal clothing, not colorful loud capes or antler hats. Had they merely changed their clothes and returned to violate, torment and kill her? As they neared, she joyfully recognized the faces of the riders. But who was the third rider? It didn't matter, and elation filled her from her toes to the top of her head. She felt as if she were swimming in joy, and uncontrollable tears poured down her cheeks. She climbed out of the rough and rocky mouth of the cave, patting the crying infant to calm his fussing. Once in the open air, Gussie drew in deep breaths and waved her left arm as high as she could to attract their notice. Her relief at being rescued made her slightly dizzy, and she had to sit down on a nearby boulder. The cold, rough surface chilled her through her skirt, bustle and undergarments, but she was too ecstatic to give it more than a moment's attention. They had seen her and were calling her name.

Samuel slid off his horse as quickly as he could when they reached her. He ran, boots beating in the dirt, and gathered Gussie and the baby in his burly arms.

"Oy, so worried I was about you, my Gussie! Are you all right? Did those monsters hurt you? Or the baby?"

"Not really," laughed Gussie, then sobbed and could not speak for a long while.

Carl called out from his mount,

"Gussie, we rode all night looking for you! Thanks to Hashem in heaven, and to Waddite, we found her! We owe them great appreciation."

Waddite then spoke up, "Help your woman up on your horse. I have a cradle board that the baby can ride in." The resourceful Quapaw dismounted, reached into his saddle bag and pulled out an elongated, woven basket with a firm back. He gently helped Gussie to place the now-squirming and screaming, red-faced David into the cradle board and tightened it just so with several polished cowhide strings.

"I will take your baby on my horse. You are shaking too much to hold him now."

Gussie nodded mutely, trying to suppress her fear of handing her infant to another person who was not a family member. She finally decided to trust the man, though, because he had brought Samuel and Carl to her. Carl dismounted and helped his trembling sister-in-law place her foot in the stirrups of Samuel's horse, then up and over its broad back behind her husband. David's screams stopped abruptly as the horses trotted along the deer paths that meandered over the hillsides and through the cottonwood trees.

When they reached the border of town marked by a cleared trail that suddenly appeared, it was almost noon. All four riders were weary, and the baby was sound asleep. Samuel turned his horse towards home. Carl continued straight toward Rabbi Schechter's house to lend a hand in the aftermath of the fire. Gussie watched him until he disappeared around a curve in the road.

22

Rabbi's Schechter's home was miraculously still standing, but the front of it lay smoldering in ashes. Carl shook his head sadly as he dismounted Strudel and walked her, now skittish as she sniffed the hazy air, slowly on a lead. He surveyed the damage and the wisps of smoke that still swooped upward from what was left of a copse of blackgum trees. The elderberry bushes that had surrounded the structure were gone as well. The fire-ravaged property appeared so forlorn and ruined to Carl, he felt a sickness in his stomach. Rabbi Schecter came around the corner of the house, his full beard bobbing and covered with ashes, and hurried over to Carl. He grabbed Carl's hand, almost twice as large as his, and squeezed it between his own two small ones.

"The bucket brigade worked very hard all night and we saved the other homes around mine. And nobody was hurt or killed, thanks be to Hashem. But more important, did you and Sam find Gussie?"

Carl nodded, unable to speak for a moment. Finally, he found his voice as the Rabbi waited patiently.

"They are unhurt, thanks to Hashem. And thanks also to my Indian friend Waddite. Do you know him, Rabbi?" – a brief nod – "He has tracking skills beyond any I could imagine. In the darkness, he knew where the attackers took her. If we didn't have him to help…." Carl could not speak further.

Rabbi Schechter wrapped his short arms the best he could around Carl's broad back and looked up into his face. His wide-set hazel eyes softened and twinkled at the same time, to Carl's amazement.

"I am so relieved and glad to hear this!" he exclaimed, then called more loudly to the congregants who were still there, "Everybody, the Gersmans found Gussie. She and the baby are safe!"

His gladdened shouts drew the attention of the people who were stirring up embers that lay buried like glowing ruby treasures beneath the debris and half-burnt tree branches and dousing them with buckets of water. There were at least twenty people from the congregation working side-by-side, and they looked up as one and waved to Carl.

"Mazel tov!"

"So happy and relieved!"

"Things could be worse!"

Carl beamed at them in relief as he heard various cheering comments from the crowd. In the midst of adversity, his soul was soothed and comforted by the outpouring of succor from his community, whether they were from Oppein or another town in Germany or elsewhere in Prussia. Townships mattered greatly in the Old Country, but here in the new one they were all simply Jews from Germany, he realized with a start. Despite this terrible attack by a handful of ruffians (not so different from the gangs of Prussian youth who ambushed wayward Jews), Carl was beginning to feel that Hot Springs was truly his home. Nonetheless, he couldn't help but ponder if this unprovoked attack on the Jews of this town was a harbinger of things to come.

⌒

Gussie's eyes fluttered half-open, but everywhere she looked was a blur. At first she thought that she was still sequestered in the cave, and she cried out in fright. A warm hand stroked her hair and a voice murmured,

"Shhhh, Gusselah my queen, you are home with your loved ones."

It was Samuel's voice. She sat up abruptly and widened her eyes, letting in the morning light. The baby was asleep in his cradle next to the bed, reddened and puffy cheeks dominating his tiny pearl face.

"You have been sleeping a very long time. Maybe ten hours or more. I think you needed that after……what happened. I need to know, my wife, did those brutes lay a hand on you?"

Gussie could hear the dread in Samuel's voice. She could sense that he had been brooding about this, no doubt all night long. She answered slowly, her voice thick with the last remnants of slumber, "No, no. Don't worry. Other than lifting me onto a horse, and taking me down from the horse, and putting me in the cave, nothing was done to me. This is the truth."

She heard Samuel sob and then sigh, and knew he was relieved. She had been violated merely by being touched by men other than her husband or relatives, according to Jewish custom. But she hadn't been raped. The men, she reflected, waking a little more from her foggy state, they need their wives to be pure and untouched by other men. Even if the woman is attacked and helpless, she pays the price of men's aggression. I thank God that nothing like that happened to me, or I would have to lie to my husband. And live with that.

Just then David awoke and squirmed for a few minutes, then let out a wail. Samuel lifted him out of the cradle and carefully placed him in Gussie's arms to nurse. He went into the kitchen and returned in less than half an hour with fresh eggs fried to perfection and a small serving of grits, which a Christian neighbor, Beulah Lee Howerton, had taught him and Gussie how to prepare. When Gussie was done nursing the baby, she helped herself to her own breakfast. There was no food like grits in Gliewitz, but with a pinch of salt and a chunk of butter they were quite tasty and went well with the eggs. She saw them being served with shrimp, bacon or pork sausage by her Christian neighbors in Hot Springs, but Jewish law forbade consumption of shellfish and pigs. Grits and eggs would have to do.

"So, the fire that those trouble-makers set," Gussie began hesitantly, fearing the worst. "Did Rabbi Schecter's house burn to the ground?"

"Not entirely. The front of the house is badly burned. The front rooms of the house are partially burnt, and there is a lot of damage from the smoke inside. We managed to save the back rooms of the house. Such a brigade of people and firemen, hauling water, throwing water. Carl and I saw them lining up and working very hard to douse the flames. But we had to search for you. My brother and I feel so badly that we couldn't toss a single bucket of water onto the fire. The Rabbi understands, though, and everyone else as well. Your disappearance, with the baby in your arms, was just as serious as the fire. We had to go looking for you immediately. Hashem must have been watching over us when He sent the Indian fellow into our path. Waddite knew how to track you down."

"Well then, we must have him to supper very soon and show him our gratitude."

"When you have recovered from this terrible event, Gussie. I won't rush you. But I agree, we must honor him in some special way for what he did."

"Who are those men that acted like *shikker* Prussian soldiers, full of liquor and spite? Why do they hate us?"

"Here the men drink whiskey, not vodka. I know why the goyim hate us in all of Europe, but not here in the land of the free and equal. All I can think is those who immigrated to America from Europe carried with them their feelings about us. And who's to stop them from acting crazy? I heard in town that the mayor of Hot Springs will hold a town hall meeting tomorrow night for everybody about the fire and those hooligans. I will certainly attend, and you can too, if you're up for it."

"You should go, Sam, and take Carl with you. But I think that I will stay home with the baby. The idea of leaving the house right now frightens me."

Samuel gazed lovingly at Gussie, and she warmed at the tenderness softening the angles and lines in his face. She also detected sadness tugging at the corners of his wide, dark brown eyes. He was clearly shaken by the ordeal they had all just endured.

"When I go to the town hall meeting, and when I go to the store, you will be alone and defenseless with the baby. It seems unlikely that you would be targeted again. I think you were taken away simply because you were alone and helpless in front of the Rabbi's house. But we must be smarter now. I will teach you how to shoot a pistol so you can defend yourself."

"This is something I never imagined learning in Germany, but many ladies who grew up here in Arkansas know how to shoot a gun. It's my turn now. *Ach,* I almost forgot! Where is Rosalia Wolfson? Has she arrived from Little Rock yet?"

"She is here, staying with Ethan Meyer and his cousins Rosa and Simon. She will move in with us in the next few days."

Gussie's eyes glistened with a few stray tears. She said softly,

"It will be very nice to have another woman here to keep me company and help with the baby and housework. I do get a little lonely at times."

"True, I am away at the store sometimes for long hours. But don't forget, Gussie, Carl and Rosalia will soon be married, and then we will lose her. Try not to get too attached. By the way, she is a *shayna maidel,* so pretty Carl is beside himself with joy after waiting all these years."

Gussie was busy settling David back into his crib to nap, as he had nursed his fill and was sleepy.

"I cannot wait to meet her, Sam. She will take my mind off the terrible memories that haunt me now."

Suddenly she broke out into fresh weeping, unable to restrain the surge of fear and residual anguish at the thought of dying with the baby in her arms. Samuel grew silent and then sat down beside Gussie, wrapping his arms around her shaking shoulders. His wide, firm hands felt comforting, and once again she prayed that he wouldn't use them in the future to strike her when he lost his temper.

The rest of the day they moved slowly in the house and the garden. Since it was a Sunday, all businesses were closed, and the Christian churches were filled with worshippers. Samuel kept his dry goods store closed as well to foster good relations with the gentile community, although he could have brought in some business with Jewish shoppers. Every few hours a friend or two would knock on the door, bringing sweet almond mandelbrot cookies or blackberry preserves, to inquire about Gussie and the baby. They would visit briefly and then leave after reassuring themselves that Samuel's wife was unharmed. Rabbi Schecter arrived midday, alternately shaking and stroking his curling gray-tipped beard as he regarded Gussie with his deepset hazel eyes softened in sympathy.

"*Oy vey,* will persecution of us ever cease?" he sighed. "Yet we see the *shvartzes* treated even worse. But I do believe that better times will come. Do not let your faith in the Almighty be weakened by evil. The Torah tells us that we have a covenant with Hashem, and we must not forget that. He will sustain us through our ordeals."

Gussie listened politely, because of course this was the Rabbi and he was owed the greatest respect, but her deepest thoughts were the opposite of his words to her. She suspected that times would be getting worse rather than better, and that this attack upon the Jewish people of Hot Springs was only getting started. The men who absconded with her and baby David in such a brazen manner would only be emboldened by their success at damaging the Rabbi's house and snatching her. She heard remarks about Jews and Negroes in town wherever she went; they hung in the air like a biting poison. More men would join them, she was convinced, and in the not-too-distant future, the attacks would grow in frequency and intensity. Just like in Germany.

"Thank you for coming, Rabbi Schecter," she replied weakly. "Your words of wisdom are comforting to me and hopefully to Samuel as well."

"You need more time to heal. We will all pray for you, Gussie. In the meantime," here he turned directly to Sam, "you should attend the town hall being convened by the mayor. We live in a country now with some similarities to the Old Country, with hatred and prejudice and injustice. But it is also supposed to be a democracy, free from kings and princes and tsars. Meetings such as this would never happen in Prussia. Let us take advantage of the freedom we have and speak our minds."

Gussie imagined showing up at the town hall meeting and speaking her mind. This wasn't something she felt capable of doing for many reasons, not the least of which was her precarious state of mind at this moment. Samuel could be her emissary, though.

23

As the hansom and horse jogged along the streets of the city, Longman took a deep breath and considered the close call. No noise arose from the depths of the trunk, so he lifted the lid a crack to check on Greta. The sudden light made her squinting emerald eyes blink rapidly until he lowered the lid again, satisfied that she was conscious and unharmed. Settling back into the leather cushioning of the cab, he became more aware of the searing pain in his wounded throat. The bleeding had stopped, but it left a trail on his clothing and skin. He replaced the reddened kerchief with another one from his traveling bag and winced. Damn that tiny devil Rosalia Wolfson! Was she in fact the daughter of a wolf? She would not get away with this. He would track her down mercilessly and steal her away from the eager groom. She would pay him back in many ways for this insulting attack.

After winding through numerous streets, the hansom stopped at the address Longman had given the driver. They both gazed up at a multi-gabled, three-story house that dominated a narrow alley. The residence had been painted a pale shade of rose with violet trim. Other than the transom over the front door and the one large casement looking out from the parlor on the ground floor, it lacked windows. The driver clambered down from his high seat and assisted Longman in carrying the trunk from the cab up the eight front steps to the lilac-painted front door.

Longman knocked, four short loud raps, and the door was soon opened by a towering, gangly, brown-skinned maid in white apron and cap. Longman stepped into the foyer.

"Mr. Longman! I declare, it be a long time. Do come in, suh. I get de mistress right away."

Longman kissed her cheek before she could get away.

"You are looking beautiful as ever, Lily Mae," he said, winking at her. She was a pleasure in bed if he brought her gold or silver jewelry.

A cloud of apricot blossom perfume and rustling of layered chiffon infused the foyer ahead of Madame Liza Meriwether. She appeared in the foyer doorway, grinning expansively at her favorite procurer.

"Welcome back, Roland dear. The girls will be so delighted to see you. Hopefully, you will stay for dinner. And what news do you bring to this part of town?"

She was not a talkative sort, Longman thought with relief. He appreciated her directness and brevity, which eased their business dealings together. He was presented to her by James Sears when they traveled together to New Orleans in 1859. For several years Roland and Liza did business together; they even had a passionate but brief love affair. Liza was born the daughter of a prostitute in this very house, and, showing an innate cleverness, was favored and groomed by the previous Madame to take over when she retired, which she did eight years ago. Business was disrupted in the South by the block-ade that the North inflicted upon it during the Civil War, and he procured girls for houses in the North only to keep out of the line of fire. He was relieved that the war was over and now he could bring girls for Liza's brothel.

"I have treasure for you in this trunk, Liza. It is filled with gold, but not the kind that the forty-niners mined from the California mountains."

He dramatically lifted the lid little by little, revealing the toes and hair of Greta Schuler peeking out from the blanket that he had draped over her. Liza gasped and stepped forward to take a closer look,

"Heavens, Roland. Don't you usually walk them in properly, like a gentleman? Granted, they're usually dosed on whiskey. But this is, well, outlandish."

"There was a bit of, er, shall we say, an incident aboard ship. I had to resort to this or there would have been some trouble. Fortunately, we both eluded the authorities. I look forward to a formal negotiation with you after dinner."

"Well, well, little ole Roland's gotten himself into a sorry plight. Stay with us here for a while, darlin', long as you need. We have a spare room in the basement, and that will have to do. But for goodness sake, let's get this poor honeychile out of the trunk and into a bath. Ooh, Lordy me, I can smell her from heah."

Liza wrinkled her nose and fanned the air in front of her, then leaned over quickly to uncover the hapless woman still lying in the trunk.

"Roland! You been standin' around lahk it is no horrible thing to be…..be imprisoned in a cedar trunk jest lahk a corpse. Help me get this poor girl out of heah."

Together they lifted Greta up and out and sat her, still bound at hands and feet, atop the trunk. Liza worked on the ropes at her wrist as Longman stood back and watched.

"Don't be lazy, Roland," Liza admonished him. "You got her into this, you should be gettin' her out. Poor dear," addressing Greta, "you must be hungry and thirsty after all your tribulations."

"Keep the ties on her feet," Longman warned. "She might try to run. And keep that scarf across her mouth, or she'll probably scream like a peacock."

"Don't you be uppity at me, Roland. This girl is gettin' a long, luxurious, scented bath and a meal like you nevah. Jambalaya and biscuits with honey."

Liza's eyes twinkled as they glanced at Greta for some expression to come to her face other than horror and utter defeat. And inevitably, Greta's features relaxed behind the scarf and her eyelids drooped slightly.

"Come, sugah, let me steer you clear of this awfully bad man and into a private room of your own. I'll draw you a bath and help you to forget about that horrid trunk."

Liza bent down and skillfully untied the ropes that bound Greta's feet. Greta took a few unstable steps and leaned against Liza, undone and exhausted. Roland had been slowly edging away from them and then quietly pushed open a swinging door that led to the kitchen. He pressed his ear to the door near the jamb where it opened to hear what he could of the two women's conversation. He knew from past experience that his presence during Greta's introduction into the brothel would only continue to upset her. They needed to get her calm and compliant, and Liza was an expert in that regard. She had accomplished such an effect upon the girls that he brought to her time and time again. Payment for the delivery would come later tonight, both in money and in carnal pleasure. He grinned salaciously, anticipating the evening ahead.

He whiled away an hour or more in the kitchen, an orderly and well-scrubbed room with a large icebox, an apron sink below a wide window, a flour drawer and smooth oak counters lined with gadgets and gewgaws that sifted, peeled, toasted and squeezed. The ladies of the night had a cook who prepared all their meals and kept the kitchen tidy and clean. There was a handmade walnut table in the center of the kitchen and two matching walnut chairs.

Longman peered inside the icebox, grabbed a glass bottle of milk and gulped down half. He rummaged around the cupboards until he found a shelf full of liqueurs. He spotted his favorite, absinthe, and poured several capfuls into the half-drunk bottle of milk. Perfection!

He sat at the table and nursed the drink for a half hour, ruminating on the adventure he had just experienced and his risk of arrest. Overall, he would have to assess the journey as a success because he had delivered the goods and would make a profit. However, he berated himself as he nursed the absinthe-laced milk, about having lost his head over the pretty Israelite, Rosalia. For the twentieth time that day, he gingerly probed the wound at his throat, now covered with a clean bandage but still delivering a sharp pain and surrounding inflammation to his neck. He recalled the ruckus she had made on the ship and knew that his business was now compromised. He would have to use other steamship lines for his abductions and ensure that nobody on the vessel knew who he was.

Again his ire rose, and he determined that he would exact revenge upon the young woman. He knew that her destination was Hot Springs, and that fit in perfectly with his plans. He had a customer, a brothel owner in that very town. He would make his way there and hunt her down like a partridge huddled under a bush. In the midst of his reverie, the swinging door glided gently inward, and Liza poked her head into the kitchen.

"Greta has had a difficult journey and still isn't feeling well. But that is to be expected, yes? She is enjoying a hot bath with attar of roses, and the other girls are comforting her. Soon she will be very happy to be here. As for you, Roland, the basement room is ready now with fresh sheets on the bed so that you can settle in and relax after your long journey. Greta is so attractive and will be even more so when we fatten her up a little with our jambalaya, beans and rice and beignets. Right now she is too thin. Why, there's nothin' for a man to grab a hold of!"

They both chuckled, and then Longman followed Liza down a hallway into a back room with its own entrance.

"This way you can avoid Greta while you are here."

They both nodded sagely at the wisdom of this strategy. Longman had forced sex upon the girl to subdue her, but now it was time to move her past that memory and into the next stage of accepting customers. That would take a little time and work, but eventually they all succumbed to the circumstance because they had nobody to turn to and nowhere to go in their new land. If an employer or relative was expecting Greta somewhere in the United States, they would never discover what happened to the immigrant girl. Roland and Liza felt safe in their dealings.

The last morning of Longman's stay in New Orleans, he informed Liza that he would be returning soon with another girl for the brothel. He did not refer to Rosalia Wolfson in the letter, but that is exactly whom he planned to provide. She would bring a handsome bounty. The very thought of it excited him as nothing else ever had.

24

The U.S.S. *Eolus* was approaching the port of New Orleans. Rosalia peered through her porthole window and stared at the pier in the distance. The breaking morning light silhouetted faint purple and gray shapes in the distance like a shimmering mantle. Perhaps the shapes were roofs or groves of trees rising on the shore. The same gold and rose rays that backlit the skyline of the land also gilded the ocean's frothy whitecaps. The ship bobbed on the rough surface of the water like a gigantic seagull, listing from port to starboard and back again. She tried to imagine hard, steady land under her feet again. She was too frightened to leave her cabin, afraid that she would catch sight of Roland Longman, but she knew that eventually she would have to disembark onto dry land, and the appeal of that helped her overcome her dread.

The long line of steerage passengers snaked around the corner of the customs office building flanked by the Port Authority of New Orleans on the left and the steamship ticket office on the right. It would take several hours of patient waiting for the steerage passengers to get through United States Customs. Rosalia was relieved to hurry past them to a section of Customs reserved for first- and second-class passengers. She silently thanked her mother, father, and Carl Gersman for putting aside as much money as they could to get her the better class ticket. As an afterthought, she thanked herself for all the English tutoring she did in Gliewitz to earn extra money for the journey as well. As she walked by the line, she could see the relief visible in the drawn and ashen faces of the immigrants who could only afford steerage tickets. As she passed the line, a distinct rank odor reached her nostrils of human sweat and urine. Unkempt hair straggled out from under shabby hats and bonnets. Many of them had held onto the ship's company-issued thin travel blankets, worn and filthy shreds.

Despite the difference in their travelling class, Rosalia shared with this group the elation of surviving and being off the steamship with solid land under their feet. Were they as filled with wonder and curiosity as she was at walking on the shores of America at last? She rejoiced quietly at every step of her booted feet on the rough cobblestone road that led her into the customs building door marked with a sign, "Second-Class Passengers". A black-skinned man in a white tailored uniform and white gloves had offered to follow her with her bags and trunk in tow on a wheeled cart. This was the first time she had ever laid eyes upon a Negro and she tried to keep from staring. A beefy, clean-shaven Customs guard, as pale-skinned as the porter was dark, greeted her immediately upon her entrance.

"Welcome to the United States, Miss. Where will you be going?"

"I go…go to Hot Springs, Arkansas," Rosalia answered awkwardly. She felt intimidated by this guard in military uniform that brought up images of the Prussian guard back home. They had been cruel and coarse whenever she saw them in Gliewitz. The dread that crept through her spine seemed to draw tightly at her mouth as well, causing her English to tumble out in accented spurts. She became furious at herself for the poor first impression she was making.

"Well, you understand and speak English, at least some. Most of the folks in steerage, we must pin destination notes on their outerwear so that they won't get lost trying to get where they're going. They can't speak a word."

He wagged his head and wrote down something in a handbook filled with lists and markings. Rosalia saw her first and last name printed neatly in a column.

"And why have you come to the United States?"

"I will marry a man." She blushed.

The customs guard tilted his head sideways and smiled.

"What I mean," she continued, "Carl Gersman will marry me in Hot Springs. I have letter to, um, prove. Will you read?" Rosalia pulled the letter of betrothal out of her small leather tote bag, strung around her wrist with a sturdy cord like a loyal companion.

"No, no, ma'am, no need. We do not need documentation for that sort of thing. Are you suffering at this time from any ailments?"

"I am healthy," Rosalia announced proudly. "Very healthy." Her pale blue eyes flashed with a spark of anger at the thought of what her condition could have been if Longman had succeeded in violating her.

"Yes, you appear to be healthy."

She held her tongue as she noticed the guard eyeing her from head to toe.

"Report to the nurse, who will take your temperature and listen to your lungs, and if all is normal, you will be sent on your way. One other thing, Miss Wolfson. Do you have anything to declare to customs that is in your baggage? Food or drink, fruits or vegetables, animals?"

"Why I would bring those?" she snapped at him. "I have enough to bring of clothes and hats and personals!"

"Calm down, little lady," the guard admonished her. "A simple 'no' will do, unless you want to spend the day in detention."

Rosalia shook her head, mute and overwhelmed with anxiety. She hadn't expected this session of questioning. Suddenly she looked around, wondering if she would spot Roland Longman in the Customs room. She nervously reached at the back of her bonnet and fussed with the hatpins. There was no sign of Longman, but she did spot an American police officer conversing in a corner of the customs room with Captain Wilkins. They both approached Rosalia before she had the chance to line up for the nurse's station. She gazed at the Captain's uniform with its crisp whiteness and blue trim, so different from any uniform she had seen in Gliewitz, and realized that they were the colors of Judaism. She shook her head; it must be just a coincidence. She tried to bolster her flagging courage with the thought that the United States military uniform was dressing a better man than the Jew-hating Prussian police. Would this captain believe her testimony about Roland Longman?

Captain Wilkins and the constable approached the Customs official standing with Rosalia, and Wilkins said gruffly,

"This young lady has been the victim of a crime upon my vessel. I am ashamed to admit it, but there it is. I feel the great onus of this happening upon my maritime command. Unfortunately, the accused has eluded me and my crew. We are missing a passenger as well and fear the worst for her. And the villain even murdered one of my officers to escape from the ship. Kindly listen to this girl's description of the man, as she spent time with him during the voyage. Perhaps he tipped her off in some way that will aid us in locating him."

The Customs official's eyes widened, and he responded,

"Sir, I will be on the lookout for the assailant. Write down his name and a description so that we don't detain the wrong man."

Wilkins addressed Rosalia directly,

"My dear, we will do what we can to nab Mr. Longman. We have not yet located the woman you observed in his clutches, a Miss Greta Schuler. She is on our passenger list, but she is not on the ship as far as we can tell. The Constabulary will do what they can to find and apprehend the criminal and make sure no harm comes to you."

"He escaped? Ach, I am very afraid he finds me once more. He will kill me, I know this! You must find him and put him in the prison."

Rosalia stamped her booted foot on the tiled floor, wishing at this moment that it were the size of a man's foot instead of the tiny thing it was.

"We cannot promise you this, but we will do everything we can to find him and lock him up. In the meantime, do you have friends or family here in New Orleans?"

Rosalia nodded. "This is a beautiful and entertaining town, but it has its dark side. Many secrets and places for bad sorts of people to hide out if you catch my drift. Walk carefully and look around, Miss Wolfson. Do not wander off alone."

Wilkins turned to the Customs official.

"The little gentlelady is stronger than she looks, Officer Mackie. And she's got a way with her hatpin. Managed to fend off the attack by Longman with it. Me and my crew saw the wound in the fellow's neck."

The immigration official glanced at Rosalia, who was taking tiny steps in the direction of the nurse's station.

"Just so you know, Miss, some places are beginning to outlaw certain hatpins of marked length. They are being used too frequently by ladies with, er, loose ways of making a living to attack customers and get more money from them. Pardon me for bringing up such a topic, Miss."

But Rosalia scarcely heard the official's last words. She hurried on to the nurse's station, trailed by the porter with her, who waited patiently outside the door. Once she was officially dismissed by the health examiner, she would be searching for her escorts, Simon and Rosa Meyer.

After the cursory medical examination, Rosalia stepped out of the building a true American immigrant, thrilled to be done with the Customs ordeal. The sidewalks and streets on the northern side of the building pointed toward downtown New Orleans, according to a street sign that she was able to read. Exhausted and forlorn-looking immigrants and travelers walked along the streets, carts laden with trunks and boxes, horses and mules jangling reins and pulling buggies.

The familiar odor of equine sweat and excrement mixed with an exotic floral scent that almost made her dizzy with its oddness. No doubt there were American blooms and plants that she had never seen before lurking in gardens and sprouting alongside the streets of this city. In the moisture-laden air above, white seagulls with black-tipped wings swooped and screeched. It was familiar to Rosalia's senses, harkening her memory back to the port in Hamburg. But at the same time, it was very different, like an altered version of a painting. Words floated by her in languages she recognized and some that she didn't. She understood the German and Yiddish of other Jews, of course. She knew what French sounded like from listening attentively to Parisian travelers who passed through Gliewitz and shopped in the open market place. English was getting easier to understand, but now she was overhearing other versions of the language that she could barely comprehend. Some of the dark-skinned people were speaking a language that sounded a little bit like French overlaid with some other language, like a verbal patchwork quilt.

Rosalia pulled a small piece of paper from her leather tote bag. Her father had written on it the name of the street corner where the Meyers would meet her in New Orleans. 'Canal Street' and 'Oak Avenue', she read her father's large and loopy writing. Just seeing the words that he had shaped with his own hands gave her a surge of homesickness. Her parents were so far away now! She wished desperately that they were by her side. She showed the porter the street corner names, and he led her there with head low and eyes down. She did not like his subservient behavior; it unsettled her. Even more disturbing, she began to observe this same bearing in all the other dark-skinned porters helping the white people with their baggage. As she waited, men and women of various skin colors walked past her. Some of them were dressed in rags, others in work clothes, but occasionally she spotted an elegantly attired almond-skinned man in a wide-brimmed straw hat or tan-skinned woman with her head held high under a feathered or flower-bedecked hat.

She waited for what seemed like an hour and then became restless. She worried that she might be in the wrong place, or that the Meyers did not receive the letter from Mama letting them know that Rosalia would be arriving on July 30, today's date. Perhaps they were expecting her another day? What would she do if they did not appear and night came? She tightened with fear from head to toe, ready to topple over at the slightest breeze. Stay calm, Rosalia, she told herself. She could feel anxiety begin to boil in her gut and transform into fierce outrage. She kicked a stray mongrel in the ribs that had wandered haplessly past her, snuffling the ground. Immediately she felt guilty and glanced sideways at the porter, who was shaking his head but stopped as soon as he caught her gaze.

Then she heard a shout in German.

"Simon, look, there she is!"

Rosalia glanced across the street and saw two people rushing towards her, puffing their full red cheeks and holding their head coverings, a respective derby and bonnet, so that they wouldn't blow away. She recognized Rosa and Simon from her childhood memories of them in Gliewitz, and a flood of relief swept across her entire body; she was no longer alone in this strange city.

Rosa got to Rosalia first, grasped her by the shoulders and gave her a resounding kiss on the cheek. She cooed, double chin wobbling as she spoke,

"You must be so exhausted from the long trip across the Atlantic. You will have a nice rest at our apartment. Are you hungry? Thirsty?"   She was chubby, short but still a few inches taller than Rosalia. A thin, black lace shawl covered her shoulders. She wiped perspiration from her brow with a white lace handkerchief. Simon added,

"We will take the streetcar back to our apartment, where you can lie down and rest. We have only a week or so to prepare for our journey together to Hot Springs."

He smiled in a kindly manner at Rosalia, a rotund fellow with a full white beard and mustache and faded mud eyes, and she felt immediately at ease in his company. Up until this moment, she had wondered if she could ever feel comfortable and trust the company of a man for the rest of her life after the ugly incident with Longman. Now she began to anticipate the next leg of her passage, boarding another steamship. That river would bring her to the Arkansas River, which would deposit her and her escorts in a city called Little Rock. She loved the name, so picturesque! Were there indeed rocks and stones decorating the land there, she wondered? A paddle wheel river boat, Simon told her, would carry them from the state of Louisiana to the state of Arkansas, but not to the town of Hot Springs. With no trains yet running in Arkansas, they would be passengers on an American stagecoach overland to her new home.

The three immigrants, followed by the porter towing Rosalia's trunk and bags, found their way to a streetcar stop and waited around a quarter of an hour for the city transport to appear. Rosalia peered down the street at the two-story clapboard buildings with filigreed wrought-iron balconies and windows trimmed with lace curtains. New Orleanians of all skin shades strolled leisurely on the cobblestone walkways, from white or pale ivory like Mama's Shabbos linen tablecloth, to the chocolate Cousin Avram had given them years ago. The women carried fanciful ruffled parasols and the men wore yellow straw hats to protect themselves from the sun's harsh rays. Rosalia paid the porter for his services, spreading the coins out in her gloved palm and picking out the little ones. She wasn't sure if this was the proper payment; however, the porter smiled, tipped his cap and hurried off.

"Here comes the tram!" cried Rosalia as a mustard yellow and deep violet-painted conveyance, longer than she'd ever seen and pulled by a pair of dun-colored mules, stopped before them. They boarded, paid and found adjacent seats.

"In America, these are called streetcars," Simon told Rosalia. "We have been living in New Orleans for three months and have learned a lot of English, right, Rosa?"

Rosa nodded vigorously, heavy cheeks jiggling.

"You arrived on an auspicious day, little Rosalia. Today there is a grand convention not far from here in downtown. It is the Louisiana Constitutional Convention. Delegates are meeting to talk about changing some laws so the *shvartzes* can vote, carry firearms, and have other freedoms they don't have yet."

"Can learn to write and read, for God's sake," Rosa added. "The goyim, the white gentiles here, they don't allow education for Negroes. That's the word they use for them, at least those with the very dark skins. The lighter skinned people are called mulattoes."

They chatted excitedly as the mules plodded down Canal Street and towed the streetcar around a corner. As the streetcar completed its slow right turn, Rosalia heard a loud report that she recognized as gunfire. She turned to the Meyers and they in turn stared out the streetcar windows. More gunfire exploded in the distance, and they and the several other passengers on board shifted nervously in their seats, craning their necks to see further out the windows. Suddenly a stream of people ran past the streetcar, all dark-skinned faces in grimaces and expressions of wide-eyed horror. Rosalia thought she detected blood spots on some of the men's clothing, and she shuddered. A few of the men limped and made their way in obvious pain, grunting and stumbling. Their friends helped them along, and several carried their companions in their arms or slung over their shoulders. The streetcar mules began to balk and twitch their long ears like living things on their heads, and the driver used his whip to urge them forward, cursing loudly. However, the snapping of his whip was drowned out by more bursts of gunfire, and now Rosalia saw white men in work clothes running after the *shvartzes*, firearms brandished and pointed toward them. She began to shiver with alarm and looked at Rosa, whose eyes were wide with fright. Simon said to them grimly,

"We are better off staying on this streetcar out of the way of these madmen with the rifles and guns. Put your heads down."

He ducked below the window, and Rosalia and Rosa did the same. It seemed like they were in that position for maybe two minutes when Rosalia heard the pounding of boots up the steps of the moving streetcar and onto the middle aisle between the seats. She looked up just as the menacing face of a thin, pale man with disheveled blonde hair appeared before her. The light blue, bloodshot eyes locked with hers, and then he moved onward. She watched as he grabbed a Negro man sitting several seats behind her by the vest with his left hand and the belt with his right, and yanked the unfortunate rider out of his seat, dragging him back up the aisle and throwing him out onto the cobbled sidewalk where he sprawled, arms and legs akimbo. The attacker leaped out of the streetcar, frizzled blonde hair flying in all directions, and loomed over his hapless victim.

"This is for Mayor Monroe!" he shouted, his eyes narrowing and his nose and cheeks flushing crimson.

Rosalia watched in horror through the streetcar window as he brandished a pistol and fired a shot into the black man's head, instantly killing him. She began to sob unrestrainedly.

"What kind of city is this?" she asked the Meyers through her tears. "Pulling a man off the streetcar and murdering for all to see? Is there no law, no police here? Have the people gone crazy?"

No sooner had she made this tearful query, when she saw a city police officer rush up to the killer, although they were now at some distance as the mules toted their heavy load further down the street. More police officers appeared ahead, and Rosalia sighed with relief. *They will stop this madness.* Suddenly at least two of them pulled out their firearms and began shooting into yet another crowd of Negro men, these ones climbing over fences to escape the hail of bullets. Some made it over and ran for cover, but the slower ones dropped back onto the public pavement, injured or dead, dark bloody puddles pooling around them.

"I have never seen a thing like this, not even in the Old Country," breathed Simon. "Now it is the police killing the *shvartzes* too! What next?"

Rosa wept along with Rosalia. She whispered,

"We must get out of here, Simon! We could be killed too! Streetcar is no protection now."

Simon held Rosa's shoulders firmly as they crouched under the windows and whispered to her and Rosalia,

"This must be the opposition to the Louisiana convention-eers. The fellows who want to keep the Black Codes, so the free *shvartzes* don't have so much freedom. They aren't looking for Jews to shoot, so we'd better just stay on the streetcar until we are some distance from the Mechanics Institute. That's where they are meeting. I wonder if they are also attacking the people inside the Institute?"

The driver called to the remaining passengers, shivering and crowded below the windows,

"We are not going straight down Canal Street past the Mechanic's Building. We will take Dauphine Street to avoid this bloodshed. Stay down and do not look out the windows!"

The minutes spent in the streetcar dragged on the hearts of the passengers as sharp reports faded in their ears. The horrible massacre of the conventioneers was still taking place as Rosalia and the Meyers rode farther and farther away from it. At last they reached a street corner close to the Meyers' home on Marengo Street. Waving for the streetcar driver to stop, they climbed off. Simon unloaded Rosalia's trunk and bags and deposited them on the stony curb. Then they waited impatiently for a small carriage for hire to load their baggage and take them to the Meyers' apartment. They tumbled through the front door tearful, trembling and ashen-faced.

For several hours they heard gunshots, yells and screams faintly in the direction of downtown. Rosalia fell asleep exhausted soon after a small but hot and fragrant dinner of Rosa's chicken soup and French bread. She dreamed that the Prussian soldiers of King Wilhelm were swarming the central market in Gliewitz and chasing her and Annaleya down a wide avenue flooded by the Neisse River.

25

After a week of resting and reviving herself at the Meyers' modest apartment in the Garden District of New Orleans, Rosalia was anxious to leave that violent town. Her first taste of America was a bitter and frightening one. Rosa and Simon were just as eager to depart rough, unprincipled New Orleans as well. They would be moving in with a cousin of Simon's who had invited them to Hot Springs to help him with his new enterprise, a restaurant called "Latke" in the heart of downtown whose Jewish cuisine catered to that small but vibrant population.

Over chicory coffee and beignets, the three of them pored over the New Orleans news journal for reports of the massacre they had witnessed. Outraged townspeople were writing in to call for the ouster of Mayor Monroe, as word was out that he had encouraged the attack. The Black Codes law was excoriated by many citizens of both races, but there was an opinion expressed by some writers who insisted the codes were necessary to keep the 'coloreds' in their places. The Negroes could not, they asserted, manage their own freedom because they had grown up without it. They were inferior and unable to blend in with the general white Christian population. He ended his written diatribe with the question, "Would you want your children to sit next to them at school?"

"Is this true, *Herr* Meyer?" Rosalia naively asked her chaperone. "Are the *shvartzes* not as smart as the white people?"

Simon smiled crookedly at her through his thick white mustache.

"They say the same thing of the Jewish people and worse. We drink blood, we have horns, we eat our babies. Lies the gentiles tell to believe they are good and we are evil. Truth is, people are people, we are very much the same on the inside. When will they learn this lesson?"

As they ate and chatted, they heard the dull thud of hammers on nails and the high whine of saws on wood from the street below. New Orleans was being rebuilt after the ravages of the war between the states had set much of the quaint city ablaze. Rosalia gazed out the front window and observed rows of streets with burnt and charred debris piled on top of rubble where there should have been houses. Then she gasped, her hand flying to her mouth.

"What is wrong? What do you see?" asked Rosa, concern creasing her brow and bunching up her chubby cheeks.

"Not….not a thing," Rosalia stammered back. She thought she had glimpsed Roland Longman turning a corner onto a side street. She recognized his long, brown leather boots and leisurely stride. But that could be another man with the same boots and similar gait, couldn't it?

"I thought a woman down there was about to be run over by a horse and cart, but it just missed her."

The Meyers seemed to accept her explanation, although she caught a worried glance exchanged between the two. Had she been acting oddly in some way that she was not aware of?

The Meyers and Rosalia spent the next few days preparing for their two-week voyage up the Mississippi River on a paddlewheel boat to Little Rock. Rosalia unpacked, shook out her clothing to freshen it up, then she washed her split bloomers and stockings and hung them to dry on a clothesline that stretched across the back balcony of the apartment. She also washed her blue taffeta travelling dress carefully in a tub of cool water with laundry soap that Rosa gave her and hung it to dry over the bathtub. When it was dry, she found the sewing kit that she had packed and carefully sewed together the fabric that Longman had ripped when he had attempted to pull off her dress. She shuddered at every stab of the needle into the sky-blue taffeta. She made the repair secretively the first night, while the Meyers were asleep.

Simon and Rosa began packing everything in their apartment: clothing, shoes, hats, documents and tickets, a small collection of dining and cookware, jewelry, candlesticks, blankets, and bottles of medicine and liniments they took for rheumatism and indigestion. Rosalia watched Simon lovingly situate his Torah book, handed down to him from his grandfather, amid shirts, socks and scarves to protect and buffer it in their travels.

The week went by quickly and the travel tasks at hand served to distract and lull Rosalia during the day, but at night as she bedded down on a small divan in the parlor, the memory of Longman's attack upon her and the helpless hostage lying on his bed assaulted her senses and thoughts. She stiffened and clenched her teeth. A headache plagued her, coming and going like bad company. Sleep was a long way from blessing her with oblivion. She imagined what would have happened if she hadn't had the hatpin or hadn't thought to use it. Sickness and shame welled up in her throat as she fantasized Roland Longman tearing off her clothing and gazing at every inch of her naked body. She could only imagine what would come next. With great embarrassment as she lay abed, she became aware that she felt sexually aroused while she was repulsed. How could this be? She repressed a sob so as not to be heard by the Meyers through the thin walls of their bedroom.

Her dear friend Annaleya and other acquaintances in Gliewitz had married long ago and knew the secrets of the marriage bed. At twenty-one, she was quite old to be single and unacquainted with a man's sexual demands. But she had her own longings, physical as well as emotional, unmet for so long that she hardly considered them real. Here they were, inching their way to the surface of her feelings, to mix with disgust and fright. This confusing amalgam of conflicting passions caused her to question her very sanity. Could she be even more damaged than she already was? To shove down the ugly, disturbing images, she turned the fantasy in a different direction. Once her hatpin had done its work and injured Longman, she imagined herself grabbing his pistol and pointing it at him. *I squeezed the trigger and the bullet in his revolver flew out and struck him in the heart. He slumped over dead, Captain Wilkins. I killed him with his own gun. He is no more.* Rather than pacifying the fury that bubbled up from her gut, it added more agitation and prolonged it as the dark minutes sagged by slowly. She knew that she would find no peace of mind fantasizing about her attacker's demise. At last her eyes, wide open and staring at the black corners of the ceiling, could stay open no longer and she fell asleep in the early morning hours, dreaming vividly.

Her cousin Daniel is staring at her in her bedroom at home. Blood dripping down his forehead from a dark hole. His coffee eyes meet hers and he laughs, a loud guffaw, "Ha! Ha! Ha!" He can't seem to stop laughing, a frenzied staccato. Terrified, she backs away. She is wearing a lavender and white floral cotton day dress which becomes soaking wet and begins to slowly dissolve, leaving her naked. She grabs a blanket off the bed and wraps it around herself, shocked and ashamed. The room disappears and she is back on the deck of the U.S.S. Eolus, still wrapped in only the blanket. She catches sight of Roland Longman, tipping his hat and smiling at her through the dining room window. A wave rushes toward the ship from the horizon, rising ominously until it becomes a towering, looming wall of water. It crashes over the ship and sweeps Rosalia overboard and out to sea. She sees deck chairs tumbling in the rough foam. Then the ocean is gone, and she is standing alone in her mother's kitchen in Gliewitz. Shadows slide around in the corners and on the ceiling above her. A great sorrow overcomes her, swelling her throat. She cries, "Mama? Mama?"

Gasping, she awoke with a start. Darkness still filled the windowpanes. An old clock ticked monotonously on top of a mahogany side table like a clucking tongue. The nightmare had frightened her, but the memory of Longman in it roused her ire and she spent the next half hour or so imagining his painful death once again. Somehow this time it managed to lull her back into a heavy sleep and oblivion. When she awoke next, daylight was streaming through the panes and she could hear Rosa bustling about in the kitchen. She slipped out of bed and joined her.

"Rosalia dear, would you like a cup of chicory and beignets before we leave for the river boat? Oh, you are still in your nightgown."

"That sounds very nice, Rosa," sighed Rosalia drowsily. She realized that she was quite hungry. "Will we have these delicious pastries in Hot Springs also?"

"Unfortunately, I don't think so. Those are foods of this town and region. You know, like the strudel in Bavaria or the hamantaschen in Germany."

The mention of Rosalia's favorite sweets, which her mother made for the Purim holiday, brought her a pang of intense homesickness. She desperately wanted to be back in Gliewitz at this moment. Even the dread of a tarnished reputation in her hometown paled in comparison with what might have awaited her had she fallen into Roland Longman's clutches. Her anger caught fire like dry tinder struck by lightning.

'This journey has been a tremendous mistake!" she shouted.

Simon and Rosa fluttered and twitched like two frightened doves.

"I never should have come here. I must go back! Not one more minute in this country for me. It is full of evil people! Why did I come here? I must have been crazy!"

She pulled herself off the divan and threw her diminutive body on the oak floor, screaming in outrage. Her nightgown billowed and crumpled around her like a wind-whipped sail. Rosa and Simon blinked and gaped, holding their ears against the piercing stabs of her screams. After several minutes of sustained outbursts, she became totally exhausted and depleted of anger, sat up and stared toward the front door with cheeks flushed a bright hue of rose.

Simon spoke then into the abrupt silence,

"Rosalia, there is something you are not telling us. Rosa and I see that you are fearful and jumpy. You keep looking over your shoulders like somebody is following you. And now this…. this tantrum! We know travel is difficult, and in a new country with different people and customs, even harder. And what happened yesterday, well, Rosa and I are just as upset as you are. But still. Tell me now, I insist. What happened to make you like this?"

Rosalia shook her head, eyes shut and tears beginning to glint at the edges of them. For a moment, the attack seemed unreal, like a nightmare. Brief vignettes of the journey across the Atlantic Ocean floated past her mind: strolling on the deck with the salt breeze in her face, visiting the steering cabin, gazing out at the endless field of dark water stretching to the horizon in every direction like an endless ruffled blanket, fondling the cold steel of the hatpin in her fingers, feeling Longman's hand yanking downward at the collar of her dress.

She became dizzy and held her head tightly in her hands. The temptation of pouring her tale out to these dear friends was powerful, but she fought it and drew her mouth in, as if she had just sucked a lemon. The memory of many years of gossip about her in Gliewitz advised and forewarned her at this moment. She could very well become defined and by and blamed for this transgression upon her in her new town in America, even though Longman was the culprit. Then, she looked at the concerned and sympathetic expressions in Simon and Rosa's eyes as they stared down at her. A flood of remorse swept through her.

"I am so deeply sorry, Herr and Frau Meyer. I have behaved very badly. It is the rigors of the travel across the sea. The journey has left me out of sorts. I am homesick and miss my papa and mama, my sister and brothers. I will do my best to calm down and become a better person. And I am so grateful to have you as escorts to keep me safe."

The Meyers' faces, alight with anticipation, drooped at the same time. The sight almost with disappointment. Clearly, they didn't believe her excuse. Rosalia almost smiled though, as they were like two bookends, so similar in their expressions and movements. She arose from the floor in as dignified a fashion as she could muster, and then stretched until she was fully awake. She slipped into the lavatory as they set out plates, spoons and butter knives for the morning meal. She hurriedly dressed, then joined the Meyers for their last breakfast in New Orleans. They gathered their baggage and Simon brought in two young men he had arranged for, one as black as coal and the other of a hue that reminded Rosalia of a walnut, to help them load all into a wagon with an old, dappled jenny hitched to it. Rosalia held back tears as she watched them work and wondered if any of their relatives had been killed in the massacre. Climbing into the wagon with the two helpers, the three travelers jounced down Marengo Street to Canal Street and then to the long wharves of the Mississippi River.

The river waters lapped at the piers and posts, and small bateaus and sailboats floated alongside the landing. Rosalia and the Meyers breathed in the fresh air and waited for the paddlewheel boat that would deliver them to Little Rock. Mid-afternoon the S.S. Sunrise appeared on the river before them. It was much smaller than the Eolus, a petite version with a paddle wheel at the stern. They boarded and Rosalia was immediately directed to the women's section of the steamer. Simon and Rosa were allowed special quarters as a married couple. Rosalia stored her trunks and bags in a large stateroom that she shared with seven other women and three little girls. Weary of ship travel, Rosalia left the stateroom for the breezy deck, reclined in a deck chair and buried her head in an English grammar book that the Meyers had loaned her. She had no desire to make acquaintance with anyone on board. She knew that the friendly and bored voyagers and crew were casting curious glances at her and wanted to chat, but she didn't care. The sturdy paddleboat plowed its way through the river with a steadiness that was crucial as it met a plethora of obstacles that the river contained. Neither the Meyers nor Rosalia had suspected that eddies, sand bars, rocks, tree stumps and thatches of debris awaited the little river steamboat in deadly ambush. Several times the crew members were sent scurrying, calling out orders to one another starboard and port, bow and stern, to steer it away from a whirlpool or a row of dark, glistening rocks, like jagged teeth poised to take a bite out of the keel of the Sunrise. After a week of steaming up the river, the boat arrived at a junction where the wide and devious Mississippi met the narrower Arkansas River. The captain of the vessel assembled the travelers topside and announced loudly,

"All those with destination to Little Rock disembark here at Helena! If the paddleboat up the Arkansas River don't show today, there's an inn at this junction y'all kin sleep in fer the night. All others with destination to Tennessee stay on the Sunrise and head up the White River."

Rosalia, the Meyers, two of the women and three men disembarked and gazed forlornly as if hypnotized at the Sunrise as it continued up the Mississippi River. When it disappeared around a bend, they turned to survey the land around them. Rosalia glimpsed a few rough lean-tos and sheds partially visible among the buckeyes and pines. Behind them stood a two-story inn lined in dusty gray water-stained clapboard that might have been white at one time.

As the sky grew dusky and the sun slid behind a range of distant mountains, there was still no sign of a river-going vessel. The group of travelers realized that they would have to stay at the inn until the next day. They followed a rough path through low-growing reeds and bushes to the front door.

The inn was comfortable and cool, built in the shade of a grove of oak trees. The innkeeper and his wife welcomed them graciously. They made their living on the tardiness of the Arkansas River paddleboats. Each passenger was charged thirty cents for the night. Rosalia dug into her leather pouch for the unexpected expense, noting that she was running low on the little she had to travel with.

The innkeeper's wife showed them to their rooms, and Rosalia was fortunate to have one to herself. She removed her hat and boots and stretched out on the clean horsehair-stuffed mattress covered by a flimsy white sheet, her body tired and achy from tension and travel on the treacherous Mississippi River. She realized with a start that she had entered the state of Arkansas, where she would be married. Her future husband, Carl Gersman, lived and breathed in this state, of all the American states. The last time she had seen him, which had been the first, she had been merely a child. Her mind churned as she imagined their second meeting. Would he judge her harshly? Would he find her unattractive now, perhaps too old? Had someone in Gliewitz written to him about her ruined reputation? She twisted in the sheets and slumber eluded her, but finally in the early hours of the morning, fatigue overtook her and she slept.

Early the next day the sojourners boarded a paddleboat that appeared as the sun began its ascent over the eastern hills that lined the horizon. Once again, Rosalia was separated from the Meyers as she was escorted to the women's quarters of the little riverboat. Although she felt lonely without them, she used the solitude to mend and darn various articles of clothing that had split their seams or developed holes in her travels.

She and the Meyers gathered for meals and daytime walks up and down the deck of the little steamer. She felt grateful for their protective presence on this leg of her journey. Another week of hazardous chugging on the Arkansas River left more than half of them travel-weary and sick to their stomachs as the boat lurched from one side to another, avoiding the dangers that lurked under those waters. The Arkansas boiled with even more perilous hazards than the Mississippi, narrowing suddenly, spilling into eddies, winding through pileups of dead cypress trunks. Meals consisted of dried beef and buffalo jerky, dried fruit, oatmeal, harsh whiskey and watered-down ale.

"I will never set foot on a boat again," moaned Simon, clutching his hefty midriff and staring bleakly at the pile of beans and ham hock that had been served for breakfast. "And the captain tells me it could be even worse, if we couldn't take the Arkansas Post Canal route which bypasses many twists and turns. Can you imagine that?"

"I will kiss the ground when we get off this floating beast at Little Rock," declared Rosa. "How is our little bride-to-be?"

"The bride sends her regrets to the groom, she died of nausea," groaned Rosalia, appearing pale and drawn. "How many more days must we endure this passage of torture?"

They were griping on the port side of the paddleboat, taking gulps of air to belay their physical woes. A ship's steward overheard Rosalia and responded,

"Tomorry or the next day we will git tah Little Rock, Miss. Hard ta say the exact tahm and day, due to the unpredictable nature of this yere rivah and the weathah. But it'll be soon."

"Not soon enough!" retorted Rosalia, leaning over the railing just in case she should lose the tiny bit of breakfast she was able to consume. She looked down into the muddied wavelets of the Arkansas River smacking the keel of the boat. They seemed to mock her in her misery, as lively as she was listless.

Two days later the river steamer chugged into Little Rock. Relieved, weary passengers gazed at the grazing cattle and clotheslines full of flapping work shirts, cotton print day dresses, bloomers and work trousers in front of small clapboard houses as they glided by. Rosalia clung to the deck railing and tried to catch a glimpse of the people living in them. She spotted roughly clad men on roofs and in doorways, looking like tiny dolls in the distance, sawing and hammering. The sounds of those tools raking and banging against wood were faintly audible over the splashing of turbulent river waves. Here another town was being rebuilt, and the devastation of America's recent War between the States was plainly catastrophic.

Still, she was elated that soon she and the Meyers would be off the river and on land again. Now they were even closer to Hot Springs and her future husband. The thought of it filled her with an indescribable mélange of hope and trepidation. She would be elevated in status to a married woman, respected as never before. She would share her life and bed with a good Jewish man, and her family's aspiration for her would come to fruition. But what if he learned about her reputation in Gliewitz? Would he reject her and strand her alone in this wild, barely civilized country that she could not yet recognize as her own? She cursed her cousin Daniel for the thousandth time and wished upon him the worst luck that life could bring.

26

Rosalia and the Meyers spent the better part of a muggy August day arranging for a stagecoach to transport them the next day to Hot Springs. One of their fellow ship passengers, a resident of Little Rock, pointed them down Main Street towards the stagecoach company of Abbott and Downing. There they secured three seats on a Concord coach leaving at the dinner hour on Wednesday. It would take about fourteen hours to reach their destination, they were told. Fortunately, it was a commonly used route and coaches frequently traveled back and forth between the city and the town. They had the option of riding in a fourteen, nine or six passenger conveyance, but the price for a seat went up as the luxury of fewer riders and less crowding went down. For the sake of frugality, they chose the fourteen-passenger coach.

They whiled away the rest of the day walking through town indulging their curiosity at the shop displays. They were glad to stretch out their legs on land after their two-week stomach-churning excursion on the Arkansas River. They strolled past one- and two-story brick buildings filled with business enterprises from guns and ammunition to barber-shops, bakeries, produce markets and dry goods. Plenty of other pedestrians were also out walking, visiting the stores for purchases and tippling shops for a midday drink. Despite the bustle of shoppers, horse-drawn buggies and mounted riders, areas of town were scarred with remnants of burnt rubble. In those sections, Rosalia watched muscular men, short and tall, lanky and stout, toting beams of lumber, wielding tools, measuring and excavating. As in New Orleans, this town was still recovering and rebuilding as a result of the war. Finally, exhausted and hungry, they sat in a small restaurant and feasted on rabbit stew with carrots and onions, and dipped freshly baked warm biscuits to soak up the gravy. This was a welcome and fresh change from the poor provender offered on the Sunrise and the smaller riverboat. Rosalia tried not to gobble the stew quickly and get a stomach-ache. She inhaled the aroma of fresh and well-cooked meat and vegetables swimming in a tomato sauce. It reminded her of the delectable lamb and beef stews her mother made.

"I cannot stop thinking about the delicious beer we always drank in Gliewitz, the best you could find in Prussia, right, Rosa?" Simon reminisced aloud. "Especially from the brewery where your Papa worked. Will we ever taste that again now that we are so far from our homeland? I wonder sometimes if we have made a disastrous mistake coming here to this wilderness and cities that are so strange to our customs. Cities without a Jewish neighborhood to raise the kinder in or a synagogue to study the Torah on Shabbos morning." He sighed so loudly that two rough-looking men at the next table turned to stare at him. Rosalia watched as they rose and approached their table.

"Y'all are some queer-lookin' folks," commented one of them, his burly shoulders hunched over and red mustache quivering as he spoke. "Where ya from?"

Rosalia shrank from both men, who loomed directly over her, men, she noted, who had weapons – 'revolvers' they called them in English – tucked into leather pouches on sturdy belts slung around their waists. Simon responded,

"Please, sir. We are visitors to Little Rock. We go to Hot Springs. We want no trouble here. Only eat lunch and find stagecoach. Then we leave."

The two burly men exchanged glances, then the man who had spoken first said, "Well, well. Not from the South or the North, eh? Welcome to our broken apart country, sir and ma'ams. Ah hope ya don't run inta any trouble because there is aplenty here. If y'all ain't carpetbaggers come to buy Southern land cheap, we ain't got no problem with y'all."

They tipped their oversized black cowboy hats and shuffled back to their table. Rosalia inhaled deeply and tried to stop trembling in fear and rage. She was ready to stick her hatpin in either one of them despite their size and armament. She wondered what these men would do to an actual 'carpetbagger'. Throw them out of the restaurant? Threaten them with their weapons, or worse, shoot them? This country was no freer of violence than her homeland, and much less orderly. But it did hold opportunities for people no matter their religion, unlike Prussia, and that thought maintained her spirits. Also, her future husband lived here, and there was nobody for her back in Gliewitz. The thought cheered and infuriated her at the same time. She had to restrain herself from laughing out loud at her own muddled feelings.

Simon and Rosa ordered four more biscuits, marmalade, and something called corn pone, for the evening meal and stagecoach ride. It would have to do until they arrived in Hot Springs, where their relatives would provide decent sustenance. Once the food was wrapped and in Rosa's travel bag, they left the restaurant and ambled along the Arkansas River, admiring the beauty of the pines and ashes that grew along its banks. They turned up Sixth Street and entered a shop filled with sweets and bakery goods and purchased some caramel candies and chocolates for their kin in Hot Springs. Rosalia commented,

"I wish to present Mr. Gersman with some of this chocolate candy to see if he will remember the first time we met. My cousin Avram brought us chocolate that evening, and we tasted it for the first time in our lives. My little brothers went crazy for it. We all did."

The sun was low in the sky when they realized that the stagecoach would be departing soon. The threesome rushed to Abbot and Downing and saw the coach awaiting its paid passengers. It stood high with huge wheels, the spokes and rim painted canary yellow and the carriage a dark crimson. Four horses were already harnessed to it, curved bars arching over their collars like wooden halos. Rosalia dreaded the long journey crowded into the coach with thirteen other passengers. She hoped that it wouldn't be completely full, but those hopes were dashed when she clambered in and every seat was filled with riders. As the group drew in and adjusted legs and arms to accommodate everybody, she became irate to find that a strange man's leg was practically in her lap.

"Take your leg off me," she scolded him angrily in English.

"Where will I put it, ma'am?" the suited gentleman answered with amusement. "I have no choice, and do apologize, but we must all be tolerant of the traveling conditions."

"This stellwagen is so crowded," Rosalia said to the Meyers in German, "I never rode in one when I lived in Germany. Are they the same?"

"We never rode in one either in the Old Country," Rosa said, "but we saw them roll through town with rich people in them. They looked much more luxurious, of course. This stagecoach is for the common people."

Several of the passengers scowled at the two women conversing in German. Rosalia stared back boldly, tempted to use a few vulgar expressions in English she had overheard on the ship while crossing the Atlantic. The scowlers looked away, and so she refrained from unleashing the coarse language that she had memorized, relishing it as one would a secret power. She had learned the English swear words listening closely to the crewmen and swabbies cursing at each other, sometimes jovially and other times angrily. They had been both accommodating and amused to explain the meaning of the expressions to her. Sometimes a sailor would leer at her as he defined the curse words, but she pointedly ignored him and pursued her purpose, determined to learn all kinds of English in preparation for her new life. She leaned against the back seat of the coach trying to relax, breathing in the leathery aroma of the interior and wrinkling her nose as it detected a mixture of human perspiration and gassy emissions. Couples were murmuring to one another and two children were arguing. An infant's mewls turned into wails. This would be her surroundings for the next day and a half. She turned her head to gaze out the opening above the carriage door at the streets of Little Rock as the horses pulled the coach slowly out of the yard and into the main thoroughfare.

Suddenly she caught sight of a familiar face across the road. The chestnut hair stylishly swept up and back, the fancy silk suit and stovepipe hat, that handsome, deceitful face! She noted a pale gray scarf wrapped around his neck, under which the wound she had inflicted was, no doubt, still healing. Looking down from a prancing palomino with flowing gold mane, his eyes swept the thoroughfare restlessly. Was he searching for her? His gaze alit upon the coach and their eyes met. She immediately felt intense sickness in her curling stomach. She resisted the urge to look away and instead delivered a withering glare, filling it with as much hatred as she could muster. He appeared to be matching her glare with his own angry one. Then the carriage was past him and on its way down Main Street towards Hot Springs. Was he pursuing the carriage on horseback? She strained her neck to look out of the window but saw only the rutted street stretching back into town. Yet, because of her indiscretion with a stranger, Roland Longman knew her final destination. Would he make his way to Hot Springs to exact revenge upon her for sticking him with the hatpin? He probably wanted to kill her for witnessing the trussed woman in his ship's cabin. The thought of it filled her mind with righteous fury, but lurking underneath was an icy block of fear.

The road grew bumpier as they exited the outskirts of Little Rock. For the first couple of hours of the journey, everybody in the carriage was politely quiet. Then some of the riders began chatting to their travelling companions. Solo sojourners either stared out at the darkness or engaged in low-pitched banter with whomever would respond. They swayed against each other every so often when the wheels rolled over tree roots or unknown debris in the dusty road. Otherwise they swung gently from side to side, and occasionally the carriage actually rode smoothly over a graded portion of road, which everyone was grateful for. The back and crown of Rosalia's head began to throb. A heavy-set, bearded gentleman in the next row of seats periodically pulled a gold watch on a chain out of his vest pocket. At one point he announced to all the passengers,

"Eight o'clock in the evening! Twelve more hours until our arrival in Hot Springs."

He continued to make this announcement every couple of hours until it grew dark and almost everybody fell into brief catnaps, lulled by the swaying of the coach on its gigantic wheels. Rosalia took offense at the time-keeper's presumptuous behavior at first, but then began to appreciate it as the hours until arrival at their destination dwindled. She could not wait to extract herself from this maddening conveyance and be free of the relentless motion, the clomping of horses' hooves, the accumulating odor of soured human perspiration. Sometime in the middle of the moonless night, she finally fell asleep for a good hour and a half, a dreamless sleep that she awoke from groggily. She tilted her head slightly to the left and saw that both Rosa and Simon were asleep, both snoring gently, heads bobbing against the seat back. The young couple seated across from her, not asleep, were leaning against each other, their right hands clinging to the brown leather straps that hung from the carriage ceiling in lieu of seat backs. They were clearly miserable, Rosalia could tell from the scowls on their faces. The stout gentleman who announced the time had fallen asleep at last, snoring loudly into his bushy brown beard.

The coach stopped periodically for calls of nature. The passengers clamored out of their seats and rushed to relieve themselves, the ladies at an outhouse of a nearby inn and most of the men behind a thicket or a copse of pines. Then they would resume the arduous journey southeast. They stopped once at a tavern for dinner, the driver joining the riders. Rosalia noticed grumbling among several of the other passengers about the driver, but she didn't know why and asked Rosa and Simon about it in German.

"Some people think the driver is too lowly and common to sit and have a meal with them," Simon answered. "He is like a servant to them. We don't see it that way, do we, liebe?"

Rosa nodded her head in agreement, mouth too full of venison stew to answer.

The outskirts of Hot Springs appeared just as orange streaks of early morning sunlight lit the undersides of thin, ragged clouds like torn laundry hanging below a dark violet sky. Quickly the light grew and spread, revealing modest one-story homes and cobbled-together huts that were sprinkled across fields and meadows that lay below wooded hills. Rosalia awoke from yet another brief doze and glimpsed the scenery through blurry, heavy-lidded eyes, knowing that this would be her permanent home. So far, the residents' homes looked frighteningly humble. But she knew that there must be grander sights in store at the center of town, and there must be a neighborhood filled with the well-to-do just like in Gliewitz. Would she ever meet the wealthy Americans of Hot Springs, Arkansas? She doubted that would ever happen, and that she would only catch sight of them in their finery and top hats as they passed by in ornate hansoms or chaises. She sensed that, despite the so-called 'freedom' of this grand new nation, the goyim, rich or poor, would not be socializing with the Jews. Deep anger welled up in her gut, although she was aware that this was foolish. Why would the huge abyss between Jews and Christians magically close from one land to another? Sighing, she shifted in the hard leather seat to ease the pressure on her hips and legs.

"Are you thinking of your betrothed, dear girl, now that we are so close?" inquired Rosa, having awoken at Rosalia's sigh.

Rosalia blushed, could feel the heat rising in her cheeks, and embarrassed by that, blushed even hotter.

"Y-y-es, I am," she stammered.

Rosa gently squeezed Rosalia's hand in hers and smiled, making the crow's feet at the corners of her black river stone eyes deepen.

"Do not worry, this will go very well. The men here long for a wife morning, noon and night. There are not so many marriageable women here as there are in Europe. We know of two Jewish men who went to the Indian people to barter and trade and married a squaw from the tribe. Squaw is the Indian word for woman. Shame, shame! Married out of the faith and now what will the children be? No Yiddisheh mama, no Yiddisheh children. But you! All the unmarried Jewish men in town, their hearts will leap for you, you will see. And you must walk carefully, modestly through town escorted by family. Carl feels extremely fortunate, I can assure you."

Rosalia nodded, unwilling to engage in conversation, still slightly sleepy from the miserable night she had spent trying and failing to plunge into oblivion while the stagecoach swung along the road. Nonetheless, Rosa's little speech did reassure her a tiny bit. Perhaps she could pull off this act of deceit, and nobody would catch wind of it, nobody would see through her. Maybe the windowpane that she felt others saw through into her dirty soul was not so clear and obvious to others as it was to her.

Now the stagecoach entered streets and left the fields behind. White clapboard buildings boasted signs for dry goods, saloons, dentist, cobbler, barbershops, even a lawyer. The streets were lined with buckeyes and dogwoods, no longer in bloom but still glorious with foliage. Rosalia spotted a bookstore and became excited. A sign of civilization! The morning sun was heating the air, and a chorus of cicadas hiding in the bushes and tree branches vibrated loudly in unison, then hushed, then buzzed again. White men dressed in work clothes walked in small groups, some quiet and others talking languidly. Negro men in much shabbier work clothing walked alone, tagging behind the white men. Rosalia spotted a fair-skinned woman with children in tow. She observed very carefully what the woman was wearing, the size of the bustle (large), the pale lavender of the skirt, the matching wide feathered bonnet, the button-down brown leather boots. She wanted dearly to fit in with her new neighbors. Behind this white woman trailed a Negro woman in a plain dun cotton dress, skin as dark as pitch and black hair braided in stiff, short columns atop her head, lugging cloth bags bulging with what must be household provisions. Suddenly several voices cried out from within her coach.

"Look! Look at that!"

"It's the hot springs! There they are!"

The riders on the eastern side of the coach were craning their necks to get a closer look at the spiraling steam arising from pools along Central Avenue and wafting uphill into the piney woods. Rosalia and the Meyers, who were now both fully awake, strained to spot the miraculous phenomenon that had put this little town on the map. They oohed and aahed with the other passengers, now all awake and alert and gawking at the mystical white clouds rising from the ground.

"How hot is the water that comes out?" mused the young husband sitting across from Rosalia.

"Sir, I have been told the water heats up to one hundred and forty degrees, plus," announced the white-bearded gentleman with the golden watch. He had it out now, prominently displayed in his palm. "Nine thirty-two in the morning."

"We do not need to know this!" chided Rosalia in his direction. He glanced back at her in surprise. Suddenly she couldn't bear sitting in the coach surrounded by these strangers for one more minute. The sour human body odors had intensified overnight, and she had no doubt that her own and the Meyers' added to the mix. The earthy odor of the horses and the reek of equine excrement from time to time had begun to sicken her as well. Despite the biscuits and cornpone she and the Meyers nibbled on to appease their hunger during this leg of the journey, her stomach was gurgling. She felt sticky and itchy on every inch of her skin and ached for a bath. She even entertained the idea of leaping from the coach and lowering herself into those springs, but instead smiled at her own impetuous, foolish idea.

"Look, Rosa," Simon spoke teasingly, "our *sheyna* bride is thinking about her groom." The two of them gazed endearingly at each other.

Again Rosalia felt mortified. Not a flicker of a thought had she spent on the upcoming meeting with her husband-to-be. But now she did and was troubled to find that she wished it were not going to happen. Her fears rose to the forefront of her mind now, and again she questioned her ability to pull the wool over Carl's eyes and present herself as a pure, virginal girl worthy of sharing a married life. Her thoughts bounced rapidly from her cousin Daniel, who had ruined her reputation in Gliewitz with his aggressive impunity, to Roland Longman, who had attempted to do the same and worse. Would Longman follow her here and finish the job of destroying her life as a respectable married woman in a Jewish community? She trembled with fear and rage, and instinctively lifted her right hand to delicately finger the pearl and steel hatpins securing her bonnet at the nape of her neck.

The team of horses was slowing, and the reins jingled and slapped the sides of the stagecoach as it pulled to a halt. Arms stretched upward and almost all the passengers groaned with stiffness and moaned with the anticipated pleasure of leaving the crowded stagecoach for good. Slowly they gathered their shawls, coats, purses, pouches and bags, and shuffled onto the platform step of the coach and to the ground. The driver untied and lowered chests and boxes from the boot in the rear of the carriage. Rosalia, Simon and Rosa were almost the last people off the stagecoach. They stood in front of the station with others who were greeting relatives, friends or business associates. Those travelers left quickly, either on foot or in a horse-drawn buggy. Rosalia and the Meyers waited quietly in front of the stage stop, an undistinguished one-story wood building with a ticket window in front and rusted iron poles alongside the right and left for the stage-coach to pull up and hitch the horses.

After they had waited for what seemed like hours to Rosalia, the sound of a horse's hooves clomping down the dusty street drew their attention. They turned their heads as one toward the sound and saw a two-seated buggy drawn by an aging chestnut mare. It was open to the sunshine, as the folding top had been pushed back. As it slowed and stopped in front of them, Rosalia recognized Carl's face from long ago, although vaguely as if she had dreamed it and now here it was in vivid detail. He set his tasseled buggy whip on the riding bench and stepped agilely down to the street.

Simon spoke first, "You are a cheerful sight, Carl my friend. We wondered if the sun would go down before you came. Your mother and father wrote me to convey their love and prayers for a healthy household to you, God willing."

They shook hands heartily, and then Rosa spoke up.

"We have been taking good care of your betrothed, and here she is. Help us to load her things into the buggy and then off you go to your brother's house. How is Samuel? And his wife and baby, nu?"

Carl was already gazing at Rosalia, who could not stop the heat from creeping up her neck and onto her cheeks. She could see from the appraising gleam in his eye that he was admiring her. Perhaps he, too, was working mentally to recall the memory of their first and only meeting so long ago at her parents' house. An entire war had taken place between their two encounters. The two of them were mute for several minutes, both unable to summon appropriate words for the occasion. Simon piped up awkwardly,

"Don't, ah, worry about us, Carl. Our cousin Ethan should be along very soon, he knew the time of our arrival as we sent word ahead from Little Rock. We will all gather to give thanks at the Rabbi's house next Friday Shabbos, yes?"

Carl suddenly jerked his eyes away from Rosalia and stared worriedly at the Simons.

"We have had some trouble here, which I hate to tell you about the moment you get to town. You will hear the details of it later. But you need to be a little more careful than you imagined. The Rabbi's house was deliberately set on fire by a band of hooligans, and that was our synagogue where we prayed. So then, Simon, your pair of hands in rebuilding Rabbi Schecter's house will be greatly welcomed as we all pitch in. In the meantime, the Rabbi is staying with the Bergauers. Their house is too small for services, but we gather under their backyard arbor since the weather is dry now."

Carl described tersely the story of Gussie's abduction. When he stopped talking, Simon almost whispered,

"Who in this country wants to do such a thing? It reminds me of the Prussian guards harassing us back in the old country. Is there nowhere safe?"

Rosalia's eyes blazed, and she frowned. The shocking news had jolted her out of the dreamlike trance of seeing Carl again.

"I will learn to shoot a rifle and show each of them no mercy!" she declared loudly. "I will teach those hooligans a lesson!"

Carl's eyes had already swung over to Rosalia's face while she was speaking. She could tell he was sizing her up and re-acting to her loud, angry words, and began to rue her out-burst as foolish and immature. Carl said to her,

"You are right to be angry. And there is more to tell that will infuriate you more. But we must proceed with caution if we are to survive here. We are the immigrants." He pointed to the ground with his forefinger. "Land is like gold, but even more of a treasure, because you grow to love it as your own. It is easy to forget that those people who have been living here before us became possessive and don't want to share it. We are interlopers in their eyes, stealing their beloved territories under their very noses. Now there are angry groups making forays into our community to scare us off. It won't work, but again we must rise above persecution in another place. Rosalia can spend a few nights at Ethan Meyer's house while Gussie revives from her terrible ordeal. We have already arranged that. Rosalia, you can ride in my buggy and we will follow Mr. and Mrs. Meyer to their cousin's house."

Rosalia was surprised and relieved at his measured response. She hoped that he was sincere in condoning her irate reaction and not just being polite. At the same time, she silently told herself to keep her tongue in check for as long as possible while she was still new in town. Still, the very outrage of what he had just said! Was this truly a free country as it was described across the Atlantic in Germany, or was that an illusion, a promise of gold that turned into dirt on closer examination?

Before anybody else could comment, Ethan Meyer, a thin, balding, man with a tufted black beard and pomaded mustache arrived in a fancy, polished black carriage. They greeted him and introduced Rosalia. He already knew Carl, who shook his hand genially.

"The whole town has been waiting for you to arrive!" He shouted.

Rosalia cringed at this man's loud voice that called attention to them on the street in a way no Jew in their right mind would do in Gliewitz, which could potentially invite danger.

"We must bring Miss Wolfson," he nodded at Rosalia, beaming, "to our house for a few days instead of the original plan to take her directly to Samuel and Gussie's house. Don't worry," he smiled, "we have plenty of room for all of you. Our house is large! Carl and I can fill you in on the terrible turn of events that befell Gussie." His grin turned quickly to a frown, the slight wrinkles on his wide tanned brow turning from cups to hills.

"I told them already," Carl explained softly. "Let's tell them about something cheery now to welcome them."

Simon and Rosa climbed clumsily into Ethan's buggy, and Rosalia hopped lithely into Carl's. After loading the luggage, Ethan and Carl urged their horses eastward down the street, and off they jangled and clomped, towing the travelers to Ethan Meyer's home and their first night in Hot Springs.

As the chestnut mare clopped along slowly with the buggy in tow, Rosalia breathed deeply and smelled a flowery sweetness in the air. Some sort of bloom was infusing a gentle breeze with a sugary scent the likes of which she had never experienced. The perfumed air and the occasional brush of Carl's arm against hers as he guided the mule rushed to her head like too much wine at a wedding. She clung to the side of the buggy with tightly clenched fists and curled fingers to keep her from floating straight up into the sky.

"......good to see you again, Rosalia," Carl was telling her, though she could scarcely focus on the words. "I have to say, you are looking a little peaked, though. Travel is wearing, isn't it? When you've rested a few days, I'm sure the color will return." She nodded, unable to speak at that moment. The trees and bushes along the streets seemed to wave at her in greeting, and the white planked storefronts grinned at her with wide door mouths and startled window eyes.

"I … I could use some time sitting in one place without moving. Please tell me, what is that wonderful scent?"

Carl tilted his head to one side to glance at her and laughed. She couldn't help but grin broadly at the sound of it. Laughter had been missing from her life for a long time.

"That is honeysuckle, white flowers that remind me of stars and grow on big bushes. You have changed very little since I shared dinner with you and your family so long ago. Except that you have grown even more beautiful."

She was grateful for his compliment and felt her neck and cheeks reddening, helpless to stop blushing. All she could do was hope that he hadn't noticed.

"You will have to tell me all about your journey. I'm sure you have had some interesting adventures."

Her heart palpitated as they jounced over the cobblestones. She would indeed tell him about her experiences travelling across the great Atlantic Ocean, up rivers and overland in a stagecoach to this American town. She would share her great emotions at leaving her family and riding on a train for the first time. She would describe her second-class cabin on the U.S.S. *Eolus*. She would relate the terrible massacre that she'd been caught in the middle of with the Meyers upon her arrival in New Orleans. She still had nightmares that woke her in a sweat about that day. But she would not tell him everything.

27

Roland Longman bided his time in Little Rock for two days. He was satisfied that since he knew Miss Wolfson's ultimate destination, he would locate her soon enough for his purposes. He spotted her in a stagecoach while he was trotting a horse around town that he had paid a rancher for a day's use. As if sensing his presence, she had turned in his direction and caught his angry glare, which he hoped had frightened her. Her stormy look in return didn't daunt him; in fact, it titillated him. She seemed to dare him to come after her, and he would oblige. As the stagecoach started moving, he rode the spirited stallion over to the stage office to ask where the coach was bound, and the grizzled, bespectacled clerk at the window told him its destination was Hot Springs. His luck had turned to success, and the horseback ride through town had paid off. He would wait patiently for her to settle into her new surroundings, no doubt meeting her future husband and his kin. Small towns were simple to maneuver in and their inhabitants easy to manipulate. He would plot a strategy to take his vengeance upon the little Jewish bride-to-be from Germany.

First he would visit the bordello there owned by his business associate, Walter Nibley. He would have resources there at his fingertips. Once again, he prodded the healing wound in his neck, still sore and red. Even more swollen and aching was his pride, which goaded him throughout the day, and sometimes invaded his nights with grim, disturbing dreams. His steely determination to exact revenge upon the haughty and wily Miss Wolfson would not be waylaid much longer. Her stagecoach had left on Monday evening, a fine day in September, so he purchased a ticket for the Wednesday morning coach. He would travel all day and arrive approximately at midnight. He deliberately chose that time of arrival because he did not want to be noticed entering town.

The Wednesday stagecoach left slightly after eleven o'clock in the morning – an hour or so late – and reached Hot Springs at one o'clock the next morning. The darkness of the street was pierced only by a single gas lamp hanging on the door of the newly built one-room station. There was just enough light emanating from the lamp to discern Missy's fancy, enclosed Rockaway buggy and spotted gelding waiting nearby. She had sent one of her lackeys to gather him and his luggage and bring them to the brothel where he would stay while he was visiting Hot Springs. The clomping of the horse's hooves and the rumble of the dray were unnerving to Longman as they pierced the quietude of the streets and woods that lined them.

Missy and Walter Nibley both greeted Roland warmly as he walked into the Rooming House. Missy planted a kiss on both of his cheeks, as usual. She had heard of the French custom and loved it, if applying it a little more boldly than the typical French peck. Walter slapped him on the back.

"Well, hardy wanderer, sit with us, share a warm bourbon and give us an accounting of your travels," he boomed, swinging his long, sturdy legs around a barstool. Roland knew that Walter was intrigued more by his procurer's business success than his tales of travel and adventure in foreign countries. If money was the root of all evil, Walter was in the field gathering those roots.

"Just came here from New Orleans via Little Rock. Delivered a pretty little package to a house there, the one on Chartres Street. Had a time getting her there, though. She put up such a fight, I had to tie her down and shove her in a trunk."

"Can you no longer seduce the ladies effectively enough to deter resistance?"

"Oh, she was plenty seduced, believe me. I had her in the palm of my hand. Still do. She wants to marry me."

"Well, then, Mr. Longman, why the sudden turn of events and attack upon your person by this rebellious girl?"

"There was another lady who became enamored of me and grew jealous of any other woman I spoke to, following me about the ship. She was a high-class lady, too rich for my blood, and nobody to procure for a brothel. She would be highly missed and her absence well-marked and noticed. Nothing but trouble, that one. But she persisted in finding any reason to chat with me, batting her eyelashes and swish-ing her silk and lace skirts as they all do, those high-class kinds. She observed me escorting the girl into my cabin and followed us. I didn't realize it until she banged upon the door, over and over, demanding to be let in. I opened my door to demand that she cease such a din and fuss. She shoved past me, entered my cabin bold as a pirate and assaulted my girl. They scratched at each other ferociously, knocked off bonnets, one pulled t'other's hair, it was dreadful. I felt that I had to intervene, and so I did, receiving this ugly wound upon my neck as a result. Which one of them did it, I cannot tell. The ladies were entwined in a raging match the likes of which I've never seen. I finally settled them down and sent Miss High Class on her way. I had to put this one, Greta, in the trunk to calm her down and get her off the ship without a ruckus. So, there it is, an adventure upon the high seas."

"I say, Longman, what a tale indeed if it did happen that way. Knowin' you, there's some twists and turns you left out. But that is fine so long as you are here safe and sound and ready to proceed with the business at hand. Specifically, I need another gal for the brothel. This town is a-hummin' like never before. The attraction of the Hot Springs bathhouses is bringin' the visitors in droves. What's more, the carpenter crews are buildin' the town again. And that is attractin' even moah business, I'm pleased to say. We don't want tah keep our customers waitin.'"

The two men smiled broadly and shook hands on the venture. Roland knew that Walter was expecting a backwoods orphaned gal, someone hungry and living in a dismal shack along the Arkansas River. That would be easy enough to provide. But the waif-like German Jew with golden hair and eyes like the summer sky he would deliver to the brothel in New Orleans, where none of her kin lived. He resisted the temptation to dream about being the first one to have her and the ruin he would inflict. He would save those daydreams for later when he was resting in solitude.

The next morning Roland awoke in the arms of Maybelle, his favorite girl. Although the customers weren't allowed to spend the night with the prostitutes unless they paid an extraordinary amount of money, he was given that privilege as a traveling procurer. His business relationship with Walter Nibley gave him special status in the Rooming House, and he took advantage of it as much as possible. Pushing the sleeping girl off him in the dim morning light that was sneaking around the edges of the window shades, he rose and stretched. He would spend the better part of the morning mapping his route with aid from Missy and Walter. The places in town frequented by immigrants and women would be his best bet for information. The immigrants would know who had most recently arrived and might let slip some information about Rosalia's residence in Hot Springs. The women – well, he knew that that they loved to gossip about other women. Perhaps he could glean something from them.

Breakfast consisted of a bowl of grits, a Southern specialty he had never tasted until he visited the South several years ago, two eggs over easy and fried to perfection by Missy herself, a cup of coffee and a shot of whiskey. The girls were all still sleeping as they had had such a busy night. He recalled some interesting sounds coming through the walls as he was drifting off: low moans, a muffled cry, murmured words, squeaking bed frames.

It was Monday morning, and the men in town who had employment were off to it for the day. The girls would have a chance now to catch up on sleep until dinnertime, with only the occasional wealthy, elderly customer coming at midday. He meticulously cleaned his mustache with a linen napkin and returned to his room to freshen up and check his appearance in the beveled and engraved mirror that hung over the scratched porcelain wash basin. Experience had taught him that people were fools who could not see past the clothes a man wore. The more gentlemanly his outer appearance, the more trust he seemed to inspire. And trust was exactly what he wanted to drum up in town. How else would he find his target? He didn't want to rely on dumb luck to stumble upon Miss Wolfson's home address. Although that could happen, weeks might pass first. He didn't have much time to procure a new girl for Walter, who didn't want to do the dirty work in his own hometown. Walter, an impatient man, would grow irate and find a new procurer for the area as quickly as he could draw a breath. He must get into town quickly today, scout around and listen.

Walter was in the back of the house harnessing Missy's spotted gelding to the carriage that would transport Roland into town. Roland boarded the box seat, doffed and waved his Stetson hat genially at his employer and headed into downtown Hot Springs. The air was cool and refreshing, a change from the muggy heat of the day before. Autumn was beckoning. Roland felt a surge of smug self-confidence and superiority as he gazed at the humble structures, the white men and women of Hot Springs in their day outfits, the smudge-skinned darkies dressed poorly and following them subserviently, heads lowered as they walked. Finding Rosalia

Wolfson would be easy once he discovered the latest news of these simple-minded townsfolk.

He halted the carriage in front of the Crabtree Inn on Central Avenue. This was an excellent jumping off point since he was friendly with the owner, William Crabtree. He would know where immigrants in town were congregating, which was typically in cafes and restaurants owned by other immigrants. He entered the cramped lobby reeking of tobacco smoke and spotted him immediately.

"Good afternoon, Willie," Roland greeted him jovially. "I just got into town and couldn't wait to stop by and see you. Maybelle sends you her best regards and hopes you'll come visit soon."

Willie, a lumbering red-haired fellow who loomed over the front desk, immediately stiffened and clenched his fists. His deep-set ebony eyes shifted from left to right under bushy carmine eyebrows that almost met above the bridge of his nose.

"Please, Mr. Longman, kindly refrain f'um mentioning the names of those sorts of women in the lobby of this hotel. It ain't propah. Ah wouldn't want mah deah wife Betsy to heah such a thing."

"All the better, as I come to ask you a favor, and it always helps to have a favor in the offing as well. Ahem, that is, to stay silent on the matter."

"Come then, suh, and speak up. What favor is this you ah referrin' tuh?" His wild eyebrows bunched together over a wrinkled brow.

"I am searching for a person who recently arrived in Hot Springs. I believe she got in just a few days ago. She is an immigrant, a young woman whom I believe plans to wed another immigrant, a man already living here. And, oh yes, she is an Israelite, name of Rosalia Wolfson. Do you know anything? Anything at all?"

Willie hung his head into his neck, appearing to concentrate, then looked up quickly and stared intensely into Longman's eyes. "Do you happen tuh know, suh, the name of the husband-to-be? That might aid me in recalling the rumors and comments ah have heard. Although beah in mind, please, due to mah position in this hotel, Ah heah a great many rumors. Ah would nevah steer ya wrong deliberately, but Ah might do just that without knowing."

This was a good question. What name had Rosalia given him on the ship when she let him know that she was betrothed? He tried to recall but could not remember. How careless of him. Finally the name popped into his head like a candle lighting itself.

"His name is Carl Gersman."

"Hmm, don't know him. Well, quite a few people arrahved in town these past few weeks, but Ah don't know of no Israelite lady. You do mean Jewish? You would be bettah off askin' the folks at the Jewish rest'rant ovah on Third Street. Let me see, what is it called? Oh yes, I believe the name is of their own peculiah native tongue. Late key. Or Light Kay. Forgive me if I cannot recall exactly. I would never frequent the place mahself."

He shook his head with a scowl, ruby locks flying like a flutter of orioles around his head.

"Much obliged for the information, sir. If this plays out the way I hope it to, I will personally arrange for you to enjoy a free night at Missy's."

Willie put a meaty finger to his lips to shush his acquaintance and glanced around to see if his wife were unluckily nearby. But she wasn't, so he breathed a sigh of relief and waved Roland toward the entry door. That turned out to be unnecessary, as he was speeding out the door already, boots echoing in the small entry and black frock coat flapping behind him.

Third Street was not far from the inn, so Longman left the horse and buggy secured to a post around the side of it and walked into town. When he came to Third Street, he glanced around to see if he could spot a café with a sign that started with the letter L and would appear to be a foreign word. Many of the establishments on Third Street were in various stages of rebuilding. A few were boarded up. One was a tippling room, and he longed to enter and toss down a few gins, but there was an important matter to attend to. The wound to his neck suddenly throbbed and bile rose in his throat as he walked. He caught sight of a modest wooden sign with a cheerful blue and white background, the words "Latke Cafe" painted in black across it. This must be the place! With any luck he might even find her there. He headed toward the sign and saw that the little cafe was open. He slipped in as quietly as possible through a slightly crooked knotty pine door and stood along the back wall. The cafe was tiny, with hard, hand-made wooden chairs and five rickety tables. A crude opening in the opposite wall revealed the kitchen, with barely enough room for one person to turn around. Two windows along the south wall let in natural sunlight, which warmed the room and made it appear a bit larger. The smell of onion, beef, potato and chicken and some unidentifiable herb wafted in the air. The restaurant was empty of patrons. Only a heavy-bosomed woman in a simple green and white checkered day dress and stained white apron occupied the premises. She was wiping her hands with a cotton rag and checking the contents of several huge, simmering tin pots on the stovetop. Longman walked over to the kitchen entrance and cleared his throat noisily. The woman whirled around in surprise.

"*Ach! Wer bist du?*

"Pardon me, madam, but I do not speak your language. I am looking for some friends."

"I am sorry, sir," the woman responded, flustered. She blinked her eyes at him and looked down, clearly embarrassed.

"I would like to find some friends who just recently moved here from Germany. Is it possible you are acquainted with a Miss Rosalia Wolfson from Prussia? And her fiancé?"

The woman's round, smooth face lightened into a broad smile.

"Yes, yes, new in town. She is very pretty, hair from gold. Carl Gersman, so happy to see her! But she get mad easy. You watch out."

"Oh, does she then?" Longman smiled, feigning innocence. "I'll bear that in mind, madam, most certainly. Do you know where they live?"

"No, I not know where these people live." She furrowed her wide brow and thought for a few moments. "So you go Rabbi. Rabbi Schecter, he know everybody, know where everybody live. He help you."

"And, if you could be so kind, where may I find this, um, Rabbi Schecter?"

"He live not far from here. You walk in twenty minutes, get there."

The woman picked up a scrap of plywood from a pile on the floor, reached for a chunk of charcoal lying on a box in a corner, and drew a crude map of lines and arrows.

Roland Longman took it from her, tipped his bowler hat and turned to leave.

"You want bowl of chicken soup with kreplach? Fifteen cent, good deal and delicious."

Longman merely shook his head as he hurried out of the Latke Café. The woman shrugged her sturdy shoulders and turned back to her stove, lifting lids and sniffing.

The Latke Café's cook wasn't the best at drawing maps. After a few wrong turns and half an hour of brisk walking, Longman literally stumbled upon the Rabbi's house. He turned a corner and tripped on a piece of lumber lying on the ground. There were other piles of lumber, sweet-smelling oak, pine and cherry wood, alongside a small pathway that led to a freshly constructed wall and doorway. Two men were arduously sanding planks that were destined for the porch. Hammer strikes echoed loudly within. Longman observed the scorching remnants of a recent fire. Burnt tree trunks, blackened leaves and earth lay before him, and a smoky scent tinged the air. However, the crew of carpenters was working quickly to restore the damage and rebuild the structure. Longman wondered at this. Could the Rabbi be so wealthy as to pay these men for their hard labor? Or were they foolishly dedicated to the religious leader and willing to work for free? He smirked inwardly at the idea. Then it dawned on him that the Rabbi might not be so willing to steer him to Rosalia and Carl. He had heard that Jews were protective of their own, like a clan in the Appalachians. How could he approach the Rabbi, gain his trust and extract from him the information that he needed?

As he was pondering this conundrum, two men emerged from the interior of the building and walked in his direction. He could see that they were Jews, their faces barely visible under long, bushy beards, full mustaches, and those odd curled sidelocks. They wore peculiar round caps on their crowns. Although he did not know what the caps signified, he had seen Jewish men wearing them in New York City as they strolled on Saturday mornings down the streets towards their temples of worship. As the two carpenters neared, he recognized the face of one of them. He searched his memory and suddenly remembered being introduced to him at Missy's place back in the spring of this year. What was the man's name? He and his companion walked past him and vaguely nodded politely and silently at him. Then it came to him: This was Carl Gersman. His face stretched into a sneer. It was the same name as the Jewess's future husband.

It couldn't be a coincidence; it must be the same man. He caught up with the pair and politely lifted his bowler in greeting.

"Pardon me, sir. Do you remember me?"

The man on the left turned in surprise and stared into Longman's face. His expression remained puzzled and blank.

"Last April or May." Longman prompted him. "At Missy's Rooming House? You are Carl Gersman, is that not true?"

When Carl heard the words 'Rooming House', his eyes widened, and his mouth compressed into a thin, hard line. The man standing next to him proclaimed,

"What, are you crazy? My brother doesn't go there. He is not that kind of man. A good man, my brother."

Ah hah, thought Longman, *they are brothers. All the better.* He suddenly noted the family resemblance: short of stature, walnut brown eyes, muscular, squared upper torsos, brawny arms.

"Yes indeed," Longman smiled, amused at the potential for conflict he might stir up. Fortune had blessed him this day. "Carl is a regular customer of the brothel. That is where we met. I just had breakfast with Betsy, your favorite, this morning, sir."

Carl looked down at his dusty leather boots and shook his head.

"You have wrong person, sir," he muttered tersely.

"Well then, how else would I know your name?"

Carl's brother glared at him and whispered in Carl's ear. Suddenly the two fellows walked briskly past him and down the street. Roland could have easily caught up with them and continued the confrontation, but it wasn't necessary or smart.

He knew enough now to make plenty of trouble for that wretched Rosalia Wolfson and her beau. All he needed to do was follow the brothers at a discreet distance to discover where they lived.

The two men were hurrying now, and he could perceive that they were having an animated discussion as they walked. They turned a corner and Roland took long strides so as not to lose sight of them. He turned the same corner and spotted them at a distance heading south on Third Street, waited a few seconds and then continued trailing them. He almost lost them when they turned down a path lined with buck-eyes and oaks. Only the sound of their steps crackling in the dry leaves guided him. He trailed them as silently as he could, hiding behind wide-trunked oaks. Past a stand of dogwoods appeared a one-room cabin, which the two men entered. As he approached the dwelling, he inhaled the aroma of freshly baked bread. He straightened his collar and smoothed his vest and jacket. Then with a steely, determined smile that spread no joy across his handsome features, he rapped loudly on the door with his gold-tipped cane.

28

Carl's face was aflame with embarrassment and self-loathing as he and Samuel hurried down Central Avenue. They planned to have Shabbos dinner together as today was Friday, but Carl couldn't imagine sitting through it now. He was dumbstruck by the incredible coincidence of running into that fellow he had met at the Rooming House. Was this castigation from Hashem for his shameful self-indulgence? Now that his brother knew about his visits, was there any chance that he would tell Gussie and Rosalia? Oy, Rosalia! He would likely lose her forever if she found out. The thought of it made his chest tighten with anguish.

"You idiot. *Shmendrick!*" Samuel hissed at him as they plowed down the street. Golden and coppery leaves fluttered down around them from nearby stands of oaks and green ashes. Samuel kicked at a few of them and continued, "You have shamed our family. You have sinned. If our friends find out, they will shun us all. And what will Rosalia think? I have half a mind to pummel you into the ground!"

They turned a corner, too engrossed in their heated discussion to discern that they were being followed. Carl shrugged his shoulders and scrunched up his face in a moue.

"Easy for you to criticize, Sam. Look at you, with a loving wife and child. I have had nobody in my bed to comfort and love me all these years. I am making a new life from the beginning again in a strange place. I left all I knew in life when I came here. It is difficult, and even though I share the love of you and your family, still I have needs, you know? I was lonely for a woman."

"Don't talk to me about your needs. Do you think of nobody else? This was a stupid idea. Did those fellows, Horace and his other two rotten friends, get you into this? I knew it! I've always had a bad feeling about those rough, unschooled gentiles. They are whoremongers, all of them. I should have warned you. I take some of the blame here."

Samuel puffed a little keeping up with his younger sibling as they walked quickly down Third Street.

"You are not going to tell Rosalia or Gussie, are you? It will be the end of everything for me. Rosalia will never marry me. I will take my own life, and Hashem do with me what He will."

Silence fell between them for a few minutes. They listened to the wind gust unexpectedly and intensify the rustling of dry leaves falling as they walked. A slight nip was in the air presaging the bite of winter. Then finally Samuel said gruffly,

"Brother, you have done wrong. But you must overcome this. Suicide would be an even graver shame to our family. And I could not bear to lose you. I will not breathe a word of this to my wife or to your intended. They need never know. Soon you will be married and have all the love you want, I hope. Just please promise me not to go to that place again."

Carl's relief at hearing Samuel's forgiving words was so overwhelming, his eyes began to water slightly. He wiped at them with the back of his roughened hand and coughed as if reacting to the gusts of wind.

"I swear to you that I will not go there again. I haven't gone since I learned that Rosalia was coming –" an angry scowl from Samuel – "and yes, I know that is not good enough. But I promise not to again. I beg of you, please keep my secret."

"Of course I will. Do you think I want to stop your wedding? No, not I. Let us just hope that we can put this behind us. We must also pray that your companions in sin, Horace and the other two, don't tell stories around town. You are in a precarious position, Carl. You have put yourself at risk and at the mercy of a few lowlifes."

Carl nodded numbly. His brother was right. He had foolishly placed himself at risk for exposure by his new, questionable friends. His only spark of hope was that they didn't want public scrutiny of their visits either. But he would deal with them later. Right now he wondered what he was going to do about the menacing Mr. Longman.

The brothers took the path to Samuel's home, ducking to avoid the low-hanging branches of the mottled pasture haw trees. The aromas of chicken roasting and potatoes boiling greeted them as they approached the house and intensified as they swung open the front door. Smoke from the fireplace danced up the chimney flue. Nights were getting chilly now. Gussie was sitting in a corner nursing the baby in a rocking chair with cotton pillows stuffed around her for comfort. She looked weary and drawn around the eyes, but her face lit up when the two men walked in.

"Wash your hands and faces, you two. The sun is about to set."

She swung David over her shoulder and patted his tiny back, waiting for a burp. The vision of mother and child gave Carl a chill. He might lose all of this for himself because of his foolhardy visits to the brothel.

Rosalia emerged from the kitchen with two large wooden carved bowls piled with potatoes and roast chicken. She wore a white cotton and lace dress, and her blonde tresses were braided and pinned up around the back of her head. Her bright smile as she greeted Carl felt like warm sunlight dancing on his face and down his chest. The men washed their hands as she and Gussie arranged the table with polished pewter candlesticks holding stubby Shabbos candles, linen napkins and china plates. Their preparations were interrupted by a soft tap at the front door. Then came a sharper, more distinct rap. Carl and Samuel exchanged anxious glances as Rosalia headed to the door. Samuel rushed to her side and said,

"Don't bother yourself. I will see who is there."

With three large strides he got there before her and cracked the door a few inches.

"Who are you? What do you want?"

"Just a word, if you don't mind, with Carl. I took the liberty of following you home, so I know that he is there."

The visitor spoke loudly enough for everybody in the house to hear. Carl blanched and grabbed onto a chair to steady himself but remained silent.

"We are preparing for Shabbos dinner. Please leave us in peace now."

"I only ask a minute of his time, sir, no more. Surely he can spare me that much?" The visitor's voice took on a slightly menacing tone, which was not lost on the listeners. Carl stepped forward shakily and found himself directly behind his brother.

"Please, Sam, let me have a word with him. Outside."

Carl stepped around Sam and faced the smooth-shaven Roland Longman. Samuel firmly shut the door behind him. Longman regarded Carl with a hint of a sneer.

"What you want?" Carl spoke softly so the women wouldn't hear.

"I am searching for a lady. Perhaps you know her? Her name is Rosalia Wolfson. She and I have some, ah, unfinished business together, the nature of which is confidential."

Longman adjusted an indigo wool ascot around his neck. Carl was stunned. What would this fancy, gentile man want with his betrothed? How would he even know her name? He sensed that Mr. Longman was registering his surprise, so he struggled to compose himself and pull together the English he would need.

"I don't know that name. Please leave."

"How can that be? I hear all over town that she is your intended and you plan to marry her right here in Hot Springs. You are lying, Mr. Gersman."

"You… you hear wrong. Now leave us alone and go away." He continued to keep his voice low, hoping desperately that nobody could listen to them from inside the house.

"Yes, you are a liar." He paused. "However, the next time you see Miss Wolfson, please extend to her my invitation to meet and settle our business."

Longman tipped his black top hat and turned on his heel, balancing affectedly on his gold-tipped cane. Carl narrowed his eyes and punched his right fist into his left palm as he watched him disappear through the pasture haws and buckeyes. What could this menacing rogue mean by unfinished business with Rosalia? His ire was matched by total confusion as he went inside to face the others.

He saw that David had been placed, sleeping, in his cradle. Samuel and Gussie were hovering over Rosalia, who was crouched in a corner, wide-eyed and motionless. Her face was as pale as the cotton dress she was wearing, and her shoulders were shaking with sobs.

Samuel turned to Carl and said harshly,

"This fellow, Longman, he seems to be bad business for her as well as you. When she heard his voice through the door, she fell into the corner and now won't tell us a thing. Maybe you can get her to explain what is going on with that man."

Carl leaned over her and said gently, "Rosalia? Please tell me, who is this man? Why does he want to see you?"

She closed her eyes tightly and shook her head, unable to speak. Gussie leaned down and grabbed her by the elbows.

"Shayna, you cannot stay in that corner all evening. Stand up and I'll help you to the table, give you a few sips of wine to steady your nerves."

Rosalia rose with help from Gussie and sat mutely at the table. She sipped on the glass of wine that Gussie quickly poured for her.

Carl stared at her mystified. There must be a story behind all of this, but how could he coax it out of her in this state of upset? They would have to talk tomorrow, but not on Shabbos. He would wait until after sunset Saturday and she had had a full day to rest and recover, and then she would provide an explanation.

They all managed to eat some of the sumptuous meal, though they said very little. The Shabbos candles flickered and lit the pots and utensils hanging on the rough walls surrounding them. Rosalia was completely silent throughout dinner, eyes cast down at her plate. Carl couldn't stop himself from glancing at her frequently, wonderingly. Samuel and Gussie chattered about the baby, supplies for the store, seeds that Gussie had traded with neighbors to plant in the garden. From time to time they glanced at Rosalia, then at Carl. Gussie brought out an apple brown betty for dessert and cut a small piece for each of them. Samuel ate his portion heartily, and Gussie ate half of hers, but neither Carl nor Rosalia touched theirs. The candles burned steadily down, and their melting wax rolled in lumpy trails to the bottom of their pewter stands. Finally, Carl rose from his seat and announced,

"It is time for me to go back to my house. I will see you all at the Bergauers' tomorrow for Shabbos service. Thank you, Gussie, for the wonderful supper."

He put on his cloth coat, a little thin for the evening chill, it occurred to him. Saying nothing to Rosalia, not even looking at her, he went out into the night lit dimly by a crescent moon, lifting a kerosene lamp Samuel gave him to see the path in the darkness. He had his own pistol by his side in the event that a wild animal might threaten him. The woods here teemed with creatures, not so evident during the day but challenging and hair-raising during nighttime travels. He shivered all the way home. Not far from his house, he heard something moving through the undergrowth, and thought he glimpsed the distant silhouette of a hulking bear in the faint moonlight. When he finally arrived home and climbed into bed, thoughts whirled in his mind, too many for him to relax and drift to sleep. Questions about Rosalia and Roland Longman plagued him, but he found no explanations that would ease his mind or even remotely make any sense. At last, towards morning he managed to fall asleep.

Pale morning light played upon Carl's sleeping face and pried open his eyes. He hadn't slumbered enough, but those few hours would have to do. He must arise and prepare for Saturday morning Shabbos services. Even though there was more work to be done at Rabbi Schechter's house, it could not be done today, or Shabbos would be broken, an offense to Hashem. He was glad of the day of rest after the turmoil of yesterday's events. He needed every bit of blessing that Hashem could spare him now as well, he realized. Thoughts of Rosalia and Roland Longman crowded into his mind and set him to tossing and turning on his lumpy horsehair mattress.

He did his best to push those thoughts aside and arose to dress for the religious service in formal black trousers that Samuel had handed down to him, arrow shirt and warm wool vest. He downed two hardboiled eggs and a thick piece of challah slathered with blackberry jam that Gussie had sent him home with last night, washing them down with hot coffee in a chipped clay cup. He grabbed his dark wool coat to ward off the morning chill and ambled lazily along the narrow path leading to Samuel's house. Why should he rush on Adonai's commanded day of rest? Instead, he breathed the fresh, aromatic air into his lungs. It was early enough to hear the rustling of birds in the nearby bushes. Perhaps a grouse or a partridge lurked under the allspice shrub, a wren fluttered in the bottlebrush buckeye. He was learning the names of plants and trees in Hot Springs from Samuel and new acquaintances. Try as he might to enjoy the stroll, dark thoughts and worries seeped unbidden into his mind like sharp daggers. It seemed only a matter of time before Rosalia would find out about his dalliances with prostitutes at the Rooming House. Too many people knew about them, and his folly at trusting Horace, Billy and Geoffrey became obvious. His impending marriage to Rosalia seemed to slip away like a golden dream forgotten. He grew sadder with each step and his shoulders began to droop.

Samuel, Gussie and Rosalia were waiting in the parlor for Carl. It had become customary for them to make their way to Shabbos services together. Since it was the day of rest, they couldn't use the horse and dray. Now there were four of them, plus an infant in a cotton sling across Gussie's chest, strolling along Central Avenue.

The Bergauers' backyard was bustling with congregants finding their seats, scooting after their running children.

Some of them greeted the Gersmans with a quick hand wave and a smile. Carl noticed curious glances being directed at Rosalia, and felt protective toward her, but dared not put his arm around her since they weren't yet wed. She and Gussie sat with the other women on the right side of a makeshift plywood divider that they couldn't see over. Carl and Samuel took their place among the men on the left. Carl made his utmost effort to focus on the Rabbi's words, the prayers, the cantor's melodic singing, but his thoughts continually strayed to the woman sitting hidden on the other side of the divider, the woman betrothed to him, at least for now.

When services were over, the men and older boys spoke solemnly to one another, mostly about the fire and the frightening attack by the strange men dressed so bizarrely on horseback. The women and girls brought platters of food to a small table covered with a white linen tablecloth and kept their eyes on the children, who raced gleefully around the Bergauers' parlor and outside around the trees and bushes in their garden. Carl spotted Rosalia in a corner with Gussie, who was looking grim. Rosalia's eyes were downcast, but every few minutes they would dart angrily around the parlor, as if trying to locate her object of ire. Their eyes met briefly, but she quickly looked away.

Carl wandered out in front of the house to breathe in the fresh air. The sun gleamed directly overhead when a large, dark shadow crept across the threshold of the garden gate. Carl noticed it at once. Behind the shadow appeared the paunchy, burly form of Constable Hargreaves, uniformed and heavy-booted. The constable nodded at Carl, motioning for him to follow as he swung open the gate and walked to the front door, knocking and then stepping in tentatively. The Rabbi, dressed in his long, black wool coat and black top hat, spotted him and wended his way through the clusters of congregants to greet him.

"Ah apologize foah interruptin', Rabbah. Ouah investigation brings us to yoah house, ta fahnd out whatevah we can about the scoundrels who set the fiyah heah. Will you kahndly allow me to speak to the crowd?"

The Rabbi nodded and gestured with his hand to the small oak dais he had been using at the far end of the garden. The constable took his place there, cleared his throat loudly, and asked for everyone's attention. It was not difficult to attain, given that everybody's eyes were glued on the city official who had entered during their time of worship.

"Pahdon me foah interruptin' y'all's holy day services. Howevah, criminal investigation of the fayah last week takes precedence since it is possible one oah moah of y'all might have infohmation impoahtant to it. Ah am heah to speak to any of y'all that witnessed the event of Friday, Octobah 20 in the evenin, pertainin' to the abduction of one Gussie Gersman and setting of a fayah at this location."

Silence descended upon the group. Carl clenched his fists at his sides and ground his teeth together. Should he step forward and tell the Constable about the leather boot he had seen? That he would even hesitate to do so shamed him. But he knew that if Horace were brought in for questioning and found out that Carl had betrayed him to the authorities, he would surely reveal their visits to the Rooming House to the entire town. Rosalia would never marry him after that. Nonetheless, he had a duty to his imperiled community. Attacks like these could increase if allowed to occur with impunity. Against his deepest desires, he raised his hand and caught the Constable's eye.

"Mr. Constable, sir, I will talk to you. I think I recognize one man from that night. It is Mr. Horace Fletcher. I say because I saw his special boot buckle, letter F for last name. I could not see his face, because it was covered. But I saw his boots with red and black leather."

Murmurs filled the parlor. Heads swiveled toward Carl like a roomful of owls. The Constable's thick white eyebrows lifted high up into a wrinkled forehead.

"Very well, and Ah thank ye kindly, sir. Please to tell me yoah full name and address so that we can contact you in the future. Any others who want to come foahwahd and be a witness to the crahm?"

Nobody else said a word. All eyes were on Carl, though. He could feel them piercing every inch of his body and spirit like invisible arrows and knew they were wondering how he came to know a man like Horace Fletcher well enough to recognize his personal boot buckles. He feared that he could be ostracized by the entire Jewish community in this little town.

"Thank you again, Mr. Gersman. If no othahs have infoahmation to offah, ah will take mah leave. Please pay me a visit at the coathouse if you do remembah something pertinent to this investigation. Good day and may the Lord bless y'all."

He stepped down from the dais and made his way through the milling crowd to Gussie, carried on a whispered exchange with her, and quickly departed. The congregation gathered around the platter-laden table to recite the kiddush over the wine. Carl lifted a thimble-sized tin cup of one from one of the platters filled with many. He could use a lot more of these today. Small platters of Mandelbrot cookies, squares of cornbread, and two sugar-glazed strudels beckoned to him as well. Rabbi Schecter led them in prayers over the wine, which they then drank, then another prayer over the ceremonial challah bread, which they broke eagerly into small pieces and ate with delight, along with the other treats. Slowly they took their leave, voices rising in discussion and comments about what had just transpired. Everybody seemed to have an opinion, and Carl fearfully listened to fragments of sentences: "…hope they catch that man and put him in jail…" "…like in the Old Country…." "…set the fire?" He was relieved that he was hearing no derogatory remarks about himself. Was it too much to hope that the people of this community wouldn't discover his wrongdoing?

On the following Monday afternoon, Carl was formally summoned to the courthouse with a subpoena. Deputy Paige read it outloud ceremoniously and then handed it to Carl at the store. Samuel was trading Mrs. Mandelbaum a fine hand shovel for a brood of chicks and two hens, and when they were done with the transaction, he joined Carl in the stock room to peruse the official document.

"You must appear at the courthouse tomorrow morning at eight o'clock. I have no idea how long they will keep you there, but I hope you can make it back to work."

Carl brooded the entire day about the looming meeting with authorities, and the hours poked along slowly for him. That night he went to bed early in edgy anticipation of his appearance, but he tossed around nervously in bed half the night. He awoke just as the sun was shooting tiny slivers of pale pink light to the undersides of streaky clouds. The clouds hung above the tree line in the broad expanse of sky like billowing sails. He admired the brief splendor through his bedroom window as he donned his best clothing: morning coat and woolen trousers, white dress shirt with arrow collar, a dark blue ascot tie. It was his only dress outfit, handed down to him recently from Samuel, and he had been saving it for his wedding. Now here he was wearing it, he wryly smiled at himself, to testify as a witness to a crime. He polished his black dress boots, laced and tied them, and rushed off to the courthouse downtown, too nervous to eat breakfast.

A fair-haired young woman escorted him into a meeting room of the courthouse. There stood Constable Hargreaves, a court recording secretary, his own brother Samuel, Rabbi Schechter, and much to his surprise, Horace Fletcher, glowering at Carl beneath furrowed, pale yellow eyebrows. Horace was handcuffed and flanked by two police officers. A judge in black robes was seated nearby at a raised desk ('bench', the recording secretary called it). Constable Hargreaves asked Carl to repeat what he had observed at the time of the incident. When he was finished, Horace burst out,

"This Jew is a lying bastard! How can you believe him 'bout anything t'all?"

"Well, Mr. Fletchuh," the judge said solemnly, "we do have anothah witness who claims you was one of the men who set fiyah to Mr. Jacob Schecter's house. Mr. Samuel Gersman, please tell the court what you know about this suspect."

"I heard his voice. He was yelling and talking to the other hooligans. Sounded like the same voice in my store when he yelled at the Biggs sisters to get out. Horace Fletcher's voice."

"Well, suh, voice identification is not enough to bring charges, nor clothing. However, puttin' the two togethah gives me enough circumstantial evidence to name Mr. Fletchuh as a suspect in the crahm. He will be released but warned not ta leave the area."

Carl grasped his brother's hand and squeezed it tightly. He looked directly at Horace as the handcuffed man glared at him. Fletcher stomped out of the courthouse, Carl noted, in the very same ornate leather boots in question.

"Constable Hargreaves, heah is the search warrant on Horace Fletchuh that you requested.

"Thank ye, Cyril, um, Judge Hayes. Ah will look foah evidence pertainin' to the crahm."

The two brothers left the courthouse quickly to get to the store. When they arrived, there was a small crowd of customers clustered at the entrance. To their surprise, Gussie and Rosalia were also waiting for them, eager to hear the news from the courthouse meeting. They had decided to take David out for fresh air. Carl's eyes widened when he saw Rosalia with the baby across her chest sleeping in the sling. He couldn't help but imagine that it was their child. Samuel unlocked the store and six customers swept in. The brothers rushed behind the counter to set up the scales and cash till and bring new inventory to the front of the store: shovels and pickaxes imported from the North, seventeen pounds of wheat flour that had to be sent for from Washington, D.C. at twenty dollars a barrel. Rosalia and Gussie rushed up to the counter together, their faces flushed with dread and excitement. The pinkness of Rosalia's cheeks, spots of rose, made her even more enticing to Carl as he gazed at both women.

"We want to hear what happened this morning," Gussie said, crossing her chubby arms tightly over her bosom and tapping one booted foot on the floor, which kicked up a small cloud of sawdust. Carl gazed at her admiringly. This was one tough lady, considering what she had just endured. The women in his hometown of Oppein were rugged in their own way, but this was several steps beyond. It began to dawn on him just how much spirit the women settlers had to muster to survive in this rugged country populated by so many kinds of people and filled with dark unknowns.

Samuel and Carl described the courtroom scene. When they told the two women that Horace Fletcher had been released, Rosalia gasped and tears came to Gussie's eyes. She brushed them away quickly, craned her neck and whispered into Samuel's ear. Samuel turned to Carl and said,

"I'm going to take Gussie home, brother. Please tend to the store alone until I get back. She is afraid. This Fletcher isn't the only guilty one. The others might come after us again."

"Might be better if she stayed here with us, where we can protect her."

"She wants to go home and feed the baby and put him to rest. Rosalia, you can stay here with Carl and help him. We're busy today, and he'll show you how to keep track of inventory and serve the customers."

Rosalia nodded and transferred David, still in his sling, to Gussie. Carl hoped that they could talk a little while they were working in the store together. They had had so little opportunity to become acquainted since she arrived in Hot Springs. It was odd to become this friendly with one's betrothed before the marriage; usually the bride and groom glimpsed each other only once or twice before the wedding ceremony, even if they knew each other already. But that was Prussia, and this was a country hardly born a couple of hundred years ago. Immigrants here were like babies in a beer garden: full of wonder and confusion. Rules of conduct, law, society, all seemed to be unwinding in unimagined directions. He smiled at his petite bride-to-be and motioned for her to join him behind the rough oak counter. She stood near him but took care not to let him touch her, forbidden by Jewish custom until they were husband and wife. Carl sighed as he weighed a quarter pound of flour into the next customer's flour bag. He longed to crush Rosalia to his barrel chest and envelope her in his arms. At the same time, her connection to the formidable Mr. Longman nagged at his mind. Could he ask her about it gently, without inspiring another emotional reaction in her? He didn't think that he was skilled enough in his conversation to broach the topic well.

A young farmer named John Golston, lean with skin tanned to leather, bellied up to the counter. He wanted fifty size 2 square head nails, so Carl directed Rosalia to the nail shelf with a small burlap bag to fill. She eagerly filled the order and brought it back. He showed her how to total up the sale and count the money, which was still foreign to her. She slowly but accurately made the correct change for Golston, who tipped his straw hat and sauntered out. Carl was secretly delighted; she was smart and quick to learn. Next in line was elderly Mrs. Mandy Wilson, skin dark as an unploughed field, a contrasting shock of white hair curling around her head like a halo, eyes bright and shiny black despite her advanced age. She requested cornmeal and sugar and handed Carl two small paper sacks. Carl showed Rosalia where those supplies were and how to fill the order. She appeared to enjoy the work, and her animated face looked lovelier than ever to him. He wondered if this was the first time she had worked outside the home and put it in mind to ask her when they had a spare moment alone together in the store. In the left corner of the store where the large bags of flour stood ready for scooping, stood the Biggs sisters patiently waiting for service.

As Mandy Wilson headed toward the door, it swung open, pushed vigorously by an unknown hand. Mandy slipped quickly out into the street. Horace Fletcher stepped inside, muttering some ugly aside at her. He strutted to the counter, staring angrily at Carl. He looked over at Rosalia beside Carl, and a slow, taut grin crawled across his face.

"Well, well, Carl mah so-called friend. The judge let me outta jail aftah Billy an' Geoffrey paid the bail bond price. Ah see you caught yersef a purty one tah marry. Yah weren't lyin'. A bride come to town!"

Carl stared back into his watery, light blue eyes, unable to speak. Rosalia glanced worriedly from one man to the other. Horace's face broke into a wide, snaggle-toothed smile.

"Now ye don't need tah visit the gals at Missy's place. It'll jest be me 'n' Geoffrey and Billy fum now on. That is, unless you decide you want a little tail other than the wife. We shore had fun tahmes there, didn't we, Carl? Ah'll give yoah regahds to Betsy, yoah favorite."

With that he tipped his dusty straw hat and marched out of the store, long beard wagging and knees pumping up and down as if he were in a parade. Silence ensued like a thick mantle across the room. Customers and, worse, Rosalia, stared at Carl as if he were a statue displayed for study. He had finally been exposed, and could it have been at a worse moment? In front of his betrothed and customers of Gersman's Dry Goods, in the middle of a workday. He glanced hesitantly at Rosalia, whose gorgeous, sky-blue eyes were wide with surprise, and then they narrowed at him.

"My English is not so good," she addressed him in German, "but I know enough to understand. You are not a good man, nor a good Jew in eyes of Hashem. How can I marry a dirty man like you?"

She grabbed a small hand shovel lying on a shelf near her reach and flung it at him. It grazed the side of his head and he winced in pain. The four customers still in the store shook their heads at the scene they were witnessing. Although Carl was relieved they didn't understand her German, nonetheless he knew they caught the gist of it all.

"You are an evil man!" Rosalia screamed, backing away from him. "I leave my family, come across ocean, you cannot imagine what happen on the ship. For you? A man that go to….?" She could not finish the sentence. Instead, sputtering with fury, she ran out of the store.

Carl felt a throbbing in the left side of his head and put his hand to it. The impact of the shovel hadn't broken the skin, but he could feel a painful lump already growing there. It was a good thing she didn't have a loaded rifle in her hands! She knew how to use one now. *This town,* he thought, even smaller than Gliewitz. *Nobody keeps a secret here.* He knew they would be talking about this to their families and friends. He shrugged his shoulders at the customers helplessly as each one came to face him for their purchases. They all had comments to make to Carl, some consoling and others judgmental. Greatly embarrassed, he remained quiet and kept his eyes on the goods and tools they were buying, the money they were handing him, the change he was making awkwardly, with trembling fingers. Even when Willie James, out of earshot of the others, commended him on his daring excursions to the brothel and admitted that he frequented the place himself from time to time, Carl said nothing and felt only shame and regret. His dream of marrying the lovely girl Rosalia, a Jewish *maydeleh* in this wilderness who would bear his children and ease his aching loneliness, seemed like an impossibility now. There was only one way he could think of to win back her heart now.

29

On a cold January morning, the steam coming off the pools of water heated in the bowels of the Earth was thicker than usual. It rolled across the hills and pathways, rising white and pure against the dark evergreens like a fluttering lace veil. Roland Longman was glad to see the steam, and his steps increased in briskness as he neared the George & Weir Bathhouse. Knowledge of the therapeutic value of the springs had spread across the states, even all the way up to New York. He was eagerly looking forward to a well-deserved soak and fingered in his pocket the silver quarter that would buy it. His earnings plus a healthy bonus for procuring a new girl for Missy's bordello had left him flush, and he aimed to enjoy himself in style.

The bathhouse was a simple wooden building painted white with dark green trim. A thin, pale-skinned fellow in a sack suit with striped suspenders took Longman's payment of two dollars at the counter and then pointed silently toward a door at the rear of the small, dark room. Longman nodded and proceeded through that door into a hallway off of which were several doorways. He was motioned into one of them by a colored attendant in a crisp, white jacket. The room was small, containing a large porcelain tub in the middle with a pipe running from it through the bottom of the back wall, and a chair upon which he folded his clothing as he undressed. The attendant wrapped him in a large, thick cotton towel and then helped him remove it at the edge of the tub. As he eased into the porcelain vessel of warm spring water, he reflected on his recent efforts. The attendant brought him a small mug of the spring water, cooled down. He sipped it; it was sweet and pure, more delicious than any water he had ever tasted. He felt the tensions easing in his back and neck muscles. As his body relaxed in the heat of the curative waters, a darkness came over his mind; yes, the same deep brooding hole that he fell into throughout his life from time to time. He pushed the darkness away yet again, refusing to fall into the black hole that yawned within. And yet the more he soaked, the dirtier he felt.

He forced himself to turn his thoughts to the success he had lately achieved. Finding a new prostitute for Nibley had been more difficult than he had expected, and the search had entailed much ginger investigation. He risked exposure and had to be on the constant lookout for anybody tailing him, even in this backwater town. Little Rock, a larger city in comparison to Hot Springs, would have been an easier location to hide in as he conducted his clandestine business. But the search in this small town was worth it, because he happened upon a beautiful flaxen-haired girl of no more than fourteen years old, caring for her three younger brothers on a tumble-down farm. They were hungry and barefoot, abandoned by their father just before their mother passed away from typhus. Clearly, they had been too poor to summon the doctor. The orphaned beauty could now make enough money to help the boys attend school, buy shoes, eat better. Both Walter Nibley and Missy had been pleased. He gloried in the memory of their glowing reaction when he brought her to them, docile and innocent. They had covered various costs he had incurred, an hourly rate that had run into almost thirty hours, plus a bonus. He now had a luxury of time to pursue his own interests, which would include getting hold of that devilish Rosalia Wolfson. His mind began to churn. He considered using a dab of chloroform in his handkerchief to render her unconscious before he made off with her. This had the added benefit of silent abduction. He would have to assure that no witnesses were nearby to point the finger at him. This was a last resort in his arsenal of kidnapping tools, as it was risky; too much could kill the girl. He rejected that option and decided upon taking her at gunpoint. Just the sight of a gun rendered anyone compliant; there would be little chance of killing her. He could almost taste the sweet revenge that he longed for once he sold her to the bordello in New Orleans. Added to that would be the reassurance that she could never bear witness to his abduction of Greta Schuler onboard the U.S.S. *Eolus.*

The attendant walked quietly over to the tub and said,

"Suh, yo' one hour is ovah. Please come wid me."

Longman rose and the delightful warm water dripped noisily off his skin and into the brimming tub. The attendant handed him the towel and then led Longman to a more public room at the end of the hall, where he could cool down with a cold water shower. The contrast made him shiver with delight and refreshed him. He realized that he had become groggy in the heated tub. The attendant followed him with his clothing into the larger shower room. Longman dried off briskly with the towel and got dressed, carefully buttoning up his trousers and straightening his suspenders. He fished in his left pocket and pulled out three pennies to tip the attendant.

Once outside, he glanced around to take stock of the other bathhouses, not nearly as well-built or fancy as the George and Weir. Some of them appeared thrown together quickly and sloppily with wide planks thatched and tarred together. They dotted the hillside surrounded by pines, blackthorns and buckeye trees. There were several small open-air thermal pools bordered by roughly hewn benches. He spotted a gathering of men, three lanky Negroes and a light-skinned Indian sporting an eagle feather in his leather headband, sitting around one of the pools and dangling their bare feet and legs in the water. Longman guessed that in this town they would not be allowed into the fancier bathhouse buildings with the white clientele. They were chatting together, animated and congenial, which piqued Longman's interest. He was always on the lookout for the goings-on about town wherever he happened to be visiting. Many a helpful comment had pointed him in the direction of folks he might be seeking or places that would serve his purpose. He sauntered over to them, stripped off his leather boots, hiked his trousers up to his knees and, much to the surprise of the group of men relaxing there, lowered himself onto the bench between the Indian and one of the Negroes, gingerly lowering his feet into the hot water. The entire group of men stared at him with widening eyes. All except the Indian, he noted, whose eyes narrowed and the thick black brows above them furrowed.

"Good morning, boys," he broke the sudden silence with as much warmth in his voice as he could muster. "I certainly do not wish to intrude upon your companionable discourse, so please continue. I will listen respectfully; make no never-mind of me."

Astonishment brimmed from every inch of their faces. No doubt they were never joined at these open-air pools by a white man, Longman smiled to himself. He caught a few suspicious looks from the colored men, but the half-breed Indian, he noticed, was guarded and passive in his expression.

The fellows sat obstinately silent, so Longman finally breached it with a question.

"So boys, what entertainment is there in the little town of Hot Springs for a visitor? I'll only be here a few more days and would like to make the most of it."

More silence. Longman exercised his tactical patience and let the proverbial penny drop. He drank in the scent of pine in the soft air. The spring water sloshed gently against the stone walls as the men shifted their legs and feet. Finally the Negro sitting closest to him, a thin older man with lips so full and thick they literally filled his face, spoke first.

"They's plenty a tipplin' rooms ta have a drink, suh."

"That is an excellent suggestion," responded Longman, "however a lonely prospect for a sole traveler. Is there some activity more……sociable-like where a crowd might gather together this coming Saturday?"

His fellow spa soakers looked down and shook their woolly heads, shrugged their bony shoulders. The Indian man continued to send sideways glances at Longman, which roused his concern. Did the fellow know something about him that he shouldn't? Suddenly another man said,

"Heah tell they's a weddin' gwine happen soon. Some Jewish folk gittin' hitched. Mebbe y'all kin go dere. Thang is, Ah don't know zactly wheah it is."

The older fellow who had spoken up first said, "Cain't be at da house of da Rabbi. You know, da place half burnt by dem crazy men riding in at night wid da torches, pract'ly set fiyah to da whole town."

Longman had heard about this incident from Walter Nibley, who made it his business to track everything going on in the community that he possibly could. The ugly incident had occurred just before Longman came to town, and he had a strange feeling that it was tied somehow to Rosalia, as it involved Jews and the house where they worshipped. Then the obvious struck him: this wedding they were talking about must be Rosalia's wedding to Carl Gersman! What better day to ruin than a bride's own? Or perhaps he would spirit her away before the wedding even took place, leaving behind a devastated groom and shattered dreams of wedded bliss for both.

"Boys, do any of you know the names of the people getting married?" he asked them. After a few moments of silence, the

Negro sitting next to him, a man with skin so dark it looked dipped in black ink, said,

"Ah don' know dey name, but ah heah tell da Hebrew wimmenfolk gwine be heah tonight at da Mitchell Bathhouse, some kine ceremony befo' da weddin'. Mah wife work dere and she tol' me. Roun' about eight o'clock."

"Is that so? Well, I do thank you all for an amiable chat, boys," Longman said, and drew his feet out of the water. He dried them off with a large kerchief from his pocket, stuck them back in his boots, and politely tipping his straw hat to them, sauntered down the pathway, grinning.

Waddite turned to look slyly at the back of the elegantly dressed stranger as he made his way down the hillside to Central Avenue. Where had he seen that fellow before? Then it came to him. He had noticed him slipping into the little Jewish café on Central Avenue. What was it called? Some foreign word. This dapper-looking white man stirred up his senses, his intuition. Some odd things like the fire and kidnapping had been happening in Hot Springs lately. There had been several lynchings in the woods as well. Waddite made a mental note to keep an eye on the Gersmans' home and the fancy gentleman as well.

He was no longer a young man, and his sinews and bones longed for the hot, sweet curative waters that rose magically up from the ground, heated by an unseen fire that no man or woman had started. Because he was part Indian, he was not allowed entrance to the bathhouse buildings, the same as the colored folks. He soaked in a small pool open to the sky with a rough bench to sit on. He would join the other Quapaws and Choctaws who congregated there, much happier to have the sky as their ceiling than an enclosed building erected by white men. Many Negroes soaked at the open pools alongside the Indian tribesmen. They were very distinct in manner and language from the white man and the Indians, but they all shared the misfortune of living outside of white society. The Negro people, no longer valuable property, were unaccepted and reviled now that the white man's war had freed them from their slave masters.

Now he firmly put aside all thoughts of the white stranger, the Gersmans, the entire town of Hot Springs, and focused on his body and the delightful spring water. Nobody knew how the water came out of the ground in a boiling state, but people told stories and myths about it. Waddite wondered if there were a drop of truth at all in any of the tales, but he doubted it. A practical thinker, he preferred to look to the ways of nature to explain the mysteries of life. But now was the time to work on the knots in his legs and back, not the knots of the puzzles of life. He put aside those thoughts and felt the sweet warmth penetrate the muscles of his legs and feet and relax them, as his darker-skinned companions were doing. Many minutes went by like this, when suddenly the face of the newly arrived Jewish girl, Rosalia, floated across his consciousness. No wonder, he smiled to himself, she is a pretty and appealing young woman. Why wouldn't his mind bring her up for the sheer pleasure of it? Except, he began to notice, this was not a vision that seemed to be luring and arousing him. Her delicate features were set in a scowl, deep-set sky blue eyes wide with fright. Her golden hair was shrouded by a rough brown net that seemed to breathe and expand around her. He felt trepidation, dread, peril lurking in the image. Then it dissolved, leaving him unsettled and alarmed. Could this be a warning that the young woman was facing danger? He shook his head to clear it, denying quietly that such a warning was possible. Yet the feeling of alarm persisted. He knew better than to ignore a powerful vision. He had absorbed his American father's practicality, but the blood of his mother's tribe ran deep within him.

Waddite rose from the tub and toweled off his feet with a rag he had packed in his leather sack. He felt soothed by the water rising deep from the bowels of Mother Earth. In this relaxed state, he renewed his determination to keep a vigilant eye out for the tiny yellow-haired woman newly arrived in town.

30

Gersman's Dry Goods store grew tinier in the distance as Rosalia hurried down the street, glancing over her shoulder. She swallowed in horror and disbelief thinking of the words that had tumbled so casually from that strange man's mouth. She had traveled so far and left much behind (both precious and intolerable, it occurred to her), and for what? She could understand enough of the stranger's English to learn that Carl, who seemed like such a decent man, a mensch, slept with evil women who sold their bodies for money. It was a sin she could hardly comprehend. Were all men like this? She began to wonder about Samuel as well. Perhaps her own father…. but no, she pushed that notion away from her mind. Isaac was devoted to her mother, hardworking and dependable. He could not possibly betray Dora that way. She hurried quickly to Gussie's house, painfully aware that she was alone and unprotected. She cast glances behind her and to the side, worried that added to everything else, Roland Longman would appear. The streets of Hot Springs were empty and silent, though, and she welcomed that hushed solitude with relief.

Gussie was washing diapers, scrubbing them hard on her metal washboard in the side garden when Rosalia arrived. She rushed over to her and tears began to stream down her face unbidden. Gussie stopped scrubbing and stared, hazel eyes widening and eyebrows arching like blackbird wings. Rosalia spoke first, struggling desperately not to sob.

"Ach! How do I say this? I just found out that Carl has been visiting the *shiksas* at a … a brothel somewhere in town. Did you even know one existed here? How can I marry him? He is filthy!"

She screamed out the last comment and stamped her foot in rage, scattering pebbles that lay on the garden path.

"Liebchen, darling, calm down. How did you discover this? Perhaps there is some mistake."

"No, no mistake!" Rosalia yelled. "A man named Horace Flesher, I think that is his name, came to the store and told us this. He is one of the men who kidnapped you, Gussie! Think of it. The judge let him go free from the jail. He came to the store and let it be known to everybody. Carl did not deny it. I am so humiliated. How can I marry him now? And yet I cannot go back to Gliewitz. I can't! But what will I be here? Still a spinster and in an even worse situation."

She began to tug at hanks of her own hair, hard enough to make her wince. Gussie dropped the diaper and washboard into the water and rushed over to stop her.

"Rosalia, please try to calm down. You must find out more about it before judging and deciding this means the end of the betrothal." She took a sterner tone. "It is time for you to grow up a little bit more. Moving to a new country, a new society, and here in the wilderness, requires being tougher than you were before in the Old Country. And that doesn't mean angrier. We will all talk to Carl and get to the bottom of this story. Perhaps some part of it is false. But I warn you, there must also be forgiveness. Are you perfect? What is the story behind you and that Mr. Longman?"

Gussie stopped and bit her lower lip, peeking sideways at Rosalia. Her words stunned Rosalia into wide-eyed silence. She was quiet for a long moment, unable to speak and suddenly dizzy. Gussie made a good argument, she realized slowly, but it was difficult to admit to her own hidden flaws, to even think about them, let alone share them with another. She had been so occupied with learning about her new surroundings, working in the store and aiding Gussie with the household, that she had managed to submerge thoughts and memories of her soiled reputation in Gliewitz and the disgusting incident on the U.S.S. *Eolus* like so much shipwreck detritus. Now, with a few words, Gussie had conjured them up again like haunting nightmares, almost unreal. Who was she to condemn Carl, when, if he knew the truth about her, he could do the same?

"Come with me into the house to sit and pray to Adonai for hope and blessings."

Gussie placed her arm firmly around Rosalia's shoulders and guided her gently into the house. They sat and prayed briefly together, reciting the *Birkhat* Kohanim, the ancient prayer of blessing others. When they were done, Rosalia covered her face with her hands and muttered,

"Forgive me, Hashem, for throwing that shovel at Carl's head."

"You did what?"

"I didn't knock him unconscious, but he'll have a lump on his temple. It was not the wisest thing to do, but I still think he deserved it."

"Then you have some making up to do with your future husband."

They busied themselves with household duties. Gussie finished the diaper wash, nursed the baby, swept the floorboards, gathered eggs in the chicken coop. Rosalia peeled potatoes and set them to boil, trimmed green beans, and plucked the hen that Carl had slaughtered for Gussie in preparation for dinner. They were thus engaged when Samuel came home from work. The sky had shifted quickly from pale light to purple darkness by then. David's whimpering cries echoed throughout the little house, and the aroma of chicken stew invaded every corner. Sam looked grim as he kissed his fingers, touched the stone *mezuzzah* on the front door jamb and walked in. At that moment Rosalia was comforting David in his crib to give Gussie a little respite from childcare, and she was making him giggle with a green carrot top that she shook in his tiny hands. She grimaced when she heard Samuel whisper to Gussie,

"Did you hear what happened at the store?"

"Yes," Gussie answer simply. "It was quite a shock for her. She was very shaken up, but we prayed and she is soothed for now. Still, there remains much to be worked out between them if this betrothal is to continue."

Samuel nodded in agreement, stroking his dark, frizzy beard with a chafed hand.

"The two of them must meet and talk. It will be difficult, but there is no other way. Carl agrees with me on this, and asked me to help him talk to her, but I will not. They need their privacy for this. You stay out of it too."

"I wouldn't think of interfering," Gussie responded briskly.

Rosalia was soothed by the baby's giggles, which became hiccoughs. At the same time she could catch a few words of Sam and Gussie's conversation floating across the room and knew they were discussing her and Carl. Sorrow and then rage welled up in her, but this time she reminded herself that she was no prize to be demanding perfection of her intended. Would he accept her knowing all of the scandals she had been caught up in, any more than she would accept him? She gave David one last kiss on his rotund tiny cheek before tucking him back in the crib and joined her future in-laws (if they were to be so) for dinner.

The next morning Rosalia awoke early feeling as glum as the shadows that slid across the walls of the parlor. She slept every night bundled in a wool blanket that Gussie had knitted and an old horsehair mattress, jammed into a corner of the room near the hearth. She arose, shivering as she changed quickly into her wash dress and brown work shoes, throwing a thick shawl around her shoulder to ward off the morning chill. She hurried outside to pump water from the well behind the garden. The water, pure and clean as a prayer, came gushing out into one bucket, then the other, and she lugged them back inside the Gersmans' cabin to start the morning wash-up and breakfast.

Gussie was now up and nursing David in a chair by the hearth. Rosalia tried to hide her sad expression, but could see that Gussie was practically looking into her as if she were the well and at the bottom was not water but tears.

"Good morning," Rosalia mumbled. "I will get you and Samuel breakfast, and then I must go help him at the store."

"Please try to cheer yourself a little today," pleaded Gussie. "Things seem very bad, true, but I have a strong feeling that you and Carl were meant to be together." Pause. "Despite the ugliness of yesterday."

Rosalia shrugged, hopelessness grabbing at her throat like a pair of choking hands. After breakfast, she and Samuel headed out together. As the store came into view, Rosalia cringed at the prospect of seeing Carl there. Samuel seemed to sense her thoughts.

"My brother will be working on his house today and doing some planting, too."

Rosalia nodded numbly, grateful to know this. They opened the store to business and Rosalia took her place behind the counter while Samuel organized inventory and loaded shelves with merchandise. The first customer of the day entered soon after, a tall, lean woman with stringy blonde hair, sharp of eye and cheekbones, a turned-up nose, almost the same age as she was. She had three children in tow behind her like a string of laundry.

"Hello, hello, who the heck is this? Some tiny thing the wind blew in?"

Rosalia found herself unable to respond. Who was she, anyway? Not yet related to the store owner. Engaged to the store owner's brother, but unable to admit it at this moment. She was merely a new employee at this time, nothing more. Suddenly Samuel popped his head out from the storeroom.

"Greetings, Beulah! We haven't seen you in a long time. Where have you been? Rosalia, this is our neighbor Beulah Lee Howerton. Beulah, this Rosalia, soon to be my sister-in-law. She is helping out at the store. Just got into town not long ago."

"So very nice ta meetcha. Ah've been sick with the galloping pneumonia, in bed for a long tahm. Henry been takin' care of me when he can. And the children too. Finally got the doctor ovah to see me. But now Ah'm out n' about, practically all recovered."

"Oy, so sorry to hear this. You should have sent Silvie to our house to fetch Gussie. She can make a chicken soup that will cure anything."

"With a newborn babe in ahms? Ah would nevah! We made do. Still, it is awful nice to be up again."

Beulah's oldest, a blue-eyed girl with freckles that reminded Rosalia of Annaleya, ran up to the counter and shoved something in front of Rosalia's face with both her hands outstretched.

"What is this?" Rosalia peered at what appeared to be a small beige and brown doll-like figure with arms splayed.

"It's my dolly! Cornelia! Ma helped me make her!"

"Stop that shoutin' raht now, Eugenia, or Ah will take Cornelia plum away."

"May I hold your doll?" asked Rosalia. She had loved dolls as a child, although her parents didn't have the wherewithal to buy her one. They saw the wealthy German children hugging their porcelain beauties with life-like tresses in town, and that's all she knew of dolls.

Eugenia nodded, so Rosalia carefully plucked the doll from the cradle of her palms. This figurine was not elegant like the ones back in Gliewitz. It was crinkly and made of layers of some kind of leaf material, with frizzy light brown hair tucked under a bonnet of the same kind of leaf. There were no facial details.

"This is a corn husk doll. The hair is cornsilk from the tassles. All the rest is corn husk leaves. If you lahk, Ah can teach you ta make 'em foah your daughters, when you get 'em."

Rosalia reddened, self-conscious of her spinsterhood and childless state at the ripe age of twenty-one. There was something about that doll, its blank countenance, its fragile dun skirt and apron, arms helplessly akimbo. She felt that she could almost crawl inside it.

"Yes, that is so nice your offer. I will be happy to learn this."

"Fine. When you have a li'l moment, come on bah mah house. We don't live too fah from Samuel and Gussie. Jest walk on ovah."

Rosalia smiled and handed the corn husk doll back to Eugenia. She realized with a start that this was the first non-Jewish woman in America that she had spoken with who was not a customer of the dry goods store. To her surprise, her spirits were considerably lifted, and she spent the rest of the day waiting on customers in a lighter mood than she could have predicted.

Several days passed during which Samuel and Carl were extremely busy at the store and worked late into the evenings. Carl couldn't help but notice that Rosalia left the store when he entered and avoided him when he called upon her at his brother's house. He finally took off a week to work on his cabin with Benjamin. Despite his misgivings about the future of his life with Rosalia, he urged himself on to complete what he had started. They applied the finishing touches to windows and doors. Benjamin sanded and polished the chest of drawers that Carl had built for Rosalia. Together they constructed a sturdy, wind-protected double outhouse, luxurious to the average resident. In exchange, Benjamin gratefully accepted cuts of beef, rabbit meat and whole hens skinned, plucked and ready for roasting. In each instance, Carl had erred in the painstaking process of kosher butchering, and so they had become treyf, inedible for the Jewish consumers, but they were still fresh and untainted and fine for the goyim. Carl paid him a dollar or two at the end of the day in addition when he was able to.

On the morning of Benjamin's final day of work, Carl stepped back to admire their handiwork. The cabin looked like a beacon of light to him with the morning sun glinting in the windows. He knew that over time it would weather and grey as the elements worked on the roof, siding and porch, but at this moment it was a glorious sight to behold. He hoped it would help him win Rosalia back and placate her ire enough to bring her to the chuppah to wed him. As the minutes marched by, sparrows and wrens chirping and tittering in the tangled tops of the silent pines, the heady scent of their needles underfoot tingling in his nostrils, he wondered where Benjamin was. The young fellow was rarely late and never showed up this late in the day. There was little left to do besides some touchup work, small adjustments here and there, some sanding.

At last he heard the shuffling of boots through the underbrush, and Benjamin's dark, smooth face appeared in the distance. To Carl's surprise, several other faces, white ones, were bobbing behind him. Immediately he recognized his former carpentry assistants and brothel buddies. He felt a pressure in his chest and anger boiled in his gut.

"Benjamin!" he called out as they approached. "Why are you bringing those scallywags here?"

Benjamin didn't reply but hung his head. Then Carl realized that his arms were tight behind his back. He felt the hair rise on the back of his neck. Something looked wrong.

"Benjamin!" he called again, although he needn't have because the four men were almost in front of him. Now he could see that Benjamin's arms were unmoving, clearly tied behind him, and Horace was holding a pistol at his back.

"Gimme a good reason not ta put a slug in this heah niggah's back!" shouted Horace, his face almost purple with rage, eyebrows scrunched into a vee. "You are *payin'* him ta work? You should be payin' us, not him. This darkie belongs back in the cotton fields, workin' for Massa. They's all kahnda sharecroppin' foah him ta do. Thas how the dahkies work foah free, jest lahk befoah the wah. But no, you givin' him a actual job?"

"Dat's right," mumbled Geoffrey.

And from Billy, "Shore 'nuf."

"Friends, put down the gun," pleaded Carl, so frightened he could hardly get the words out of his mouth. "First, I pay Benjamin mostly in meat, not money, as I haven't much to spare. And second thing, there are no more slaves now. You know that. The war is finished, and the *shvartzes* do not work for free anymore."

"Oh, is that right, Jew-boy?" Horace sneered. "Well, well. Ya seem ta know more about this here nation than we do. But something you don't know, we whites will nevah let the darkies go free. No sir. We'll kill 'em all first. And I mean ta start with this one." He brandished his .38 caliber pistol like a hidden treasure revealed and pointed it at Benjamin's head. Carl could see the perspiration dripping from the poor man's temples and upper lip.

Billy pulled a looped rope from the pack he had slung over one shoulder. "It's hangin' time," he grinned, and ran toward Carl. "You first, then the niggah."

Carl waited until Billy was almost upon him and then slid his hunting rifle out from under a canvas tarpaulin at his feet. He always kept it near him in case the grizzly bear with cubs should emerge from the forest and come after him. Billy was suddenly looking down the double barrel.

"We make the deal," Carl called to Horace, keeping his eyes on Billy. "You untie Benjamin and don't hurt him. Then I don't shoot Billy. We have the deal?"

Horace stared wildly at Carl and Billy, his right hand wagging the pistol back and forth. After a moment of silence, he said, "Goddammit, Carl, Ah can't stand ya! Ya see, men? This is why Ah hate the Jews jest as much as the darkies. They below us, but clever lahk a fox." He lowered his weapon and quickly untied Benjamin's wrists. Benjamin immediately ran for the woods and disappeared. Carl kept the rifle pointed at Billy, who was shaking like the mouse he'd cornered just this morning in the new outhouse.

"No lynching today, fellows. Y'all go and take your rope and gun, put them away. And let Benjamin be. He has a wife and child. And he is a good man, no matter his color."

Carl lowered his rifle slowly, keeping his eyes on Billy, a large, muscular man who could easily overpower him. He reminded him of a tiger, bright green eyes slightly tilted in a wide face.

An uncomfortable silence hung over the men like a pall of invisible smoke. Horace finally shuffled his feet awkwardly, bringing Carl's attention to his boots. Those unique red leather boots that he always wore, that singled him out as one of the cloaked men who set the Rabbi's house on fire and kidnapped Gussie and David. There they were again. He had to fight the urge to swing his rifle upward again and take deadly aim at him. As if sensing Carl's impulse, the three interlopers hurried off back on the path through the verdant pines and black gums draped in orange and gold autumn leaves, muttering and swearing and taking turns dragging on a flask. Carl shook his head with relief. They didn't know what a terrible shot he was.

Winter was drawing near, and the townspeople were stocking up on supplies in anticipation of bad weather. Samuel was investigating the import of cocoa powder and chocolate, a persistent request from Rosalia. Carl was honing the butchering skills that he had learned in Oppein on animals that hunters brought to him. He wouldn't prepare them if they had been shot with bullets or arrows, so the animals, generally small ones, were brought alive to be put to death kosher-style with a quick slice of an exquisitely sharpened butcher knife. He had set up a fenced yard and stretched a mesh screen over a pit behind Sam's store to skin the carcasses, drain the meat, and finally slice and wrap it in scraps of clean cloth.

Gussie was laying in apple preserves and blackberry jams. Rosalia refused to go to the store, moping around the house instead. Her moods swung from irate to depressed to fearful, and she dreaded seeing Carl again. However, underneath the emotional turmoil lay an awareness in her that she had to bare all, becoming as vulnerable to him as he now was to her. The secrets in their lives must be laid out like roots dug up from the dark earth and cleaned off. She knew that, and yet couldn't quite imagine how such a discussion could possibly happen.

A raw, damp wind swept through the town, woolen overcoats were drawn up to the ears and chin, and dark clouds flowed across the sky. By the look of it, a huge nor'easter was blowing through, so Gersman's Dry Goods closed after opening only briefly on Thursday morning. Samuel had used the dray that morning to get to the store. Now he and Carl rode home in it, transporting some kitchen supplies that he knew Gussie would want, feed for the horse, and a new shovel that had come in from the East Coast. Samuel led the mare into the barn and shut her in with plenty of water in her trough and feed for the day. Then the two brothers walked into the house together, surprising Gussie and Rosalia, who were both knitting. The long steel needles continued clicking along as the women manipulated them expertly. The two women were wrapped in warm blankets to ward off the chill in the house. David, also bundled up, cried out gaily when he spotted his father. Rosalia focused on her stitches, keeping her head down and shoulders bent over. The wind was howling now as it whipped past the house. The sound of it echoed in every bone of her body. Gussie spoke first.

"Done for the day early? I should have known. It's looking stormy outside. Nobody's going to shop today. We will be fixing some knishes and kasha in a little while for a midday meal. I'm going to teach Rosalia how to make hot sassafras tea like the gentile ladies do here. It will warm us all up."

Rain began to patter on the rooftop. Samuel and Carl piled kindling and sturdy oak logs that were stacked in the corner into the hearth. Soon a small fire was dancing with flames that infused the room with welcome heat. As they all warmed up, Carl glanced timidly at Rosalia every now and then. Gussie said firmly,

"The two of you need to talk. Rosalia has told me many things these past few days, and it's time that all of this comes out on the table."

Rosalia smiled weakly and responded,

"Yes, I agree. But I must say what I have to say privately to Carl."

"Then go into the bedroom and close the door."

Samuel shook his head.

"This is not proper. Unmarried man and woman alone together in the bedroom. No."

"Yes," insisted Gussie. "You know your brother and I know Rosalia well enough. They need to talk privately, and that is the only place. I would suggest the garden on a pleasant day, but today is anything but that. Only a trout would want to be outside today. Besides, nobody will know but us. And Hashem, who sees into all hearts."

As if to confirm Gussie's words, the pattering rain transformed into a noisy cloudburst. Samuel shrugged his shoulders, which Gussie knew meant he conceded the argument. They watched as Rosalia and Carl stood up and closed themselves together in Samuel and Gussie's bedroom.

31

Rosalia and Carl stood on opposite sides of the bed, both gazing down at the stitched sunflower and green vine quilt that covered it. After a considerable amount of silence textured with the pounding of rain on the roof, Carl spoke first to Rosalia's relief.

"What Horace Fletcher said is true. And I am ashamed. I am not worthy of you. But I have not gone there for a long time now, since I heard that you were coming here to marry me. I was very lonely. Still, I know it was wrong. Can you find a way to forgive me? Can you still marry me? I will be the best and most loyal husband that any man can be, and the best father. I will protect you more than the wild bear protects her cubs. I will provide for you and our kinder, our children, always. That I promise you."

Rosalia had to fight her fury. Here he stood confirming the accusation of going to brothels. What kind of a person was this man? Then Gussie's words drifted into her mind, unwanted and painful. What kind of a person was she? There was an answer, hidden like the half matzoh cracker on Pesach that the children of each family sought for after the ceremonial meal, and like the cracker, it became stunningly apparent. She was an innocent, still pure, and he was not. She had been ambushed, attacked, and betrayed; he had not. She hadn't sought the violations that a boy and a man inflicted upon her. He had deliberately and repeatedly pursued the sexual pleasures illicitly that belonged only in the matrimonial bed. The gall rose in her throat. She watched Carl furl and unfurl his fingers, in and out of his palms. Heard his breath, hard and ragged. She sucked in her breath, then let it out slowly. She blinked away tears, wondering if this was really happening. The two of them, alone together in a bedroom, confiding like a married couple, but so far from it. She took another breath for bravery and answered him,

"You are not worthy of me? That is exactly what I thought when I heard that horrible man's words come out of his mouth about you. I could not imagine ever marrying you or even speaking to you again."

Carl hung his head. He looked like a defeated man. Not even a man, a boy. His broad shoulders and stocky torso belied a weaker, softer person inside. She continued,

"Carl, there are things about you that I know now, ugly things I do not like. But at the same time, there are things about me that you do not know."

He stared at her in astonishment.

"You?" he asked incredulously. "You are an angel, tiny and beautiful. A good woman, more rare and precious than a ruby, like the Torah says."

Rosalia straightened her spine, stood as tall as she could.

"That is true, I am a good woman, but I have been violated in certain ways."

He nodded mutely. She could see gratitude exuding from his soft eyes. He did not know what was coming. She was certain that he couldn't imagine what she was going to tell him about herself. She motioned for them to sit on either side of the bed, as she felt a little silly standing. An unexpected thrill lit through her body as they sat together on a marital bed, even though the entire breadth of the horsehair mattress was between them. She could sense that Carl was experiencing something similar. His eyes were now brighter than a moment before, his face full of longing for her. She opened her mouth to speak just as the room flashed white with lightning and thunder cracked overhead. They paused to listen as the roar faded.

"That man, Roland Longman. I met him on the ship taking us across the ocean. He was very charming, very polished and gentlemanly. We spoke a few times. Then he lured me to his room and attacked me. Yes, I was touched by a stranger, a man not related to me. I fought back and got away from him, but not before he tore my dress. I will show you where although I have since mended it the best I could. And he had another woman in the room, tied up like a barnyard animal about to be butchered. I stabbed him with my hatpin and escaped before he could do what he intended. I ran for help, but when the crew came to his room, the woman was gone. I fear that I caused her death. He must have thrown her overboard somehow, into the water. Still I see her in my nightmares, drowning. I do not sleep easily now."

She could feel the tears welling into her eyes. Carl was staring at her, his eyes even wider than before. She allowed him to take in this story and the silence between them was filled with rain popping on the roof, intermittent lightning flashes and explosive thunder. He finally cleared his throat and responded,

"Rosalia, my dear wife-to-be," he began in a tender tone. She did not allow the hope rising in her breast to take flight, because all was not yet revealed. "Mr. Longman is an evil man and is employed by the owners of the brothel. To tell you what I know, I must damn myself even more. But you deserve to be relieved of your guilt. The woman you saw tied up in his ship cabin, she was not drowned at sea. She was surely too valuable to him for such a fate. He took her to a brothel in New Orleans, I am sure. Somehow he smuggled her off the ship. She is alive, although not living a good life."

Rosalia covered her gaping mouth with a delicate hand. "How do you know this?"

Carl winced and his cheeks flushed red. "I saw him at the brothel several weeks ago, just before you came to town. He related this story to the owner while I was there, listening. He also mentioned another lady who attacked him out of jealousy."

"That was me. But I felt no jealousy. That was an outright lie. Well, this means that you visited the brothel recently, and have been lying to me," Rosalia sputtered at him. "How can I trust you? You are a liar!"

"I must ask you for forgiveness. That place will never see me again, whether you have me for a husband or not. I am ashamed. But I know that we were meant to be together. Here we are, miles from our parents and grandparents, thousands of miles away in fact. We are in a new country with more freedom for the Jews than ever in the Old Country. Even with those crazy hoodlums harassing us, it is still better. I own land. Imagine! Our children will be allowed to study for any profession they want. We can move to a big city, even New York, if we want to. All of this is denied us in Germany."

"I realize that we are both in a new land that offers more freedom, but also it seems, more danger too," Rosalia countered. "And I have more to tell you. This is even harder to say, but I must."

She paused, wondering if she had gone insane to be telling him. This could spell the end of her life with Carl. But she knew that she couldn't enter into a marriage with him and continue to hide the ugly secret she harbored. It dragged at her soul like a thick rusted anchor.

"When I was younger, only just thirteen, my cousin and his friend grabbed me in the barn and…." She stopped abruptly, overcome with the pain and humiliation that memory brought her.

"Oy, did they violate you?" Carl asked, banging his open palms on his knees and rocking on the edge of the bed.

"No, now I realize and know a little more, they did not rape me. But they, they…. touched me. Between the legs. My father came into the barn and scared them off before they could finish with me. But then they spread the rumor that they had succeeded in violating me. I do not know why a relative would want to spoil my chances for marriage in Gliewitz, but he did. People believed them, and I could say nothing about it without humiliating myself. That is why I have come all these many miles here to marry you. No self-respecting Jewish man in Gliewitz would have me for a wife."

"Well, well," Carl breathed almost to himself. "So that is why the *sheyna maydeleh* has traveled so far. I thought I was just lucky, but I should have suspected something."

His words pierced into her heart. But she bravely continued.

"So you see, Carl, we must forgive each other if we are to exchange vows under the chuppah. I was a helpless child when this happened. You are a grown man, and what you did was far worse."

Carl nodded and looked out the window at the blackness that the storm had brought. Rosalia pulled her hatpin in and out of her bonnet with shaky fingers, studying every twitch and line in his face, every muscle movement in his husky neck and arms.

"This cousin, he must have been in love with you and knew he could never have you. What he did was very wrong. You had no guilt there, either. You were just a little girl. There is nothing to forgive here. Your secrets are nothing like mine which show my weakness of character. Your beauty attracts trouble wherever you go. But that trouble will end when we marry." He peered at her nervously and added, "If you do still want to marry me."

Rosalia smiled and nodded at him, slipping the hatpin firmly into the threads of the bonnet and leaving it there. The storm had subsided, the crackle and rolling roar of thunder more distant now. They smiled at each other, rose awkwardly from the opposite sides of Sam and Gussie's bed and returned to the parlor. Samuel and Gussie were just arranging generous slices of apple strudel for dessert. Rosalia and Carl sat across from each other at the table and dug in heartily, and Sam and Gussie exchanged relieved glances. Rosalia caught Gussie's eye and gave her a little smile, which Gussie returned. As the torrent of rain turned to showers, the four of them discussed Carl and Rosalia's upcoming wedding. Gussie exclaimed,

"Rosalia must have a *mikvah* before the wedding. It will take place at the Mitchell Bathhouse, as they all do."

"Oy, Gussie," Rosalia protested, "won't that water be too hot? I see it steaming as it rises from the earth when I pass by. It will burn me."

Samuel and Carl both laughed. Samuel explained,

"You can soak in a spa without danger. The water is piped in and cooled to a comfortable temperature. The Rabbi approved the water for a mikvah, as it fulfills all the requirements of Jewish law. And you will have a lot of company because many of the married women here love to accompany the bride-to-be in the *mikvah* ritual."

"Samuel will order from New York a very nice fabric to make the wedding dress and veil."

Rosalia immediately thought of her well-tailored blue silk traveling frock, a hand-me-down from Great Aunt Eva, which would have been perfect for the wedding except that now it was tainted with both a mended seam and the ugly memory of Roland Longman ripping it down the front. She was grateful for her generous and loving future in-laws and their generous offer to help her make a wedding gown.

The rest of that week was stormy and windy, heralding in the winter ahead. Carl applied himself to the painstaking task of perfecting the exact art of kosher butchering. Rabbi Schecter oversaw the slaughtering, cleaning and cutting of the hens, partridges, and rabbits that the townspeople brought to Carl. He wanted to start with smaller animals, but after several days of this was ready to move on to a deer or large sections of beef that hunters brought to him. The word spread quickly among the Jews of Hot Springs that a bona fide kosher butcher with blessings from the Rabbi was available. Many of them braved the weather and paid a visit to the rear entrance of Gersman's Dry Goods, where Carl had set up a separate counter and scale. Frequently a gentile would come to ask him for pork loin or cutlets, which he had to refuse since the Jewish laws forbade the eating of pigs. Some of them left disgruntled, and others were simply bemused, having never heard such a thing.

"Well, now they know," Carl called to Samuel one morning from his counter to Samuel's in front. The two areas were only divided by a partial wall lined with shelves laden to the ceiling with inventory. That made it easy for them to banter, discuss or argue good-naturedly all day. Carl had been inundated with customers all that blustery morning, and finally there was a lull.

"Sam, I must find an engagement ring to give to Rosalia and decide on a wedding date with her. But I don't know where I would find such a piece of jewelry that would be worthy of her in this little town. Maybe in New Orleans or New York City I could find a solid gold ring set with a pearl or even a diamond. And even if I found one, how could I pay for it? In kosher meat? I have very little money saved yet."

"That is true. You will have a hard time finding real jewelry here, and it will take quite a lot of time for you to travel to those cities and select one, not to mention the expense. I'll talk to a blacksmith friend of mine, Chester Williams."

"How can he help me with a ring for Rosalia?"

"He can make you a 'prairie ring'. It's just a metal nail bent into a circle to put on the finger, and it substitutes for a real ring until you can get one. Men travelling west give them to their women out on the prairies."

"Well, my bride deserves better than that, but for now I will go to this Mr. Williams myself and ask him for one. Maybe he will trade me a ring for a cutlet."

Samuel burst out laughing. "Maybe he will! But the cutlet is worth more."

"Not to me."

Both brothers strolled over to Chester Williams' smithy after they closed the store for the day. The old fellow had extinguished the large forge and was just about to smother the smaller one when they stepped in. Carl tipped his straw hat and handed the blacksmith a bundle, which he refused.

"My hands are dirty from the day's work, so whatever that is, set it over there. What do you two Hebrews want?"

"For you there is a delicious cut of beef, fresh from today's butchering. In exchange, I would like a prairie ring for my betrothed so that I may set a date with her formally for the wedding."

"Oh! Lucky man, are you? And will you be marrying a colored girl? I hear tell y'all let 'em in your store, so why not get hitched to one?"

Carl glared at him, and Samuel made a low, waving gesture with his hands to calm his brother down.

"No, sir. I will marry a beautiful Jewish girl and you are invited to the wedding ceremony and festivities if you will do this one thing for me."

Chester grinned, showing a hint of his scraggly brown teeth, reached into a small wooden box and drew out a long, dull metal nail with a square head. He cranked the fan to blow the forge fire back to life and dropped the nail onto the anvil. When the nail was glowing red, he used a pair of tongs to bend it into a circle, the square head resting on the end of the nail. It looked quite large for fingers as tiny as Rosalia's, Carl thought, so he asked for a smaller one. Chester obliged with a shorter nail, and soon Carl was on his way home with the dull, curious prairie ring for Rosalia. He decided to propose to her formally in front of his family and present the ring as a substitute until he could purchase a more elegant one later.

The following evening, at Samuel and Gussie's dinner table, Carl presented Rosalia with the prairie ring and explained its purpose as a temporary stand-in. Rosalia blushed and stammered as she accepted the leaden ring, the nail curled around itself like a coiled snake. She placed it on the finger to the left of her left middle finger, where she had seen her own mother wearing her simple gold wedding band. December was almost at an end, and they all agreed that January of 1867 would be a fine time for a wedding celebration. The blessed event would cheer the Jewish community in the midst of bleak winter.

32

The wedding was only a few days away, on the second to last Saturday in January 1867. Rosalia and Carl had written their respective parents and advised them of the date even though none of them could possibly make such a long and costly journey.

In Sam and Gussie's bedroom, Rosalia carefully fingered the lace edging of the cloud-white wedding gown, slipping it over her head and fluffing it out. Carl had saved money to buy the fine satin fabric that Samuel ordered from New York and had also included elegant silk-wrapped buttons and fine silk thread for bobbin lace at the collar and sleeve cuffs. Rosalia and Gussie had tailored laboriously to design a wedding gown and make it fit perfectly. Their heads bent over the gleaming material day after day, yellow gold abutting raven black. Samuel would walk by clucking like a hen just to get a rise from them, but even his juvenile antics weren't strident enough to break their concentration.

"Try it on now," said Gussie, a big smile lighting her face. "Let's see how it drapes on your tiny figure."

Rosalia slipped the smooth silk gown over her head, then twirled around so that it swung open at the hem. She gazed at herself in Gussie's wood-framed full-length mirror. Gussie's full lips parted in a broad smile, and she exclaimed,

"This is magnificent, Rosela, just perfect, or almost. I still have another twenty inches of lace to sew onto the bodice. And we must make sure that the bustle fits properly under the skirts."

Members of the congregation were making other preparations for the nuptials as well. The most important one, however was the *mikvah*. Rosalia had never taken the ritual bath, but she had heard of them from her mother. The bride must be submersed in fresh, flowing water the night before the wedding. Some of the more pious women took a *mikvah* after their menstrual cycles ceased every month, and a man could take a *mikvah* a week or so before the wedding if he so desired. It was a purifying ritual and required complete nudity, no jewelry, not even a braid or knot in the hair, to ensure that every millimeter of the human body was touched by water.

Rabbi Schecter had arranged for Rosalia's *mikvah* at the Mitchell Bathhouse the evening before she was to be wed, a typical tradition. Several women of the congregation volunteered to stand watch and make sure that no men entered the area, as proscribed by Jewish law. As preparations developed and friends of the Gersmans pitched in, it began to dawn on Rosalia how strongly this wedding ceremony would solidify and legitimize her standing in Hot Springs. She would no longer be an émigré from another country, alone and at odds, fearing her past reputation. She would be a wife and eventually a mother, and hopefully, find a way to be a teacher, a dream that had grown in her heart the longer she lived her and saw how poorly educated many of the children were, especially the girls. Her thoughts were whirling so quickly in anticipation of what was to come, and what she could imagine for her life, that at moments she would clench her teeth. At other times she would hum an old folk tune that her father sang to her when she was a young child, 'Chad Gadya'. *My father bought a kid, then came the cat and ate the kid, then came the dog and bit the cat, then came the stick and beat the dog, then came the fire and burned the stick.* The family sang it at Pesach seder, although nobody knew what it had to do with the enslaved Jews of ancient Egypt being set free by Moses. Sometimes she would sink her face into the rough, blank face of her corn husk doll, relieved to be marrying a man from whom she had no secrets or fears to hide.

On the night of the *mikvah*, Rosalia and Gussie gathered up their cotton drying cloths and lanterns. Rosalia gingerly placed her pistol in the bottom of the bag. Since learning how to use it, she took it with her whenever she went to town or to Gersman's Dry Goods, always looking over her shoulder for the familiar, dreaded face of Roland Longman. Then she removed the gun and replaced it with her corn husk doll.

"I prefer a gun to a doll for protection," she whispered to the ragged piece of corn fluff styled into the likeness of a person. "But I must not break Hashem's commandments, so you will come with me to the *mikvah* instead of an instrument of death. Besides, what can happen there? I will be with four other ladies, and I know that Hashem will watch over me."

While they got ready to leave for the bathhouse, Rosalia and Gussie could hear the chatter of women outside waiting for them. Rosa Meyer greeted Rosalia immediately with a tender hug when they finally left the house. Three other women, Talia, Julia and Naomi, whom Rosalia knew only from Shabbos services, also accompanied them. She thought of her dearest friend in Germany, Annaleya, and it shocked her to think how long it had been since they had seen each other. How she longed for Annaleya to be here now, and her mother and sister. The pain of her loss put a damper on her joyful mood, and she began to feel sullen. Couldn't she have stayed in Gliewitz and lived as a spinster? At least then everything would be familiar, with her family and friends close by. Ach, it was too late for that regret now. She strolled with a clutch of women on the city streets to the bath-house in the dark lit by lanterns casting bobbing and shifting shadows. She forced herself to put aside the thoughts of the past and be grateful that she was marrying a man whom she could truly love.

Rosa and Gussie stayed in the *mikvah* room with Rosalia. The three other women remained outside in the dim hallway with their lanterns stationed on chairs to assure that no men approached.

In the *mikvah* room, Rosalia shyly removed her shawl and slipped her cotton work dress slowly over her head. Gussie took the articles of clothing as they came off, one by one, placing them in a neatly folded pile in a tow sack. When Rosalia was finally naked, Rosa and Gussie searched for rings, bracelets, necklaces, earrings, ribbons, anything that could be removed from her now-quivering petite body. She had none of those items on her, so Gussie took a small wooden comb out of her dress pocket and combed through Rosalia's blonde tresses to ensure there were no knots or snarls and every hair could then be soaked. Rosalia tried to stand still, but quickly became impatient and shifted her weight from one foot to another. She felt embarrassed that the women could behold her nude body this way and was glad for the darkness of the room punctuated only by shafts of soft, flickering light from the three lanterns. It occurred to her that this ritual was not only a purification but also a maturing experience for her. After all, very soon, her husband Carl would be allowed to gaze upon her bare body just this way. That would be far more mortifying, although she was keenly aware that her own lust, held in abeyance for so many years, would yearn for him to look and touch.

Rosalia was now ready to submerge in the *mikvah*. For the first time she was going to enjoy the wondrous waters she had heard so much about since coming to Hot Springs. Now her feet were on the second step down and she was ankle-deep. The warmth of the water seeped into her cold toes and made her smile. Third step and she was knee-deep. The last step down was the bottom of the pool, and she slowly and deliciously slid to her neck into the enveloping heat. Rosa said to her from her perch at the edge of the pool,

"Say a prayer for your new life with a husband and children to come and bless your future."

The words to the morning prayer came to Rosalia's mind. Would Hashem object if she said it at the wrong time of day?

"Modah ani l'fnecha…." She murmured, the Hebrew rolling off her lips easily after so many years of recital at dawn. *I am thankful to you, Lord of the Universe.* It was the right prayer because she was filled with gratitude at this moment. She was glad to be alive after having come so close to suffering the fate of the red-haired woman on the ship. At the thought of her, she began to pray fervently for the poor woman, hoping that she had not been killed and could somehow be rescued and safe. But deep in her heart she dreaded the horrible, more likely outcome.

Rosa said, "Dunk down all the way, *maydeleh*. Soon you will be a married woman."

Rosalia held her breath and thrust her face and head down into the water. It was so warm and comforting that she welcomed it and felt like she belonged underwater with the stone walls surrounding her. She prayed underwater in thought alone, asking Hashem to protect her from evil. Somehow Roland Longman's visage appeared in her mind. Gussie's hands were above her, pressing strands of her hair down into the water. Rosalia came back up, drawing in a breath and shaking the water out of her eyes and off her face.

"Mazel tov!" Gussie and Rosa crowed in unison.

"You are now purified and ready for marriage," Gussie beamed. "Whatever sins and wrongdoings you have committed, they are cleansed. Did Carl take a *mikvah*?"

Rosalia nodded as she climbed out of the pool, a tiny, naked goddess swaddled in drops of water that rolled down from her blonde wavy tresses to her feet. "Last week. He felt the necessity, you know."

Everybody in the community knew of Carl's visits to the brothel in the woods; it had become juicy fodder for gossip.

And gossip spread like wind-blown dandelion seeds in Hot Springs. However painful and humiliating this was for Rosalia, she kept her outrage in check.

As Rosalia dressed, the three women chatted about the preparations for the wedding the next day. She was borrowing Gussie's dress boots even though they were slightly too large, as her only pair had been badly scuffed in her sojourn to America. The Rabbi's front parlor was sparkling clean, although the wreckage of the fire left some searing and smoke damage to the walls and windows. Jewish women throughout the town had been cooking all day today for the feast the next day. They were making knishes, dough briming with ground beef, onions and potatoes, and the aroma infused the neighborhoods. Mountains of crisp mandelbrot cookies, many braided challah loaves, kreplach packed with sauerkraut and roast chicken were being prepared. The men oversaw the wine and beer for celebration and toasting. Carl had the rugged and inelegant prairie ring polished and ready to bestow upon her. Rosalia smiled at the thought of it.

"Hopefully Carl will remember to put my beautiful wedding ring in his dress trousers pocket tomorrow."

"I'll have Samuel remind him. A ring of the wild west you will receive."

Rosalia hadn't seen Carl for the past seven days, as ordained by Jewish law. He was carefully avoiding his brother's house, taking a circuitous route to work through the buckeyes on an old deer path to town. She wasn't going into Gersman's Dry Goods and remained at home. This was a time to enjoy being a single individual before the bride and groom would be a wedded couple for life. She realized that this week of separation would have been a lonelier time for her back in Gliewitz before she left her parents' home. After the long, solitary and treacherous journey she had undertaken to get to America, a week without seeing Carl was a simple thing. She had needed the time to work on the wedding dress and helped Gussie organize the feast. At home in Gliewitz, her parents would have provided the entire feast with contributions from aunts, uncles and cousins, but this was not Gliewitz. Here on the edge of wilderness, with little extended family, every soul pitched in for one another, family or not, and especially for a blessed occasion like a wedding.

Gussie was helping Rosalia dress when they heard loud voices echoing down the hall. Rosa, who stood guard at the entrance to the pool, peered down the empty hallway. The noise became louder, a commotion of voices, female and male. The three women glanced at each other in stunned surprise. Then there was silence. Relief flooded through Rosalia like a gentle wave. A man's presence was forbidden and could corrupt the holiness of the ritual bath. Somebody must have stumbled upon the women guarding outside and spoke with them. She and Gussie were tying their bonnets under their chins. Rosalia grabbed her linen bag and they walked down the hallway to join Talia, Julia and Naomi.

"A man wanted to come in," Talia exclaimed excitedly. "We had to explain to him about the bride's *mikvah* and then we sent him away."

They headed in a disorderly bunch down the hillside path toward the street. Rosalia allowed the cool night air to refresh her after the hot soak and tilted her head toward the sky. The next thing she knew, a heavy, firm arm wrapped around her waist and pulled her away from her friends. A broad hand clamped tightly over her mouth. She tried to whirl around and struggle out of the grip to no avail. Whoever was behind her had her securely pinned against him. The other five women whirled around and found themselves facing the barrel of a .22 revolver gleaming in the waxing moonlight. Behind the revolver Rosalia squirmed with her eyes wide and alarmed. She stared helplessly back at them, moaning under the pressure of the hand across her waist.

"Evenin', ladies," the man spoke pleasantly. Rosalia immediately recognized Roland Longman's voice. "Do as I say and she won't get hurt and neither will you. Turn around. I want to see your backsides only. If I see a face, I will shoot it."

They obeyed, crying and sobbing now. Rosalia stiffened with outrage, providing as much resistance as she could, but in vain. Longman dragged her quickly into the black tangle of forest.

33

The moon was almost full, just a sliver off the top side missing, and seemed to be closer to the Earth than usual. It bathed in glimmering light the treetops, roofs and chimney flues of Hot Springs. Carl gazed out the front window at the wonderful sight of it, marveling how like daytime it seemed and contemplating his impending wedding the next day. He still needed to wipe down his only pair of decent shoes and rub oil into them for luster. He had traded blacksmith Chester Williams a haunch of venison for them. He laid out his wedding clothes on a chair: black button trousers, a blue and white ascot that matched his prayer shawl, warm vest, and the required black fur top hat. His father had bestowed the prayer shawl upon him at his Bar Mitzvah, and he had brought it with him to the New World. His thoughts turned to Rosalia, and he was immediately aroused by the prospect of spending the night with her after they married. He laughed joyfully out loud. They would share a solid companionship that would ease their solitary lives. They both carried troubling secrets and shared them with each other, which had imbued their friendship with an intimacy he never imagined could exist between two people. Even though they had only had one genuine conversation from the depth of their feelings, it equaled a thousand others.

Carl's reverie was interrupted by the rustling of bushes and the clopping of horse's hooves approaching the cabin. Carl peered out the front door and saw Waddite perched on his Appaloosa horse. His Quapaw friend's brow was furrowed like a dark ditch in the road. The Indian swung down from his saddle and tied the Appaloosa to a nearby tree limb.

"Waddite, you come to pay respect to me, the groom, tonight?" Carl asked jovially, hoping to charm him out of his apparent bad mood.

"I fear trouble is coming, Carl," said Waddite worriedly. "I heard a white man talking in the corn hole pool where I was soaking. He started asking questions about your wedding, and one of the men told him about the ritual bath tonight at Mitchell's Bathhouse that your woman must undergo. I saw this man sneaking around your house and your brother's house. We should go and find the women at the bathhouse tonight, and make sure they are safe."

Carl shook his head in wonder. The white man Waddite saw must have been Roland Longman. It seemed that Rosalia wouldn't be safe from this madman until somebody put him in jail. He grasped the handle of his rifle, and the firm sleekness of it reassured him.

The two men headed toward the center of town, following the road easily with the stream of full moonlight upon it. They started at a walk and then trotted their horses as quickly as they could. The Mitchell Bathhouse wasn't far, Carl realized, but every minute counted now. He fought a sudden nausea rising in his throat. He tried to steady himself by glancing over at Waddite from time to time, who was relaxed and stoic in the saddle.

At the end of Whittington Avenue, just up ahead they spotted a group of people running toward them. As they came closer, he recognized Rosa Meyer. When they finally met, Carl strained to see Rosalia among them, but she wasn't there. Rosa was the first to speak, shouting in English when she saw Waddite.

"A man took Rosalia with a gun! We can do nothing! Nothing! He will shoot us all!"

The women broke into tears afresh, and Gussie looked ready to faint, pale as paper in the moonlight. Carl and Waddite spurred their horses to a gallop toward bathhouse row. The streets were empty and the air was chilly and clear, stinging Carl's eyes as he rode. When they arrived at the Mitchell Bathhouse, they hopped off their mounts and quickly tied them to nearby trees. They ran to the front door and finding it locked, banged on it with clenched fists, but only the echoes of their pounding greeted them. They ran around the building, Carl to the left and Waddite to the right. Carl's eyes swept back and forth through the trees, straining to catch sight of Rosalia. He met Waddite at the back of the building, who told him,

"I see no people, but I do see horse and buggy tracks, fresh ones, leading down to Central Avenue. He must have taken her that way."

They ran back to their horses and started out slowly so that Waddite could track the ruts made by the buggy wheels. When they got to Central Avenue, they continued to follow the tracks eastward out of town. The road stretched before them deserted and lit by the moon. They urged their horses to gallop as fast as they could, and their speed soon paid off. Around a bend in the road they spotted a silvery dot moving away from them. They gained on the glinting speck and Carl now knew they were coming up behind a familiar Rockaway buggy. He had his rifle in one hand, reins in the other, just like Waddite. When they were within shooting distance of the horse and buggy, it slowed down and then turned sideways in the road. A bullet whistled past their ears. Carl's heart began to pump so maniacally, he thought it would leap out of his chest. Strudel followed the Appaloosa off the road and into the shadowy woods. Another bullet flew and landed near Strudel's feet, causing her to rear. Damn this bright moon, now it is a detriment, Carl thought, hanging onto the reins and calming Strudel. Then he realized that it worked both ways, and quickly lifted and aimed his rifle at the buggy. Waddite raised his arm and hissed at Carl,

"Don't shoot. You might hit your woman. We don't know where she is. It is quiet now, so the man is either reloading his gun or trying to sneak up on us."

"What we do now? We can't let him take her away."

A shadowy figure ran from the buggy into the trees. They couldn't discern whether it was Rosalia or Longman, but all too soon they knew. Another bullet whistled past Waddite's shoulder from the direction of the woods.

Suddenly the two men heard another sound, the unmistakable growling of a bear. Strudel and the Appaloosa snorted and began to rear. Waddite quieted his horse and began to back him up slowly. Carl did the same, and the hairs on the nape of his neck stood up like frightened little soldiers.

A piercing scream, then another one, rent the silence. More screams commingled with ferocious growls. The horrific din went on for what seemed like an hour, though Carl knew it was only a matter of minutes. Finally the screaming stopped, but they could hear faint snuffling and snorting through the dogwood trees. Carl didn't need to be a genius to figure what had happened. He sent a prayer to Hashem that Rosalia wasn't in the woods with Longman. They could hear the beast crash through the bushes and moonlit dogwoods and pines away from them. Then eerie silence fell on the woods again, broken by a cry from the buggy.

"Help, please help me!"

It was Rosalia's voice filled with panic. The two men raced their mounts to the buggy and her face, pale as parchment, appeared in the window. Carl could see her eyes blazing like never before, almost dark violet in the moonlight. He dismounted and saw that her hands and feet were tied with a thick, braided rope. He flung open the buggy door and climbed in to untie her. As Carl worked on the knots around her wrists and ankles, they both began to sob.

"We must find his body," Carl choked out shakily.

"No! Leave him there. What if he is still alive and can shoot us?"

"That isn't possible. No man could survive what we heard."

"Let's just go into town and find the constable, please. I could not stand to look upon that man alive or dead."

Finally she was free from the rope. Carl said,

"I want to hold you so badly. I see you are trembling from head to toe."

"Let me tremble. You can hold me all you want after we are married."

Waddite interrupted their conversation with a wave of his hand. Carl had forgotten about him entirely in his rush to recover Rosalia. He must have been searching through the trees for Roland Longman's body. Waddite announced to them, almost formally,

"I found the man's body lying in much blood, and he wasn't moving. He is most surely gone. We will leave him there for the constable and deputy to take back. It is better this way because they will see exactly how he died."

They left the buggy in the road, but Carl removed the traces and reins from the horse. Rosalia climbed onto Strudel using a step stool stored behind the buggy box, and Carl mounted the buggy horse. Together the three of them rode slowly back into town shivering from the night chill.

Constable Hargreaves' station was tiny and unlit, a one-story brick building with a tiny ticket window to the right of the front door. The three riders dismounted and Carl banged on the splintered pine door until his fists ached. By then the immense moon was low in the sky. An owl hooted intermittently and coyotes yipped and howled in some distant canyon. Constable Hargreaves eventually cracked the door open, bundled against the frosty January night in a gigantic wool blanket, and stared at the three weary faces that greeted him.

"What y'all doin' this tahm a naht?" the Constable croaked, not fully awake. "Does this have somethin' ta do with the gunfiyah Ah jest heard. Hitch up them horses and come in outta the cold. Ah'll heah your story at the woodstove."

When Carl described what had transpired, the constable, cottony eyebrows twitching, declared,

"Ah gotta round up Deputy Paige foah this one."

The bedraggled threesome entered his parlor and, as if on cue, his wife Mary appeared, stoked the dying embers in their Franklin stove and added kindling and a few pieces of split oak. She quickly boiled water on top of the stove in a tin pan and made cups of tea for them. Then she wrapped them each in a warm woolen blanket. Rosalia stuttered out her tale of abduction at the Mitchell Bathhouse. Carl related his and Waddite's pursuit, and the kidnapper's demise by a wild creature, no doubt a black bear. Waddite leaned in, listening closely and nodding. Constable Hargreaves, now fully awake, responded,

"If that is true, then it is very strange. We have many black beahs heah in Hot Springs, but rarely do they attack a person. And in January most of 'em ah hibahnatin'. But once in a while a beah comes out of its den in the wintah and we jest don't know why. Theah must be an investigation. But seems to me y'all got plenty enough witnesses to a crime of abduction. We need ta git out theah immediately, find the man and hep him if he survived the beah attack. Meantahm, y'all git back home to sleep because Ah know they's a weddin' tomorrah. Town's small, everybody knows everybody's business."

Rosalia looked at Carl in horror and cried out to him in German,

"We cannot marry tomorrow! We can't see each other for another week, and we must change the wedding date. Not only that, but I must also have another *mikvah* to purify myself."

Carl ached to think that he couldn't have his bride tomorrow.

"Rosalia, did you forget? As the bride, you are freed of all wrongdoing on your wedding day, as this day you are closer to Hashem than anybody else. You do not need another *mikvah* unless you desire it in your heart. We won't let that villain ruin the *mikvah* or the wedding. Because then he will win, living or dead, yes? Let's win this time, eh?"

"We must go to the Rabbi's house. Samuel, Gussie and the other women who attended me at the *mikvah* will probably be there. They will want to know that I'm safe. And we can ask the Rabbi to delay the ceremony when we get there."

34

Carl, Rosalia and Waddite bid goodbye with many thanks to Mary for the warm fire and tea. Cyril Hargreaves kissed Mary's cheek and braced himself for the winter air. He didn't know how long he would be, or whether he would be surveying the remains of a body or a live person wielding a shotgun. He had viewed and cleaned up the results of plenty of brawls, gun fights and animal attacks, and occasionally the 'dead' man was still very much alive.

Hargreaves stopped at the cabin of the town's deputy, Harmon Paige, a gangly, towering, long-faced fellow with a thatch of rust-colored hair that people only caught sight of when he doffed his brown slouch cowboy hat, which wasn't often.

"This was a shootout," Hargreaves informed Paige, "*and* a bear attack. All started by an abduction of that new Jewish gal jest came in from Germany, Rosalia Wolfson."

Deputy Paige nodded solemnly, grabbed his hat and placed it firmly on his head. They raced their horses down Central Avenue and into the highway, which was just lighting up with the first rays of sunrise. They reined in alongside the buggy, forlorn and abandoned with neither reinsman nor wheeler, the lines and traces trailing on the ground. Swinging off their mounts and tying them securely to a dogwood tree, Hargreaves and Paige crept furtively among the tall green ashes and stubbier rusty blackhaw trees, both relieved that the increasing daylight allowed them to survey the undergrowth for a distance. A half hour of stepping over rocks and stones brought them to an inert body huddled on the ground.

"Ah'll take a closer look heah," murmured Hargreaves to Paige. "You jest keep a'peekin' through the trees foah that beah. Might come back, you nevah know."

Paige averted his eyes from the gruesome remains lying at his feet and stared in all directions, pointed slowly with his .38 revolver and rotated slowly. Hargreaves bent down and examined the corpse, for it was all too obvious this man was beyond reviving. He tried to avoid stepping in the blood that pooled around the body, but that was impossible. The man's shirt was raked and torn, and his abdomen was pretty much gone. There were deep gashes on his head and face. The dead man's revolver, Hargreaves made a mental note, was a Colt Navy six-gun, light and easy to transport, same kind that General Robert E. Lee had carried as a sidearm during the War between the States. It was useless now, fallen onto the dead leaves near the victim's right leg.

The two lawmen rolled the corpse onto a linen tarpaulin that Hargreaves had packed, then lifted it and backtracked to the buggy in the road. Paige stared thoughtfully at the black conveyance for a moment and then blurted out,

"By golly, that's Missy Lanford's Rockaway carriage and gelding! And there's her initials carved into the boot. What's it doin' heah?"

Hargreaves glanced sideways at his deputy and said,

"Hmm, and how would you know that?

"Nevah mind, "retorted Paige, blushing furiously. "Let's jest git this thing outta the roadway and return it to its rightful ownah."

"This man's gonna come back ta town same way he left. In Missy Lanford's carriage. Hep me lift him in."

Hargreaves tied the reins and traces of the buggy to his paint. By the time they left the forest with the shrouded body ensconced in the buggy, dawn was erasing the night shadows. They were greeted by a handful of people milling along Central Avenue.

"We heard shots, a lot of em, middle of the night, Constable!" called out Arthur MacDougal, his face crosser than usual. "I get up early, but it was dark out when that dang commotion woke me."

Others in the crowd called out to the constable, talking over one another.

"Was there a shootout?"

"Anybody get hurt?"

"Are you and the deputy all right, Cyril?"

Constable Hargreaves motioned with his arms outstretched and palms down for everybody to get calm.

"We are not exactly sure what happened heah, and Ah will not trah ta guess. Please give us some tahm ta talk with the people involved and find out exactly what occurred and why."

"At least tell us who's the stiff in the buggy!" cried Zeke Braeburn, the editor of the Hot Springs *Beacon*. The nosy fellow had run up to the buggy and was peering inside.

"That we do not as of yet know. Now if you please, we must get to the coroner's office."

The crowd made way and the two lawmen spurred their mounts on, Deputy Paige on his huffing chestnut and Constable Hargreaves driving the buggy with his paint in the traces. Once they had deposited the remains of the dead man plus the buggy at the coroner cum town doctor's receiving parlor, they turned their horses towards Rabbi Schecter's residence. Rosalia had told them that the women who attended her at the evening bath ritual (Hargreaves couldn't remember the foreign word for it) would probably be there awaiting word along with the Rabbi. Sure enough, there was a group of women in Rabbi Schecter's sitting parlor. He could see them through the windows weaving amongst one another. Hargreaves rapped on the door roughly with his knuckles and waited. Rabbi Schecter, wearing a dark navy morning coat with a thick woolen vest underneath, opened the door and motioned him in with a wave of his hand.

Gussie stood behind the Rabbi with her mouth half open and tears running down her face. Behind her milled the women who had attended Rosalia's *mikvah*. Their husbands were also there, having lingered after Shabbos dinner to wait for their wives to return from the *mikvah*. The candles had long ago burned down into their pewter holders, and remnants of a delicious rabbit stew and small bits of challah loaf dotted a floral porcelain platter on a wide table.

"Did you find her?" cried Gussie, clutching Samuel's hand tightly.

"Everybody, you will be happy to heah that Rosalia Wolfson is safe," proclaimed Hargreaves. "She is unhahmed by the hooligan who took her, as far as Ah kin tell."

The women chattered excitedly, and Talia and Julia burst into tears. Gussie remarked,

"She is almost my sister. I must go to her now."

"I will go also because she is like a daughter to me," said Rosa Meyer firmly.

Constable Hargreaves stopped them mid-step with a beef palm stretched out.

"Sorry, ladies," he wagged his balding head at them, "Ah must ask y'all some questions about what transpiahed at the time of Miss Rosalia Wolfson's abduction. If y'all ah witnesses, and if there ah othahs, y'all must stay in this room while Ah heah your accounts."

Gussie and Rosa looked at each other balefully, then sat together primly on the Rabbi's sofa. Talia, Julia and Naomi, wiping tears from their faces, joined them. The five women related what had happened at the *mikvah* and Constable Hargreaves scribbled notes in a thin, leather-bound book. The details were fresh in their minds, so they were able to describe the man who had kidnapped Rosalia, each filling in details that the others left out: clothing, appearance, weapon, his actions and the words he spoke that had terrorized them like hot coals flung in their faces. Hargreaves concluded,

"Your descriptions match closely the man that Deputy Paige and I found killed bah the beah in the woods. Thank y'all foah your hep."

His booted steps shook the new plank flooring of Rabbi Schecter's parlor as he retreated, leaving the remaining congregants to their sorrows and consolations.

By the afternoon of that endless morning, the rumors among the Jewish community had been dispelled, and the actual story was known. Nonetheless, Carl fretted constantly that people would want to know more about the whys and wherefores. The link between him, the now-deceased Roland Longman, and the brothel could be discovered. The disastrous story of Rosalia and Roland Longman during her steamship voyage could be revealed as well. His mind worked to come up with the most superficial but acceptable explanation for Rosalia being stolen away at gunpoint by Longman. 'I don't know why' just wasn't going to sit well with the members of the congregation. Try as he might, he couldn't come up with an alternate story that would satisfy their curiosity. If Constable Hargreaves made those connections in his investigations, he doubted that it could be hushed up. The Hot Springs *Beacon*, always hungry for sensational local stories, would splash it on the front page as soon as a journalist wrote it up.

The following day, Constable Hargreaves came to the back of Gersman's Dry Goods dragging a large doe tied down in a travois hitched to the flanks of his chestnut horse. Both horse and rider were sweating and breathing heavily despite the coolness of the sweet January air. Cyril Hargreaves wore a red knit hunting cap, and the fringe around his bald pate stuck out from under it in wispy gray strands. Carl stared at the deer and then at Hargreaves' jowly, pale face. There was a droopy expression to the edges of his eyes and mouth that signaled a nuanced warning to Carl. He wished the man would take his dead animal and go away, but he knew that wasn't going to happen.

"Constable, good afternoon," he addressed Hargreaves politely. He peered at the doe and noted that she had been killed with at least two gunshots to the head and neck. A cruel and painful death, this one, and not kosher for butchering. He hoped the Constable was planning to take her to the gentile butcher in town.

Hargreaves nodded at Carl and then leaned forward until his face was close to Carl's.

"Ah have spoken with Rosalia and the ladies who were at the Mitchell Bathhouse with her the night of the crahm. None of them had any kahnd of explanation foah why Roland Longman abducted her."

Carl listened intently, dark brown eyes narrowed, full lips pressed together anxiously. He started to ask if Rosalia had told him anything about Roland Longman, and then thought better of it. Mutely he nodded his head in understanding.

"Now, many of us are aware that you and Rosalia are getting' married this comin' Satahday." His deep, rumbling voice was beginning to lull Carl into a trance. He pinched himself in the arm to stay awake. "Ah will do mah best ta keep all of this outta the *Beacon*. At least, until the weddin' is ovah and done with. Y'got that?"

Carl nodded again. Silence fell between them for a few seconds. Then Carl caught on. Like a Prussian official, the

Constable wanted his wheels greased. People were not hugely different from one continent to another.

"I thank you very, very much, sir. Please, give me deer. I will skin, clean, and make steaks all for free. My gift to you."

A smile lit up Hargreaves' countenance, spreading his frosted mustache apart under his nose like a dangling snowflake.

"Well, Ah thank yah kahndly foah that, Carl. Very generous, indeed. Mary will be glad to get those steaks. Yah have a fahn reputation foah butcherin', sir, all ovah town. Ah'll be back foah the meat tomorrah."

The two of them untied and lifted the luckless doe out of the travois and placed her carefully in the side yard on a net suspended on six posts. Normally, Carl wouldn't accept an animal shot to death, but circumstances now were not normal. He would pray over the beast, that its suffering had been brief. He hoped that Hashem would forgive him. The meat would certainly not go to a Jewish family.

When Hargreaves was gone, Carl sat for a moment and took stock of his situation. He wasn't planning to butcher anything three days before the wedding and was accepting only hens and small game that would take little time, but this man had dropped a mouse into the challah batter, his mother's favorite expression. Fortunately, he had already prepared for the wedding that didn't happen the week before. Rabbi Schecter had bestowed a tallis upon him the night before the first wedding date, a dark blue and white striped shawl that he would wear to religious services as a married man. The prairie ring for Rosalia was in a small box in the cabin awaiting her finger. His high lace-up boots were already polished, and his dress trousers were clean and pressed. The ascot tie and high fur hat that his brother had lent him were also clean and on hand in his bedroom. Rabbi Schecter had prepared the marriage ketubah for the bride and groom, the promises written on fine parchment that would always hang on a wall in their home.

He realized that he had better start on the doe right away. She must be carefully opened, salted, and stripped in the rear to allow all the blood to drain from her body and onto the ground while she lay in the netting. That way none of her blood would be consumed. She would drain overnight in a covered and reinforced corral to protect her from wild predators. Carl rolled up his sleeves, muttered a prayer asking forgiveness for the dead doe, and grabbed his sharpest knife to begin.

It was late when he started for home, and he longed to wash up with a basin of warm water and wash rags. He had been careful, as usual, to keep the animal's blood from splattering him, but the salt and guts inevitably flew upward from time to time as he skinned the animal. His own sweat had turned pungent as well. The thought of his marriage day sweetened his walk home in the dark night, the moon a fingernail sliver hanging above the purplish-gray tree line, with only a lantern to light his way. He fervently hoped that the *Beacon* would never get wind of what had happened between Rosalia and Roland Longman on the ocean voyage.

35

Rabbi Schecter insisted on delaying the wedding until the following Saturday so that the prenuptial couple could honor the tradition of one week apart before reciting their vows. During that time, they recuperated from their ordeal. Rosalia was grateful for the interval, during which she napped often, sometimes with David sleeping in her arms. The infant was growing like a seedling into a budding rose of a boy. Once again, she and Carl were obliged to avoid one another and remain separated until the ceremony. This time it was more difficult, as Rosalia longed for his strength and comfort after the shock of being taken at gunpoint by the seemingly unstoppable Roland Longman. It was like a recurring nightmare, only now that he had perished, there would be no third time.

During that week of suspended nuptials, on Tuesday morning, Constable Hargreaves sent his deputy to summon Rosalia to the courthouse.

"We have a visitor come to see you. A ship's captain. Will ya fancy that?"

Deputy Paige was chattering away in Rosalia's ear as they hurried down Central Avenue toward the courthouse on foot. She felt the blood drain from her face and began to shake, tripping every few steps.

"Whoa, steady! You feelin' all right, ma'am? You ah lookin' a trifle peaked.

Rosalia could not speak. It was as if her tongue was glued to the top of her mouth. Was this the start of another one of those nightmares she had from time to time? They usually started in the halls of the U.S.S. *Eolus,* as she careened crazily from one side to the other and ran from pursuit by a menacing shadow. Sometimes before the dream ended she would bump into Captain Wilkins or Ensign Hastings, or both, who appeared as fragile and helpless as the corn husk dolls she had strung together with her neighbor Beulah Lee. But no, the ground felt solid and undisturbed beneath her boots, the winter sun glanced between clouds, the morning smells of the town, pine needles, baking bread and fried eggs, tickled her nostrils. She was wide awake.

Captain Wilkins stood immediately when she entered the room, towering over her. Constable Hargreaves was at his side. The captain, trim in a white and navy uniform with gold tassels, bowed briefly in her direction.

"I understand you are to be wed come next Saturday," he began. "May I offer my congratulations. I imagine you are wondering why I would appear in Hot Springs six months after you disembarked from my vessel in New Orleans."

Rosalia nodded mutely and tugged at the tips of her knitted gloves.

"The investigation of one Mr. Roland Longman has been ongoing since that time. Resources are limited, and we did our absolute best, but have come up empty. The woman that you claim he held in his cabin and who then disappeared, we have not been able to locate her. She has a brother who is quite irate and demanding answers. Regretfully, we cannot give him one. Through U.S. Customs I tracked you to this lovely town," a glance at the constable, "and now Constable Hargreaves informs me that Roland Longman took you at gunpoint and is now expired. This same man murdered one of my crew. Were you aware of that, Miss Wolfson?"

"No. Oh, how horrible." Rosalia's eyes filled with tears, try as she might to stop them. "But Mr. Longman is dead now and will not hurt or kill others again."

"Killed by a wild animal!" interjected Constable Hargreaves. "An appropriate end to a lawless man. The captain was hoping against hope you would have heard something about the lady missing from his boat."

"Greta Schuler was her name," Captain Wilkins reminded her. "It is quite possible that her body is in the ocean and irretrievable. However, I have crew members stationed on all sides of my ship to spot a person overboard, and they swear to this day they saw nobody go over. It is a mystery. We were hoping Mr. Longman might have said something to you about her that might help us locate her."

"I am so sorry. He…he said nothing about her." She could not stop the tears now, and they flowed down her reddening cheeks. Her guilt at not saving the woman when she was just a few feet away from her felt like a log lying across her shoulders. The men shifted uncomfortably on their feet. She wanted to relieve them of their confusion at losing a passenger but couldn't bring herself to relate the story that Carl had told her of the unfortunate Frau Schuler's true fate.

"Please sit, Miss Wolfson." Constable Hargreaves set a chair near her, and she sat as she wiped the tears from her face with a small linen handkerchief he handed her.

"You can stop yoah frettin," Constable Hargreaves spoke soothingly. "Roland Longman is no longer a threat to y'all."

He didn't realize that she was weeping from guilt, not fear for her own safety. She blew her nose self-consciously and cleared her throat.

"Captain Wilkins, I will be honored if you come to my wedding on Saturday. You also, Constable. And of course your wife."

"Ma'am, I would be delighted to attend. Unfortunately, my stage for Little Rock leaves tomorrow and my ship sails the next day. I must be on it, of course."

Constable Hargreaves, however, agreed to attend.

"Ah have nevah been to a Jewish weddin'. Ah didn't even know Christians was allowed to attend. But Mary and Ah will be theah. Thank you kindly."

Saturday morning arrived astonishingly fast. In Samuel and Gussie's bedroom, Rosalia carefully slipped the white satin and lace wedding gown over her head and fluffed it out. Today all eyes would be upon her and this beautiful dress. Gussie was nursing the baby in the other room, but suddenly she appeared to aid Rosalia in attaching the veil in her fine blonde hair and draping it neatly down her back. It would stay behind her until Carl lifted it over her head to cover her face during the ceremony. This would avail Rosalia a certain privacy while surrounded by intense scrutiny on such an important day. She thought that the veil would be a nuisance, but in fact she relished the feel of it against her skin and the gentle pressure of it on the crown of her head. It made her feel like a Malka, a queen. Next she slipped her already-stockinged feet into gray leather boots to her knees. A row of buttons lined up like little white eyes along the outsides, waiting to capture her lower legs in their grip. She had borrowed these from Gussie, grateful not to have to walk to the chuppah in her dark, heavy traveling boots. They fit slightly too large, but she would gladly tolerate the looseness in her toes for one day. She decided to stuff some wads of coarse cotton in the tips of the boots to keep them from slipping around on her feet.

She carefully extracted from the lining of her travelling blanket the golden chain with the ruby pendant that her mother had sewn into it. Dangling it from her fingers, she untangled it and hooked it around her neck. It accented her dress most beautifully but added sorrow to the moment. Her mother was far from here and wouldn't be at her wedding, and the jewelry, she discovered, made a poor substitute. She would have traded the necklace for Dora's presence in an instant. There would be no gold band to place on her finger during the ceremony; she would have to accept the rustic prairie ring, merely a curved nail, for now. Suddenly the lack of a proper wedding ring seemed irrelevant to her, and the prairie ring more fitting for this union in the wilderness. Grabbing her grey wool winter cape, she followed Gussie into the parlor, ready to walk with her to the Rabbi's house. Samuel grinned with unusual *bonhomie,* clearly delighted by the vision of two beautiful women in their finery. He made admiring noises as he gazed at Gussie's full, curvy figure nicely accentuated by her new yellow chintz dress trimmed in white lace. Then the three of them walked to the Rabbi's house, Rosalia flanked by her future in-laws.

As they strolled, the women carefully lifted their fine dresses to keep the hems clean. Aromas drifted and wafted up and down the streets. Jewish women throughout the town had been cooking the day before and all morning for the feast. Knishes had been made, a hundred or more, dough stuffed with ground beef, onions and potatoes. The aroma of them was infusing the neighborhoods where they were being baked. Mountains of mandelbrot cookies, many braided challah loaves, kreplach packed with sauerkraut and roast chicken were also being prepared. The men oversaw the delivery of wine and beer for celebration and toasting.

When they arrived, Rosalia was relieved to observe that all the fire damage had been removed, sanded over or covered with small woven mats. People she recognized, and some she didn't, were also walking to the wedding because it was Shabbos, but those who were elderly, infirm or just recovering from the recent epidemic of influenza that had swept the town were slowly climbing out of buggies and drays. Their younger relatives had them by the elbows and helped them to hitch their horses or mules to the Rabbi's side fence. They entered the Rabbi's front parlor, which had been bedecked by a bouquet of white and burgundy lenten roses and graceful emerald pine boughs on the oak mantel. Congregants were taking seats in the parlor and every possible space of the house. It was too cold a January day for the wedding to take place outdoors where the congregation could spread out, so people were bunched up together like peaches in a jar. Young children were squirming on their parents' laps. People dressed in their taffetas, satins and wools were lining the hallway that divided the parlor from the Rabbi's living quarters. Only the elderly were assured a seat. Voices floated and echoed through the parlor, murmuring, admonishing children, an occasional laugh punctuating the low hum.

Rosalia leaned shakily on Gussie's arm. Together they stepped back outside to the veranda, where they would wait in the nippy winter weather until it was time for the bride to enter. Rosalia and Carl had met with Rabbi Schechter twice in December to learn what was expected of them during the ceremony. Rosalia felt a wave of nausea rise in her throat, a fluttering in her stomach. What if she forgot to do or say something important for the ritual? Did Carl remember to bring the wine glass to crush underfoot? Did he remember the ring, that steel nail tortured into a circle by the blacksmith's flames? Would Rabbi Schecter remember her name?

"It's time," Gussie hissed in her ear, startling her from her waterfall of cascading thoughts. As they entered the parlor, a murmur of appreciation and delight went through the crowd. Immediately her anxiety subsided. The many pairs of eyes gazing at her were filled with warmth and happiness from smiling faces. Any troubles they might be suffering, she imagined, – illness, winter freezes, struggles to provide a living, marital disputes – they had put aside at this moment. Her veil floated about her like a spun silk cloud. She willed herself to relax and look straight ahead so as not to stumble. The chuppah beckoned to her from the bimah, draped in multi-colored silk ribbons, hellebores and pine boughs. The rabbi and his congregants had taken the time and trouble to assemble, set up and decorate the symbolic arch for her wedding.

She caught sight of Waddite, who was outfitted in full ceremonial Indian garb and taking in everything attentively. His tan and pearl-hued eagle feathers appeared incongruous poking out above the crowd, but Rosalia loved the way they looked. The sight of him mysteriously soothed her. She clutched Gussie's dry hand with her own clammy one and held on tightly during this endless, short walk across the Rabbi's sitting parlor, now arranged as a place of religious service, toward the chuppah. Its four fir poles were draped with a rough linen canopy, a symbol of the home she would share with Carl. For a moment she thought somebody else would be standing under that canopy to get married, not her.

Rabbi Schecter stood at the back of the parlor with the cantor at his side, the folds of their blue and white tallis shawls draped around them like matching flags. Rosalia could feel their eyes upon her as she moved in tiny steps down the aisle lined with benches and chairs. Rosa Meyer beamed at her as she approached the bimah. From the corner of her eye she saw Beulah Lee Howerton standing in the women's side of the room, looking around with wonder in her eyes. She glimpsed the three black sisters that she had waited on in Gersman's Dry Goods standing against the back wall, near the entrance. Carl had insisted that they invite them. They were wearing huge wide-rimmed, ruffled hats, each a different color: plum, apricot, strawberry. She knew that Carl's helper, their nephew

Benjamin, would not be here because he and his family had fled for the North after he was almost lynched. How Carl had thwarted the brazen attempt had become fodder for gossip throughout Hot Springs, not just among the Jews but spreading beyond to both the white and colored communities. Rosalia tried to suppress the great pride blooming in her at marrying such a man, but it was a challenge while Samuel and Gussie kvelled to everybody who came near them. Zeke Braeburn had written up the story in the Hot Springs *Beacon*. Arthur MacDougal, the surly cobbler, had issued Carl a spoken death threat. Carl had become briefly famous, and that had its darker side.

All too quickly she was standing under the chuppah, its curved wicker dome casting a shadow on her veil and dress. Samuel stepped aside, a huge smile stretching his face. Carl faced her in the finest clothing she had ever seen on him. She smiled slightly knowing that he had borrowed items of apparel from Samuel and Simon Meyer. He looked more handsome to her than he ever had in the dark wool trousers and matching jacket sporting a shiny grosgrain lapel, with the white collared arrow shirt setting off those chocolate eyes. His new tallit, a blue and white striped woven prayer shawl, was draped across his shoulders, bestowed by the Rabbi to honor his upcoming status as a married man of the community. She knew that the inelegant prairie ring was clutched tightly in his right fist.

There were two matching pine chairs for the bride and groom on the bimah, ornately hand-carved by a master woodworker in town. Rosalia and Carl sat side-by-side as

Rabbi Schechter began to intone the prayers and blessings of Shabbos morning services, followed by the marriage blessings and vows. More than an hour passed as the parlor grew warm with body heat. Congregants began peeling off their outer layers and laying them on their laps. Finally Rabbi Schechter turned to Carl and instructed him to veil the bride. Rosalia stood and Carl reached over to cover her face with the veil. This was the bedeken, the veiling ritual that would imbue modesty and privacy upon the bride.

"A shame to cover your gorgeous punim, the finest face I have ever seen," he whispered so that none other could hear. Rabbi Schechter heard the comment, though, and beamed despite himself. Rosalia was filled with so much joy at that moment, she could not keep a grin from dancing across her face. But at this point it didn't matter because nobody could see that grin behind her veil now. After a brief, silent pause, Carl began singing to her, a Hebrew strain that switched from wistful to happy. He danced a little jig around her as the crowd clapped to urge him on. She had seen this before at other girls' weddings in Gliewitz, and so it was familiar to her. What was unfamiliar was being the center of loving attention. She was grateful to be veiled as it eased the intensity of the moment by providing a hiding place for her joy, a long-deserted emotion since her childhood. Tears began coursing down her cheeks, try as she might to stop them.

Then it was time for Rosalia to circle Carl seven times to symbolize the breaking down of barriers and walls between them. *The biggest walls have come down already.* Rosalia counted the rounds, getting a little dizzy. *We told each other our darkest secrets. Things can only get better from here.*

Gussie and Rosa Meyer broke a plate together to seal the ceremony, a task usually shared by the mothers of the bride and groom. Since neither mother was present, the two women closest to them had volunteered happily to do so. Rosalia smiled wistfully at the thought of her own mother breaking the plate for Edith at her wedding ceremony. It must have brought Dora so much pleasure, and Rosalia couldn't help but grieve for a moment that her parents weren't with her now. Then came the shared sip of wine, the coarse prairie ring upon her finger, the pounding of the hapless wine glass into the floorboards by Carl's boot, and they were now married. Rosalia thought she heard sobbing behind her as she faced the Rabbi (*oy, probably Gussie*), and then a noisy rain of "Mazel tovs", good luck blessings cried out by everybody in the room.

She felt Carl's rough, broad hand on hers as he led her through the clapping, chattering crowd to the *yichud* for fifteen minutes of privacy together as husband and wife. The Rabbi's small study next to the kitchen had been designated for this ritual, his leather-bound tomes lined on the wall their only companions. In those fifteen minutes, Carl lifted Rosalia's veil from her face and kissed her on the lips. Even though they were now allowed to touch one another, Rosalia could not keep from trembling with fear. So far, sex had been a violent and violating experience, and ironically, she was still a virgin. How would it be different with Carl? She had to resist the urge to slap him, and in fact had to resist the impulse to reach for one of the lustrous pearl hatpins that her father had given her. She had used them to pin her veil to the cotton band so that it wouldn't fly upward during the wedding. He kissed her again, sweetly and gently, and her arms and hands went limp.

"Are you frightened, *beshert*? True love of mine?" asked Carl. "Don't be. We will discover together the right way to do this. We are both roughened by the ugly side of it, and it is for us to discover the beauty of love, *nu*?"

"Yes, I agree," sighed Rosalia. "It will not be easy for me to allow you to … to touch me. I have found only threats and unhappiness there, with boys and men. At least you know and understand what I have been through. With nothing to hide, I feel freer with you than any other person I have known, man or woman. It will be easier to be a good wife to you. This I promise."

"No, Roselah, you are always a fine person. I am the one who must now be good and live the life of an honorable married man here in Hot Springs. I have done wrong and will be making it up to you forever. We will do this slowly, and we will be careful with each other. How does that sound?"

Rosalia could not speak. She leaned forward and kissed him now, allowing her desires to well up through her body for this man who was now hers. She didn't even know the words for those sensations, but they were strangely familiar because she had been pushing and shoving them away from herself for many years.

When they emerged from the yichud, they saw that the chairs had been pushed against the walls and three long tables covered with white linens had been arranged in the center of the parlor. Rabbi Schechter was waiting for them with Carl's round, high beaver fur hat. The newly married couple would be treated as a king and queen for the next year, in a manner of speaking, and this was Carl's crown. The younger men were eagerly waiting to hoist both Carl and Rosalia above the crowd in the carved pine chairs and parade them around the parlor. The guests were milling around and murmuring in anticipation. Rosalia clung desperately to the arms of the chair as the hoisters bounced them precariously through the front door and out into the fresh, chilly air, around the front yard once and then back inside. Carl grasped his new beaver hat tightly to keep it from falling off.

Gussie, Rosa, and several other women brought out trays of potato kugel, mandelbrot cookies, a huge brisket, roast chicken, homemade applesauce and bottles of wine and beer. Rosalia joined the women along the western wall of the parlor and watched Carl cavort and twirl with the men on the eastern side of the room to the cantor's violin playing one familiar song after another. Gussie slipped up beside her and said,

"Do you see Waddite? He's dancing with the fellows but doing his own kind of dance. It must be a Quapaw dance. And he looks so happy! I'm glad he's here. I owe him my life."

"He appears regal, decked out in beads and feathers. When I see him, I realize all over again that I'm in America, not Germany. Nobody like that would ever show up to my wedding in Gliewitz."

They both giggled at the thought of it.

"Gussie, it must have been so awful to be thrown up on a horse with the baby by those ruffians and left in a cave. Will you ever be able to get over it?"

"Liebe, I could ask you the same question. You know, about the man on the ship who attacked you. We must get over these things somehow, or they will take the joy from our lives. We are living in strange, rough times. I can only hope that life will be a little easier for our children, and even easier for theirs."

Another violinist struck up a traditional dance tune. Men with men and women with women, they whirled around one another, in large and small circles, in snaking lines, pushing inward to meet in the middle and pulling out to form a large wheel of dancers. Rosalia found herself gently shoved into the eye of the human vortex as the women, girls and children danced and curled around her, swinging their feet to the left and to the right. Some of the men were in a dancing frenzy, leaping and twirling in pairs. A marriage was no small thing in the Jewish community, and in this corner of the Wild West where they had settled, they were reminded of their enduring heritage, customs and beliefs. Rosalia couldn't help but feel gratitude toward the many women who grasped and squeezed her hands and the men who bowed to her from across the room like lords addressing the *Malka*, the bridal queen. Constable Hargreaves caught Rosalia's eye and waved from the back of the room. Mary had taken her place among the women and seemed at ease among them.

Many hours of celebration marked the typical Jewish wedding, and this one was no exception. The elderly guests were out of breath from dancing and now sat. Eyes were glistening, faces were sweaty and many congregants were swaying and unsteady as the wine disappeared from their cups. Slowly they bid farewell and a final mazel tov to the newly married couple and gradually filed out of the Rabbi's sitting parlor and kitchen.

Unable to speak they were so exhausted, the groom and his bride leaned against one another as they walked home. Rosalia had danced with the other ladies and girls so many hours that her boots were pressing against her ankles and hurting them. She suspected a blister was forming on her right foot. She wished it weren't Shabbos so that they could ride in the buggy. She was forced to lift her satin bridal gown as she walked so as not to dirty the lace hem on the road. As the sun began to fade behind the western hills and darkness gathered at the edges of the forest, they tottered into Carl's cabin, now Rosalia's as well.

The air inside the cabin was almost as chilly as the weather outside, but Carl did not stop to make a fire in the hearth. He ushered her into the master bedroom. It was sparsely furnished, with only a short, wide horsehair bed, a pine chest of drawers and a spindly pine chair. A small, square window opposite the bed looked out onto darkness. Atop the bed lay a thick quilt patterned with salmon-pink and orange flowers entwined in dark green ivy. This was Rosa Meyer's hard work, her wedding gift to them. Carl started a fire in the brick fireplace he had installed in the corner of the bedroom to warm them on their wedding night. Soon it was crackling, and the scent and heat of burning walnut wood filled the room. Rosalia allowed him to undress her, slowly and carefully, until she was shed of every item of clothing. Never before naked before a male, she instinctively wanted to grab the brightly colored quilt lying on top of the bed and cover herself. She resisted the impulse and instead watched curiously as Carl undressed himself. She had never seen a man fully naked. They smiled self-consciously at each other, then climbed into bed.

Rosalia never forgot the woman on the U.S.S. *Abraham Lincoln* whom she witnessed tied up in Longman's ship cabin. She pleaded for months with Carl to help her rescue the girls from the bordello in Hot Springs. He repeatedly refused, not wanting to revisit the site of his indiscretion and shame, nor did he want to draw the town's attention to himself in that way. However, in May of 1868 he buckled and agreed to accompany her, but only if Samuel and Rabbi Schechter joined them. Together the four of them knocked at the brothel door and met with Missy and Walter J. Nibley, who did not ask them in.

"Well, well, lookie heah," Missy said with a slight titter, glancing from left to right and back again at the four of them, all dressed in black and clustered like a murder of crows. "Y'all heah to enjoy the girls, or y'all gonna try to convert us to religion? We get those visits from tahm to tahm."

Rosalia noticed that both her husband and brother-in-law were clenching their jaws, and Carl averted his eyes altogether. She, however, had no trepidation about her role in this confrontation. Rabbi Schecter was the first to speak, as Samuel and Carl had designated him spokesman for the group.

"Madam, we are here for the young *maydelehs,* the girls. In our congregation, we have a group of women who will house them if they leave this sinful occupation. There they can learn to farm and grow food, knit and embroider, and care for themselves without having to resort to…" The rabbi peered past Missy and Walter into the sitting parlor.

Rosalia piped up, despite the butterflies in her stomach, "I can teach them to read and write, to do addition and subtraction. They will get education for free."

Missy and Walter stared at them speechlessly, as the visitors stood, shifting awkwardly, on the front porch. Then, almost as one, the brothel owners burst out laughing. They called the girls out of their bedrooms (one customer scurried off red-faced) and asked the rabbi and the Gersmans to repeat the request. None of the girls ever accepted their offer.

Epilogue

Carl and Rosalia Gersman lived in the house on Whittington Avenue for most of their lives. Rosalia bore ten children, four girls and six boys, two of whom died before the age of five. Nathan, their second child and first boy, died at the tender age of two. During that time, Carl's kosher butcher business grew quickly as more Jews immigrated to Hot Springs from Prussia and then Eastern Europe. He developed a reputation for generosity and kindness because he often donated cuts of beef, lamb, or an entire chicken or turkey to the poor and hungry, both White and Black. Rosalia tutored children in English grammar and reading whenever she could take time from raising children and household duties.

A genuine synagogue, Congregation House of Israel, was built in 1885, just in time for an influx of Jewish émigrés from Eastern Europe. Townspeople and visitors alike took curative hot springs soaks for pleasure and as prescribed by medical doctors for everything from catarrhs and influenzas to consumption, yellow fever, gonorrhea, syphilis and arthritis. They drew enough visitors to the area to keep Hot Springs' economy solvent in contrast with many other cities of the Deep South that struggled with the Reconstruction plan after the Civil War. The Mitchell Bathhouse and Weir & George Bathhouse stayed in business for decades until they went out of business, possibly due to the discovery and medical use of penicillin, which replaced hot springs soaking in doctors' prescriptions everywhere.

Men like Roland Longman continued to prey upon young women immigrating from Europe to the United States on ocean-going steamships. They snatched them away from their intended trajectory toward citizenship in the New World and sequestered them against their will in brothels. These 'houses of ill repute' spread like a malignant fungus in the streets of New York, New Orleans, and other cities where customers were guaranteed to patronize them. The kidnapped girls and women were almost never heard from again by the families that they left or the relatives and friends awaiting them in America. Despite official complaints to the police and customs officials, they were rarely found.

Afterword

From the tattered remnants of family memory, an old sepia photograph, and the 1920 United States Census, I wove a tale of Jewish immigrants surviving in one of the most violent periods of American history, the Reconstruction Era. If my great-grandparents hadn't had the gumption to leave the familiarity of their family, friends, hometowns and culture to settle in America, I wouldn't exist. This story is an homage to them. They left precious few records behind, no journals or diaries, no letters or notes, and only two photographs that I know of.

The story is based on historical research that revealed the following: The Pale of Settlement that was enacted against the Jewish population in Eastern Europe and Prussia forced them into poverty and deprivation. At times there was relief from restrictions, but by the late 1800's the oppression was so severe that there was a Diaspora of Jews from Europe to the United States. My great-grandfather arrived in 1859, and my great-grandmother in 1866. They married in 1867. Women rarely traveled alone, and they were targeted by human traffickers on the ships that came over the Atlantic. The New Orleans Massacre took place the same year that my great-grandmother arrived in the United States. The Garland County Courthouse, seat of Hot Springs, Arkansas, burned to the ground in 1903 along with most of the official public records of marriage, divorce, death and deeds. With so little to go on, I created a fictionalized version of my ancestors' immigration to America.

Acknowledgments

I drew from many sources to write Fire in the Springs. Many thanks go to Garland County Historical Society for answering my questions about the history of Hot Springs. Thanks also to National Park Ranger Mark Blaeuer of Hot Springs, Arkansas, for his illuminating information about the Indian tribes in the area, which were expanded upon in his book, *Didn't All the Indians Come Here?* I am indebted to the Civil War Historian presiding over the Memorabilia Room in the lobby of the Arlington Resort Hotel in Hot Springs. I appreciate the historical horse and mule knowledge that equine expert Priscilla Alden Johnson shared with me. Ardenwood Farm in Fremont, California, where I performed as a docent at the Patterson House, was a valuable font of details about the lifestyle of people living in the 19th century, including the corn husk doll. The same goes for the Empire Mine Regional Park Blacksmith Shop in Grass Valley, California, whose blacksmith told me about prairie rings and then made me one.

Thank you to the Mormon Temple Family Visitor Center for its many historical books, newspapers, newsletters and records. I am forever grateful to Donna Lewis for her gift to me of *Island of Hope, Island of Tears* by Brownstone, Franck and Brownstone. Without the insights I gained from this work, *Fire in the Springs* might still be just an idea. Thanks to my travel companion, Roberta Maisel, who accompanied me to the city of Hot Springs for a week of exploration, interviews and photography. I must also acknowledge Wallace Stegner, whose brilliant 1971 novel, *Angle of Repose,* was my first inspiration in writing about my ancestors that lived in the American frontier.

Other Sources:

James G. Hollandsworth, *An Absolute Massacre: The New Orleans Race Riot of July 30, 1866* (Baton Rouge: Louisiana State University Press, 2004)

Giles Vandal, *The New Orleans Riot of 1866: Anatomy of a Tragedy* (Baton Rouge: Center for Louisiana Studies, 1994)

John Kendall, *History of New Orleans* (Chicago: The Lewis Publishing Company, 1992)

www.ingramcontent.com/pod-product-compliance
Lightning Source LLC
Chambersburg PA
CBHW051254130726
47987CB00004B/1527